School, Family, and Community Partnerships

Second Edition

School, Family, and Community Partnerships

Your Handbook for Action

Second Edition

Joyce L. Epstein, Mavis G. Sanders,
Beth S. Simon, Karen Clark Salinas,
Natalie Rodriguez Jansorn,
Frances L. Van Voorhis

CORWIN PRESS, INC.
A Sage Publications Company
Thousand Oaks, California

For information:

 Corwin Press, Inc.
A Sage Publications Company
2455 Teller Road
Thousand Oaks, California 91320
www.corwinpress.com

Sage Publications Ltd.
6 Bonhill Street
London EC2A 4PU
United Kingdom

Sage Publications India Pvt. Ltd.
M-32 Market
Greater Kailash I
New Delhi 110 048 India

Printed in the United States of America

Library of Congress Cataloging-in-Publication Data

School, family, and community partnerships: Your handbook for action /
Joyce L. Epstein ... [et al.].— 2nd ed.
    p. cm.
Rev. ed. of: School, family, and community partnerships / Joyce L.
Epstein.
Includes bibliographical references and index.
  ISBN 13: 978-0-7619-7665-3 (c) — ISBN 13: 978-0-7619-7666-0 (p)
 1. Community and school—United States. 2. Home and school—United
States. 3. School improvement programs—United States. I. Epstein,
Joyce Levy.
  LC221 .E68 2002
  371.19'0973—dc21   2002003384

This book is printed on acid-free paper.

07 08 09 10   10 9 8 7 6

Acquisitions Editor:	Robb Clouse
Editorial Assistant:	Erin Buchanan
Copy Editor:	Toni Williams
Production Editor:	Diane S. Foster
Typesetter/Designer:	Larry K. Bramble
Proofreader:	Scott Oney
Indexer:	Teri Greenberg
Cover Designer:	Michael Dubowe
Production Designer:	Sandra Ng

Contents

Acknowledgments

The authors are grateful to many researchers, state and district leaders, teachers, administrators, parents, grandparents, community partners, and students who have worked with us for many years to increase knowledge on partnerships and to design and test ideas for applying research results in practice.

Special thanks are due to Lucretia Coates, now principal of Dr. Bernard Harris, Sr., Elementary School in Baltimore, who was a coauthor of the first edition of this *Handbook;* the Fund for Educational Excellence in Baltimore, which collaborated on early efforts to link research to practice; and the Baltimore City Public School System, whose district leaders and school teams helped us learn how to change old ways of thinking about parent involvement to new ways of conducting programs of school, family, and community partnerships.

Thanks are due, too, to over 1700 schools, 150 school districts, and 20 state departments of education that have participated in the National Network of Partnership Schools at Johns Hopkins University. Annual data from these partners have increased knowledge on partnerships, raised new questions for research, and contributed to the development of tools in this *Handbook* for creating and sustaining programs of family and community involvement.

We recognize, in advance, the efforts of thousands of educators, parents, and other family and community members who will use this edition of the *Handbook* to improve their partnership programs. We look forward to working with you to learn more and better ways of organizing and sustaining programs of family and community involvement that contribute to students' success in school.

Finally, we greatly appreciate the grants that supported the work on this edition of the *Handbook.* We thank the U.S. Department of Education's Office of Educational Research and Improvement (OERI) for grants to the Center for Research on the Education of Students Placed at Risk (CRESPAR) and Disney Learning Partnership and the Wallace Reader's Digest Funds for grants to the Center on School, Family, and Community Partnerships at Johns Hopkins University. The research summaries and tools in the *Handbook* have been developed by the authors and do not necessarily reflect the positions of the funding sources.

About the Authors

Joyce L. Epstein, Ph.D. in sociology from Johns Hopkins University, is Director of the Center on School, Family, and Community Partnerships and the National Network of Partnership Schools, Principal Research Scientist in the Center for Research on the Education of Students Placed at Risk (CRESPAR), and Professor of Sociology at Johns Hopkins University. She has over 100 publications on the organization and effects of school, classroom, family, and peer environments, with many focused on school, family, and community connections. In 1995, she established the National Network of Partnership Schools to demonstrate the important intersections of research, policy, and practice for school improvement. She serves on numerous editorial boards and advisory panels on family involvement and school reform and is a recipient of the Academy for Educational Development's 1991 Alvin C. Eurich Education Award and the 1997 *Working Mother's Magazine* Parent Involvement in Education Award for her work on school, family, and community partnerships. Her most recent book, *School, Family, and Community Partnerships: Preparing Educators and Improving Schools* (Westview Press, 2001), aims to add the topic of family and community involvement to courses for future teachers and administrators.

Mavis G. Sanders, Ph.D. in education from Stanford University, is Assistant Professor of Education in the School of Professional Studies in Business and Education, Research Scientist at the Center for Research on the Education of Students Placed at Risk (CRESPAR), and Senior Advisor to the National Network of Partnership Schools at Johns Hopkins University. She is the author of many articles on the effects of school, family, and community support on African American adolescents' school success, the impact of partnership programs on the quality of family and community involvement, and international research on partnerships. She is interested in how schools involve families that are traditionally hard to reach, how schools meet challenges for implementing excellent programs and practices, and how schools define "community" and develop meaningful school-family-community connections. Her most recent book is *Schooling Students Placed at Risk: Research, Policy, and Practice in the Education of Poor and Minority Adolescents* (Lawrence Erlbaum, 2000).

Beth S. Simon, Ph.D. in sociology from Johns Hopkins University, is a social science research analyst at the Centers for Medicare and Medicaid Services, U. S. Department of Health and Human Services. She conducts quantitative and qualitative research to improve the quality of services and communications for health care beneficiaries. Previously, she was Associate Research Scientist at the Center for Research on the Education of Students Placed at Risk (CRESPAR) at Johns Hopkins University, where her research focused on family and community involvement in high schools and the effects of partnerships on high school student success. She also served as Dissemination Director of the National Network of Partnership Schools and as developer of the Network's website.

Karen Clark Salinas, M.S.W. in social work from the University of North Carolina, Chapel Hill, is Senior Research Assistant at the Center on School, Family, and Community Partnerships at Johns Hopkins University. As Communications Director of the National Network of Partnership Schools, she is editor of *Type 2*, the Network's newsletter, and coeditor of the annual collection of *Promising Partnership Practices*. She also coordinates workshops and provides technical assistance to members by phone, e-mail, and website. She is coauthor of the inventory *Starting Points* that helps schools identify their present practices of partnership; the *Measure of School, Family, and Community Partnerships;* and materials for the *Teachers Involve Parents in Schoolwork (TIPS)* process. She is also coproducer of the video *National Network of Partnership Schools: Working Together for Student Success.*

Natalie Rodriguez Jansorn, M.A. in education from University of Maryland Baltimore County, is State and District Facilitator of the National Network of Partnership Schools at Johns Hopkins University. In this capacity, she assists state, district, and organization leaders in establishing school, family, and community partnership programs to support students' school success. She is an experienced speaker at conferences on partnerships. Previously, she served as the Network's Middle and High School Facilitator and devoted particular attention to urban schools. She has developed workshops, tools, and publications to help middle and high schools implement effective partnership activities that are linked to school improvement goals. She is coeditor of the annual collection, *Promising Partnership Practices.*

Frances L. Van Voorhis, Ph.D. in developmental psychology from the University of Florida, is Associate Research Scientist at the Center on School, Family, and Community Partnerships and TIPS Coordinator of the National Network of Partnership Schools at Johns Hopkins University. She is the author of research articles on the *Teachers Involve Parents in Schoolwork (TIPS)* interactive homework process, including a study of the effects of TIPS science in the middle grades on family involvement and students' science skills. In addition, she conducts research on the progress in partnership program development of states, districts, and schools in the

National Network. She designs materials to help members conduct work-shops on TIPS Interactive Homework and on the National Network of Partnership Schools. She also develops and coordinates the Network's annual collection of new TIPS activities.

**CORWIN
PRESS**

The Corwin Press logo—a raven striding across an open book—represents
the happy union of courage and learning. We are a professional-level pub-
lisher of books and journals for K-12 educators, and we are committed to creating and providing resources that embody these qualities. Corwin's motto is
"Success for All Learners."

Introduction

There is no topic in education on which there is greater agreement than the need for parent involvement. Teachers and administrators want to know how to work with families in positive ways and how to involve the community to increase student success. Families want to know if their schools are providing high-quality education, how to help their children do their best, and how to communicate with and support teachers. Students want to succeed in school and know that they need guidance, support, and encouragement from their parents, teachers, and others in the community. Despite strong agreement on the importance of these goals, most schools, districts, and states still need help in developing comprehensive programs of school, family, and community partnerships.

For over 20 years, researchers at Johns Hopkins University have worked with educators, parents, students, community partners, and other researchers to learn how elementary, middle, and high schools develop and maintain excellent programs of partnership. We also have worked with district and state education leaders to understand how they write and support policies and facilitate schools' work on partnerships. With all of these partners, we have learned how programs of school, family, and community partnerships can be organized to improve schools, strengthen families, and help students succeed.

This *Handbook* translates the lessons learned in research and fieldwork into practical approaches for program development. We present a research-based framework and field-tested tools to help leaders understand the six types of family and community involvement, create an Action Team for Partnerships, plan and implement family and community involvement activities to reach school goals for student success, mobilize community resources, encourage progress, evaluate results, and continue to improve plans, practices, and programs over time.

The first edition of the *Handbook*, published in 1997, used the best knowledge at that time to guide schools, districts, and states to design and conduct productive partnership programs. Data collected over the past five years reveal that progress on partnerships is more likely when there are eight essential elements: strong leadership, good teamwork, annual written plans, well-implemented activities, adequate funding, thoughtful evaluations, strong collegial support, and continuous planning for improvement. The new *Handbook* provides step-by-step strategies so that every program will include these essential elements.

What's New in the Second Edition?

The second edition of this *Handbook* is, indeed, new and improved. In addition to basic information on the framework of six types of involvement, challenges to meet for excellent partnership programs, and results for student success, it includes new research, strategies, and tools to help leaders in schools, districts, and states learn

- How to involve the community in school, family, and community partnerships

- How to organize more effective Action Teams for Partnerships

- How to strengthen partnership programs in middle and high schools

- How to implement interactive homework for students to show and share their work with family partners

- How to organize a program of volunteers in the middle grades

- How to conduct state and district leadership activities to assist schools with programs of partnership

The chapters also include new examples of successful partnership activities from schools, districts, and states; improved planning and evaluation tools for effective partnership programs; and additional guidelines and materials for conducting effective training workshops on partnerships.

Overview of Chapters

Ten chapters offer step-by-step strategies to establish, strengthen, and sustain excellent partnership programs.

Chapter 1: A Comprehensive Framework. This chapter summarizes the theory and research on which the *Handbook* is based. The first article describes the framework of six types of involvement, identifies challenges that must be met, and provides results of well-implemented programs of school, family, and community partnerships. It also discusses an action team approach for developing comprehensive partnership programs. The second article presents an overview of how connections with the community can be organized to strengthen partnership programs.

Chapter 2: Using the Framework in Practice: Stories From the Field. Examples from elementary, middle, and high schools illustrate how the six types of involvement and action team approach work in various schools and communities. The stories from the field also feature state and district leadership activities that promote partnerships.

Chapter 3: Taking an Action Team Approach. Twelve common questions are addressed on organizing effective Action Teams for Partnerships. Several tools and guidelines are included to help develop strong and successful teams.

Chapter 4: Conducting Workshops. Agendas are provided for state, district, or school leaders to conduct Team-Training Workshops and End-of-Year Celebration Workshops for schools' Action Teams for Partnerships. The chapter includes suggested scripts and activities to help workshop leaders cover key topics, themes, and activities. Workshops to prepare educators, parents, and community partners to work together to initiate and improve partnership programs are important new professional development activities.

Chapter 5: Selecting Materials for Presentations and Workshops. Charts and diagrams are supplied which may be reproduced as transparencies, handouts, and activities for the workshops described in Chapter 4 and other presentations. These materials enable workshop leaders to present and discuss the framework of the six types of involvement, challenges to meet, results of partnerships, team structures, and how to write a One-Year Plan for partnerships.

Chapter 6: Strengthening Partnership Programs in Middle and High Schools. Three articles summarize research and practical approaches to family and community involvement in secondary schools. Reproducible materials are included to use in workshops attended by middle and high school Action Teams for Partnerships and in presentations to leaders who will assist middle and high schools with their partnership programs.

Chapter 7: Developing State and District Leadership for Partnerships. State and district leadership activities are outlined to increase expertise on school, family, and community partnerships. Information is included on the costs of partnership programs and sources of funds. Checklists are provided to help state and district leaders organize their partnership programs.

Chapter 8: Implementing Teachers Involve Parents in Schoolwork (TIPS). Two research-based partnership approaches are described. TIPS interactive homework increases family involvement with students at home in positive conversations about schoolwork. TIPS Volunteers in Social Studies and Art increase family and community involvement at school by organizing volunteers to present art masterpieces linked to units in history to increase students' art appreciation. The chapter includes sample interactive homework assignments for the elementary, middle, and high school grades and a sample social studies and art presentation.

Chapter 9: Planning and Evaluating Your Partnership Program. This chapter includes essential tools that help elementary, middle, and high schools set long-term goals for school, family, and community partnerships; write One-Year Action Plans; conduct End-of-Year Evaluations; and assess the progress of their partnership programs.

Chapter 10: Networking for Best Results on Partnerships. Information and resources are provided to enable readers of this *Handbook* to join other schools, districts, and states in the National Network of Partnership Schools at Johns Hopkins University. The National Network provides ongoing professional development on school, family, and community partnerships to school, district, and state leaders and many ways to share ideas and progress.

Time for Action

The chapters in this *Handbook* show that there is now more and better evidence of the importance of school, family, and community partnerships for student success from elementary school through high school. There are now more systematic strategies for planning, implementing, evaluating, and improving effective programs of family and community involvement. It is time for action.

1

A Comprehensive Framework

This chapter includes two summaries of research and practical approaches that will help school, district, and state leaders develop and sustain excellent programs of school, family, and community partnerships.

Reading 1.1: School, Family, and Community Partnerships: Caring for the Children We Share by Joyce L. Epstein. The first article summarizes the theory of overlapping spheres of influence to explain the shared responsibilities of home, school, and community for children's learning and development. It also charts the research-based framework of six types of involvement, the challenges each type poses, and the expected results of well-designed and well-implemented practices.

This article outlines important structures and processes to develop effective partnership programs. The workshops, tools, and guidelines in the rest of the *Handbook* have been designed to help schools implement these strategies. For example, one key structure is an Action Team for Partnerships (ATP) of educators, parents, and others who plan, implement, evaluate, and improve school programs of partnership. Other sections of the *Handbook* include the tools needed to help elementary, middle, and high schools organize effective ATPs and to conduct active, goal-oriented partnership programs.

Reading 1.2: Community Involvement in School Improvement: The Little Extra That Makes a Big Difference by Mavis G. Sanders. The second article summarizes research on school-community linkages in comprehensive programs of school, family, and community partnerships. In addition to families, businesses, organizations, groups, and individuals in the community offer many resources and opportunities to improve schools, strengthen families, and increase student success.

This article provides examples of student-, family-, school-, and community-centered activities. Four factors have been found to support school-community partnerships: high commitment to learning, principal support, a welcoming climate, and two-way communication between partners. The article also emphasizes the importance of reflection and evaluation for sustaining effective community partnerships.

The two articles in Chapter 1 provide background information, research, and practical strategies to help you understand the big picture of positive school, family, and community partnerships.

1.1 School, Family, and Community Partnerships: Caring for the Children We Share

Joyce L. Epstein

The way schools care about children is reflected in the way schools care about the children's families. If educators view children simply as *students*, they are likely to see the family as separate from the school. That is, the family is expected to do its job and leave the education of children to the schools. If educators view students as *children*, they are likely to see both the family and the community as partners with the school in children's education and development. Partners recognize their shared interests in and responsibilities for children, and they work together to create better programs and opportunities for students.

There are many reasons for developing school, family, and community partnerships. Partnerships can improve school programs and school climate, provide family services and support, increase parents' skills and leadership, connect families with others in the school and in the community, and help teachers with their work. However, the main reason to create such partnerships is to help all youngsters succeed in school and in later life. When parents, teachers, students, and others view one another as partners in education, a caring community forms around students and begins its work.

What do successful partnership programs look like? How can practices be effectively designed and implemented? What are the results of better communications, interactions, and exchanges across these three important contexts? These questions have challenged research and practice, creating an interdisciplinary field of inquiry into school, family, and community partnerships with "caring" as a core concept.

The field has been strengthened by supporting federal, state, and local policies. In the 1990s, the Goals 2000: Educate America Act set partnerships as a voluntary national goal for all schools. Title I specifies and mandates programs and practices of partnership for schools to qualify for or maintain funding. Many states and districts have developed or are preparing policies to guide schools in creating more systematic connections with families and communities. These policies reflect research results and the prior successes of leading educators who have shown that these goals are attainable.

Underlying these policies and programs is a theory of how social organizations connect; a framework of the basic components of school, family, and community partnerships for children's learning; a growing literature on the positive and negative results of these connections for students, families, and schools; and an understanding of how to organize good programs. In this chapter, I summarize the theory, framework, and guidelines from our research that should help elementary, middle, and high schools and education leaders take similar steps toward successful partnerships.

Overlapping Spheres of Influence: Understanding the Theory

Schools make choices. They might conduct only a few communications and interactions with families and communities, keeping the three spheres of influence that directly affect student learning and development relatively separate. Or they might conduct many high-quality communications and interactions designed to bring all three spheres of influence closer together. With frequent interactions among schools, families, and communities, more students are more likely to receive common messages from various people about the importance of school, of working hard, of thinking creatively, of helping one another, and of staying in school.

The *external* model of overlapping spheres of influence recognizes that the three major contexts in which students learn and grow—the family, the school, and the community—may be drawn together or pushed apart. In this model, there are some practices that schools, families, and communities conduct separately and some that they conduct jointly to influence children's learning and development. The *internal* model of the interaction of the three spheres of influence shows where and how complex and essential interpersonal relations and patterns of influence occur between individuals at home, at school, and in the community. These social relationships may be enacted and studied at an *institutional* level (e.g., when a school invites all families to an event or sends the same communications to all families) and at an *individual* level (e.g., when a parent and a teacher meet in conference or talk by phone). Connections between educators or parents and community groups, agencies, and services can also be represented and studied within the model (Epstein, 1987, 1992, 1994).

The model of school, family, and community partnerships locates the student at the center. The inarguable fact is that students are the main actors in their education, development, and success in school. School, family, and community partnerships cannot simply produce successful students. Rather, partnership activities may be designed to engage, guide, energize, and motivate students to produce their own successes. The assumption is that if children feel cared for and are encouraged to work hard in the role of student, they are more likely to do their best to learn to read, write, calculate, and learn other skills and talents and to remain in school.

Interestingly and somewhat ironically, studies indicate that students are also crucial for the success of school, family, and community partnerships. Students are often their parents' main source of information about school. In strong partnership programs, teachers help students understand and conduct both traditional communications with families (e.g., delivering memos or report cards) and new communications (e.g., interacting with family members about homework or participating in parent-teacher-student conferences). As we gain more information about the role of students in partnerships, we are developing a more complete understanding of how schools, families, and communities must work with students to increase their chances for success.

How the Theory Works in Practice

In some schools there are still educators who say, "If the family would just do its job, we could do our job." And there are still families who say, "I raised this child; now it is your job to educate her." These words embody a view of separate spheres of influence. Other educators say, "I cannot do my job without the help of my students' families and the support of this community." And some parents say, "I really need to know what is happening in school in order to help my child." These phrases embody the theory of *overlapping spheres of influence.*

In a partnership, teachers and administrators create more *family-like* schools. A family-like school recognizes each child's individuality and makes each child feel special and included. Family-like schools welcome all families, not just those that are easy to reach. In a partnership, parents create more *school-like* families. A school-like family recognizes that each child is also a student. Families reinforce the importance of school, homework, and activities that build student skills and feelings of success. Communities, including groups of parents working together, create school-like opportunities, events, and programs that reinforce, recognize, and reward students for good progress, creativity, contributions, and excellence. Communities also create *family-like* settings, services, and events to enable families to better support their children. *Community-minded* families and students help their neighborhoods and other families. The concept of a community school is reemerging. It refers to a place where programs and services for students, parents, and others are offered before, during, and after the regular school day.

Schools and communities talk about programs and services that are family-friendly—meaning that they take into account the needs and realities of family life, are feasible to conduct, and are equitable toward all families. When all these concepts combine, children experience *learning communities* or *caring communities* (Brandt, 1989; Epstein, 1995; Lewis, Schaps, & Watson, 1995; Viadero, 1994).

All these terms are consistent with the theory of overlapping spheres of influence, but they are not abstract concepts. You will find them daily in conversations, news stories, and celebrations of many kinds. In a family-like school, a teacher might say, "I know when a student is having a bad day and how to help him along." A student might slip and call a teacher "mom" or "dad" and then laugh with a mixture of embarrassment and glee. In a school-like family, a parent might say, "I make sure my daughter knows that homework comes first." A child might raise his hand to speak at the dinner table and then joke about acting as if he were still in school. When communities reach out to students and their families, youngsters might say, "This program really made my schoolwork make sense!" Parents or educators might comment, "This community really supports its schools."

Once people hear about such concepts as family-like schools or school-like families, they remember positive examples of schools, teachers, and places in the community that were "like a family" to them. They may remember how a teacher paid individual attention to them, recognized their uniqueness, or praised them for real progress, just as a parent might. They might recall things at home that were "just like school" and supported their work as a student, or they might remember community activities that made them feel smart or good about themselves and their families. They will recall that parents, siblings, and other family members engaged in and enjoyed educational activities and took pride in the good schoolwork or homework that they did, just as a teacher might.

How Partnerships Work in Practice

These terms and examples are evidence of the *potential* for schools, families, and communities to create caring educational environments. It is possible to have a school that is excellent academically but ignores families. However, that school will build barriers between teachers, parents, and children that affect school life and learning. It is possible to have a school that is ineffective academically but involves families in many good ways. With its weak academic program, that school will shortchange students' learning. Neither of these schools exemplifies a caring, educational environment that requires academic excellence, good communication, and productive interactions involving school, family, and community.

Some children succeed in school without much family involvement or despite family neglect or distress, particularly if the school has excellent academic and support programs. Teachers, relatives outside the immediate family, other families, and members of the community can provide important guidance and encouragement to these students. As support from school, family, and community accumulates, significantly more students feel secure and cared for, understand the goals of education, work to achieve their full potential, build positive attitudes and school behaviors, and stay in school. The shared interests and investments of schools, families, and communities create the conditions of caring that work to "overdetermine" the likelihood of student success (Boykin, 1994).

Any practice can be designed and implemented well or poorly. And even well-implemented partnership practices may not be useful to all families. In a caring school community, participants work continually to improve the nature and effects of partnerships. Although the interactions of educators, parents, students, and community members will not always be smooth or successful, partnership programs establish a base of respect and trust on which to build. Good partnerships withstand questions, conflicts, debates, and disagreements; provide structures and processes to solve problems; and are maintained—even strengthened—after differences have been resolved. Without this firm base, disagreements and problems about schools and students that are sure to arise will be harder to solve.

What Research Says

In surveys and field studies involving teachers, parents, and students at the elementary, middle, and high school levels, some important patterns relating to partnerships have emerged.

- Partnerships tend to decline across the grades, *unless* schools and teachers work to develop and implement appropriate practices of partnership at each grade level.

- Affluent communities currently have more positive family involvement, on average, *unless* schools and teachers in economically distressed communities work to build positive partnerships with their students' families.

- Schools in more economically depressed communities make more contacts with families about the problems and difficulties their children are having, *unless* they work at developing balanced partnership programs that also include contacts about the positive accomplishments of students.

- Single parents, parents who are employed outside the home, parents who live far from the school, and fathers are less involved, on average, at the school building, *unless* the school organizes opportunities for families to volunteer at various times and in various places to support the school and their children.

Researchers have also drawn the following conclusions:

- Just about all families care about their children, want them to succeed, and are eager to obtain better information from schools and communities so as to remain good partners in their children's education.

- Just about all teachers and administrators would like to involve families, but many do not know how to go about building positive and productive programs and are consequently fearful about trying. This creates a "rhetoric rut," in which educators are stuck, expressing support for partnerships without taking any action.

- Just about all students at all levels—elementary, middle, and high school—want their families to be more knowledgeable partners about schooling and are willing to take active roles in assisting communications between home and school. However, students need much better information and guidance than most now receive about how their schools view partnerships and about how they can conduct important exchanges with their families about school activities, homework, and school decisions.

These results are synthesized from Ames, Khoju, and Watkins (1993), Baker and Stevenson (1986), Bauch (1988), Becker and Epstein (1982), Booth and Dunn (1996), Clark (1983), Dauber and Epstein (1993), Dornbusch and Ritter (1988), Eccles and Harold (1996), Epstein (1986, 1990), Epstein and Lee (1995), Epstein and Sanders (2000), Lareau (1989), and Scott-Jones (1995).

The research results are important because they indicate that caring communities can be built intentionally; that they include families that might not become involved on their own; and that, by their own reports, just about all families, students, and teachers believe that partnerships are important for helping students succeed across the grades.

Good programs will look different at each site, as individual schools tailor their practices to meet the needs and interests, time and talents, and ages and grade levels of students and their families. However, there are some commonalities across successful programs at all grade levels. These include a recognition of the overlapping spheres of influence on student development; attention to various types of involvement that promote a variety of opportunities for schools, families, and communities to work together; and an Action Team for Partnerships (ATP) to coordinate each school's work and progress.

Six Types of Involvement— Six Types of Caring

A framework of six major types of involvement has evolved from many studies and from many years of work by educators and families in elementary, middle, and high schools. The framework (summarized in the accompanying tables) helps educators develop more comprehensive programs of school and family partnerships and also helps researchers locate their questions and results in ways that inform and improve practice (Epstein, 1992; Epstein & Connors, 1995; Epstein & Sanders, 2000).

Each type of involvement includes many different *practices* of partnership (see Table 1.1.1). Each type presents particular *challenges* that must be met to involve all families and needed *redefinitions* of some basic principles of involvement (see Table 1.1.2). Finally, each type is likely to lead to different *results* for students, parents, teaching practices, and school climates (see Table 1.1.3). Thus, schools have choices about which practices will help achieve important goals. The tables provide examples of practices, challenges for successful implementation, redefinitions for up-to-date understanding, and results that have been documented and observed.

Charting the Course

The entries in the tables are illustrative. The sample practices displayed in Table 1.1.1 are only a few of hundreds that may be selected or designed for each type of involvement. Although all schools may use the framework of six types as a guide, each school must chart its own course in choosing practices to meet the needs of its families and students.

The challenges shown (Table 1.1.2) are also just a few of the many that relate to the examples. There are challenges—that is, problems—for every practice of partnerships, and they must be resolved in order to reach and engage all families in the best ways. Often, when one challenge has been met, a new one will emerge.

The redefinitions (also in Table 1.1.2) redirect old notions so that involvement is not viewed solely as or measured only by "bodies in the building." As examples, the table calls for redefinitions of workshops, communication, volunteers, homework, decision making, and community. By redefining these familiar terms, it is possible for partnership programs to reach out in new ways to many more families.

The selected results (Table 1.1.3) should help correct the widespread misperception that any practice that involves families will raise children's achievement test scores. Instead, in the short term, certain practices are more likely than others to influence students' skills and scores, whereas other practices are more likely to affect attitudes and behaviors. Although students are the main focus of partnerships, the various types of involvement also promote various kinds of results for parents and teachers. For example, the expected results for parents include not only leadership in decision making, but also confidence about parenting, productive curriculum-related interactions with children, and many interactions with other parents and the school. The expected results for teachers include not only improved parent-teacher conferences or school-home communications, but also better understanding of families, new approaches to homework, and other connections with families and the community.

Most of the results noted in Table 1.1.3 have been measured in at least one research study and observed as schools conduct their work. The entries are listed in positive terms to indicate the results of well-designed and well-implemented practices. It should be fully understood, however, that results may be negative if poorly designed practices exclude families or create greater barriers to communication and exchange. Research still is needed on the results of specific practices of partnership in various schools, at various grade levels, and for diverse populations of students, families, and teachers. It will be important to confirm, extend, or correct the information on results listed in Table 1.1.3 if schools are to make purposeful choices among practices that foster various types of involvement.

TABLE 1.1.1   Epstein's Framework of Six Types of Involvement for Comprehensive Programs of Partnership and Sample Practices

Type 1 Parenting	Type 2 Communicating	Type 3 Volunteering	Type 4 Learning at Home	Type 5 Decision Making	Type 6 Collaborating With the Community
Help all families establish home environments to support children as students	Design effective forms of school-to-home and home-to-school communications about school programs and their children's progress	Recruit and organize parent help and support	Provide information and ideas to families about how to help students at home with homework and other curriculum-related activities, decisions, and planning	Include parents in school decisions, developing parent leaders and representatives	Identify and integrate resources and services from the community to strengthen school programs, family practices, and student learning and development

Sample Practices

Type 1 Parenting	Type 2 Communicating	Type 3 Volunteering	Type 4 Learning at Home	Type 5 Decision Making	Type 6 Collaborating With the Community
Suggestions for home conditions that support learning at each grade level Workshops, videotapes, computerized phone messages on parenting and child rearing for each age and grade level Parent education and other courses or training for parents (e.g., GED, college credit, family literacy) Family support programs to assist families with health, nutrition, and other services Home visits at transition points to preschool, elementary, middle, and high school; neighborhood meetings to help families understand schools and to help schools understand families	Conferences with every parent at least once a year, with follow-ups as needed Language translators assist families, as needed Weekly or monthly folders of student work sent home for review and comments Parent-student pickup of report cards, with conferences on improving grades Regular schedule of useful notices, memos, phone calls, newsletters, and other communications Clear information on choosing schools or courses, programs, and activities within schools Clear information on all school policies, programs, reforms, and transitions	School and classroom volunteer program to help teachers, administrators, students, and other parents Parent room or family center for volunteer work, meetings, and resources for families Annual postcard survey to identify all available talents, times, and locations of volunteers Class parent, telephone tree, or other structures to provide all families with needed information Parent patrols or other activities to aid safety and operation of school programs	Information for families on skills required for students in all subjects at each grade Information on homework policies and how to monitor and discuss schoolwork at home Information on how to assist students to improve skills on various class and school assessments Regular schedule of homework that requires students to discuss and interact with families on what they are learning in class Calendars with activities for parents and students to do at home or in the community Family math, science, and reading activities at school Summer learning packets or activities Family participation in setting student goals each year and in planning for college or work	Active PTA/PTO or other parent organizations, advisory councils, or committees (e.g., curriculum, safety, personnel) for parent leadership and participation Independent advocacy groups to lobby and work for school reform and improvements District-level councils and committees for family and community involvement Information on school or local elections for school representatives Networks to link all families with parent representatives	Information for students and families on community health, cultural, recreational, social support, and other programs or services Information on community activities that link to learning skills and talents, including summer programs for students Service integration through partnerships involving school; civic, counseling, cultural, health, recreation, and other agencies and organizations; and businesses Service to the community by students, families, and schools (e.g., recycling, art, music, drama, and other activities for seniors or others) Participation of alumni in school programs for students

TABLE 1.1.2 Challenges and Redefinitions for the Successful Design and Implementation of the Six Types of Involvement

			Challenges		
Type 1 Parenting	Type 2 Communicating	Type 3 Volunteering	Type 4 Learning at Home	Type 5 Decision Making	Type 6 Collaborating With the Community
Provide information to all families who want it or who need it, not just to the few who can attend workshops or meetings at the school building	Review the readability, clarity, form, and frequency of all memos, notices, and other print and nonprint communications	Recruit volunteers widely so that *all* families know that their time and talents are welcome	Design and organize a regular schedule of interactive homework (e.g., weekly or bimonthly) that gives *students* responsibility for discussing important things they are learning and helps families stay aware of the content of their children's classwork	Include parent leaders from all racial, ethnic, socioeconomic, and other groups in the school	Solve turf problems of responsibilities, funds, staff, and locations for collaborative activities
Enable families to share information about culture, background, and children's talents and needs	Consider parents who do not speak English well, do not read well, or need large type	Make flexible schedules for volunteers, assemblies, and events to enable employed parents to participate	Coordinate family-linked homework activities, if students have several teachers	Offer training to enable leaders to serve as representatives of other families, with input from and return of information to all parents	Inform families of community programs for students, such as mentoring, tutoring, and business partnerships
Make sure that all information for families is clear, usable, and linked to children's success in school	Review the quality of major communications (e.g., the schedule, content, and structure of conferences; newsletters; report cards; and others)	Organize volunteer work; provide training; match time and talent with school, teacher, and student needs; and recognize efforts so that participants are productive	Involve families with their children in all important curriculum-related decisions	Include students (along with parents) in decision-making groups	Ensure equity of opportunities for students and families to participate in community programs or to obtain services
	Establish clear two-way channels for communications from home to school and from school to home				Match community contributions with school goals; integrate child and family services with education
			Redefinitions		
"Workshop" to mean more than a meeting about a topic held at the school building at a particular time; "workshop" also may mean making information about a topic available in a variety of forms that can be viewed, heard, or read anywhere, anytime	"Communications about school programs and student progress" to mean two-way, three-way, and many-way channels of communication that connect schools, families, students, and the community	"Volunteer" to mean anyone who supports school goals and children's learning or development in any way, at any place, and at any time—not just during the school day and at the school building	"Homework" to mean not only work done alone, but also interactive activities shared with others at home or in the community, linking schoolwork to real life	"Decision making" to mean a process of partnership, of shared views and actions toward shared goals, not a power struggle between conflicting ideas	"Community" to mean not only the neighborhoods where students' homes and schools are located but also neighborhoods that influence student learning and development
			"Help" at home to mean encouraging, listening, reacting, praising, guiding, monitoring, and discussing–not "teaching" school subjects	"Parent leader" to mean a real representative, with opportunities and support to hear from and communicate with other families	"Community" rated not only by low or high social or economic qualities, but also by strengths and talents to support students, families, and schools
					"Community" means all who are interested in and affected by the quality of education, not just families with children in the schools

TABLE 1.1.3 Expected Results for Students, Parents, and Teachers of the Six Types of Involvement

Results for Students					
Type 1 Parenting	Type 2 Communicating	Type 3 Volunteering	Type 4 Learning at Home	Type 5 Decision Making	Type 6 Collaborating With the Community
Awareness of family supervision; respect for parents Positive personal qualities, habits, beliefs, and values, as taught by family Balance between time spent on chores, on other activities, and on homework Good or improved attendance Awareness of importance of school	Awareness of own progress and of actions needed to maintain or improve grades Understanding of school policies on behavior, attendance, and other areas of student conduct Informed decisions about courses and programs Awareness of own role in partnerships, serving as courier and communicator	Skill in communicating with adults Increased learning of skills that receive tutoring or targeted attention from volunteers Awareness of many skills, talents, occupations, and contributions of parents and other volunteers	Gains in skills, abilities, and test scores linked to homework and classwork Homework completion Positive attitude toward schoolwork View of parent as more similar to teacher and home as more similar to school Self-concept of ability as learner	Awareness of representation of families in school decisions Understanding that student rights are protected Specific benefits linked to policies enacted by parent organizations and experienced by students	Increased skills and talents through enriched curricular and extracurricular experiences Awareness of careers and options for future education and work Specific benefits linked to programs, services, resources, and opportunities that connect students with community
Results for Parents					
Understanding of and confidence about parenting, child and adolescent development, and changes in home conditions for learning as children proceed through school Awareness of own and others' challenges in parenting Feeling of support from school and other parents	Understanding school programs and policies Monitoring and awareness of student progress Responding effectively to student problems Interactions with teachers and ease of communications with school and teachers	Understanding teacher's job, increased comfort in school, and carryover of school activities at home Self-confidence about ability to work in school and with children or to take steps to improve own education Awareness that families are welcome and valued at school Gains in specific skills of volunteer work	Know how to support, encourage, and help student at home each year Discussions of school, classwork, and homework Understanding of instructional program each year and of what child is learning in each subject Appreciation of teaching skills Awareness of child as a learner	Input into policies that affect child's education Feeling of ownership of school Awareness of parents' voices in school decisions Shared experiences and connections with other families Awareness of school, district, and state policies	Knowledge and use of local resources by family and child to increase skills and talents or to obtain needed services Interactions with other families in community activities Awareness of school's role in the community and of community's contributions to the school
Results for Teachers					
Understanding families' backgrounds, cultures, concerns, goals, needs, and views of their children Respect for families' strengths and efforts Understanding of student diversity Awareness of own skills to share information on child development	Increased diversity and use of communications with families and awareness of own ability to communicate clearly Appreciation and use of parent network for communications Increased ability to elicit and understand family views on children's programs and progress	Readiness to involve families in new ways, including those who do not volunteer at school Awareness of parent talents and interests in school and children Greater individual attention to students, with help from volunteers	Better design of homework assignments Respect of family time Recognition of equal helpfulness of single parent, dual income, and less formally educated families in motivating and reinforcing student learning Satisfaction with family involvement and support	Awareness of parent perspectives as a factor in policy development and decisions View of equal status of family representatives on committees and in leadership roles	Awareness of community resources to enrich curriculum and instruction Openness to and skill in using mentors, business partners, community volunteers, and others to assist students and augment teaching practice Knowledgeable, helpful referrals of children and families to needed services

The tables cannot show the connections that occur when one practice activates several types of involvement simultaneously. For example, volunteers may organize and conduct a food bank (Type 3) that allows parents to pay $15 for $30 worth of food for their families (Type 1). The food may be subsidized by community agencies (Type 6). The recipients might then serve as volunteers for the program or in the community, thereby perpetuating Type 3 and Type 6 activities. Or consider another example. An after-school homework club run by volunteers and the community recreation and parks department combines Type 3 and Type 6 practices. Yet it also serves as a Type 1 activity because the after-school program assists families with the supervision of their children. This practice may also alter the way homework interactions are conducted at home between students and parents (Type 4). These and other connections are interesting, and research is needed to understand the combined effects of such activities.

The tables also simplify the complex longitudinal influences that produce various results over time. For example, a series of events might play out as follows. The involvement of families with children in reading at home may lead students to give more attention to reading and to be more strongly motivated to read. This in turn may help students maintain or improve their daily reading skills and then their reading grades. With the accumulation over time of good classroom reading programs, continued home support, and increased skills and confidence in reading, students may significantly improve their reading achievement test scores. The time between reading aloud at home and increased reading test scores may vary greatly, depending on the quality and quantity of other reading activities in school and out.

Consider yet another example. Studies using longitudinal data and rigorous statistical controls on background and prior influences found important benefits for high school students' attitudes, behaviors, and grades as a result of continuing several types of family involvement from middle school through high school (Lee, 1994; Simon, 2001). However, achievement test scores, stable by 12th grade, were not greatly affected by partnerships at the high school level. Longitudinal studies and practical experiences that are monitored over time are needed to increase our understanding of the complex patterns of results that can develop from various partnership activities (Epstein, 1991; Epstein & Dauber, 1995; Epstein & Sanders, 2000; Henderson & Berla, 1994).

The six types of involvement can guide the development of a balanced, comprehensive program of partnerships, including opportunities for family involvement at school and at home, with potentially important results for students, parents, and teachers. The results for students, parents, and teachers will depend on the particular types of involvement that are implemented, as well as on the quality of the implementation.

Action Teams for Partnerships

Who will work to create caring school communities that are based on the concepts of partnership? How will the necessary work on all six types of involvement get done? Although a principal or a teacher may be a leader in working with some families or with groups in the community, one person cannot create a lasting, comprehensive program that involves all families as their children progress through the grades.

From the hard work of many educators and families in many schools, we have learned that, along with clear policies and strong support from state and district leaders and from school principals, an Action Team for Partnerships (ATP) in each school is an essential structure. The action team guides the development of a comprehensive program of partnerships, including all six types of involvement, and the integration of all family and community connections within a single, unified plan and program. The trials and errors and the efforts and insights of many schools across the country have helped identify five important steps that any school can take to develop more positive school, family, and community connections (Burch & Palanki, 1994; Burch, Palanki, & Davies, 1995; Connors & Epstein, 1994; Davies, 1991, 1993; Davies, Palanki, & Burch, 1993; Epstein & Connors, 1994; Epstein & Dauber, 1991; Epstein, Herrick, & Coates, 1996; Johnson, 1994).

Step 1:   Create an Action Team

A team approach is an appropriate way to build school, family, and community partnerships. The Action Team for Partnerships (ATP) can be the "action arm" of a School Council, if one exists. The action team takes responsibility for assessing present practices, organizing options for new partnerships, implementing selected activities, evaluating next steps, and continuing to improve and coordinate practices for all six types of involvement. Although the members of the action team lead these activities, they are assisted by other teachers, parents, students, administrators, and community members.

The action team should include at least three teachers from different grade levels, three parents with children in different grade levels, and one administrator. Teams may also include at least one member from the community at large and, at the high school level, at least two students from different grade levels. Others who are central to the school's work with families also may be included as members, such as a cafeteria worker, a school social worker, a counselor, or a school psychologist. Such diverse membership ensures that partnership activities will take into account the various needs, interests, and talents of teachers, parents, the school, and students.

The leader of the action team may be any member who has the respect of the other members, as well as good communication skills and an understanding of the partnership approach. The leader or at least one member of the action team should also serve on the School Council, School Improvement Team, or other such body, if one exists.

In addition to group planning, members of the action team elect (or are assigned to act as) the chair or co-chair of one of six subcommittees for each type of involvement. Alternatively, members can serve as chair or co-chair of three to five committees that focus on family and community involvement for school improvement goals (e.g., improving reading, math, behavior, partnerships). A team with at least six members (and perhaps as many as 12) ensures that responsibilities for leadership can be delegated so that one person is not overburdened and so that the work of the action team will continue even if members move or change schools or positions. Members may serve renewable terms of two to three years, with the replacement of any who leave in the interim. Other thoughtful variations in assignments and activities may be created by small or large schools using this process.

In the first phase of our work in 1987, projects were led by "project directors" (usually teachers) and were focused on one type of involvement at a time. Some schools succeeded in developing good partnerships over several years, but others were thwarted if the project director moved, if the principal changed, or if the project grew larger than one person could handle. Other schools took a team approach to work on many types of involvement simultaneously. Their efforts demonstrated how to structure the program for the next set of schools in our work. Starting in 1990, this second set of schools tested and improved on the structure and work of action teams. Now, all elementary, middle, and high schools in our research and development projects, and in other states and districts that are applying this work, are given assistance in taking the action team approach.

Step 2:   *Obtain Funds and Other Support*

A modest budget is needed to guide and support the work and expenses of each school's action team. Funds for state coordinators to assist districts and schools and funds for district coordinators or facilitators to help each school may come from a number of sources. These include federal, state, and local programs that mandate, request, or support family involvement, such as Title I and other federal and state funding programs. In addition to paying the state and district coordinators, funds from these sources may be applied in creative ways to support staff development in the area of school, family, and community partnerships; to pay for lead teachers at each school to serve as ATP chairs or co-chairs; to set up demonstration programs; and for other partnership expenses. In addition, local school-business partnerships, school discretionary funds, and separate fundraising efforts targeted to the schools' partnership programs have been used to support the work of ATPs. At the very least, a school's action team requires a small stipend (at least $1,000 per year) for time and materials needed by each subcommittee to plan, implement, and revise practices of partnership that include all six types of involvement and that promote school improvement goals.

The action team must also be given sufficient time and social support to do its work. This requires explicit support from the principal and district leaders to allow time for team members to meet, plan, and conduct the activities that are selected for each type of involvement. Time during the summer is also valuable—and may be essential—for planning new approaches that will start in the new school year.

Step 3:   Identify Starting Points

Most schools have some teachers who conduct some practices of partnership with some families some of the time. How can good practices be organized and extended so that they may be used by all teachers, at all grade levels, with all families? The action team works to improve and systematize the typically haphazard patterns of involvement. It starts by collecting information about the school's current practices of partnership, along with the views, experiences, and wishes of teachers, parents, administrators, and students. See *"Starting Points"* (pp. 208-211) and *"Measure of School, Family, and Community Partnerships"* (pp. 330-335) for two ways of assessing the nature and extent of present practices.

Assessments of starting points may be made in a variety of other ways, depending on available resources, time, and talents. For example, the action team might use formal questionnaires (Epstein & Salinas, 1993) or telephone interviews to survey teachers, administrators, parents, and students (if resources exist to process, analyze, and report survey data). Or the action team might organize a panel of teachers, parents, and students to speak at a meeting of the parent-teacher organization or at some other school meeting as a way of initiating discussion about the goals and desired activities for partnership. Structured discussions may be conducted through a series of principal's breakfasts for representative groups of teachers, parents, students, and others; random sample phone calls may also be used to collect reactions and ideas; or formal focus groups may be convened to gather ideas about school, family, and community partnerships at the school.

What questions should be addressed? Regardless of how the information is gathered, the following areas must be covered in any information gathering:

- *Present strengths.* Which practices of school, family, and community partnerships are now working well for the school as a whole? For individual grade levels? For which types of involvement?

- *Needed changes.* Ideally, how do we want school, family, and community partnerships to work at this school three years from now? Which present practices should continue, and which should change? To reach school goals, what new practices are needed for each of the major types of involvement?

- *Expectations.* What do teachers expect of families? What do families expect of teachers and other school personnel? What do students expect their families to do to help them negotiate school life? What do students expect their teachers to do to keep their families informed and involved?

- *Sense of community.* Which families are we now reaching, and which are we not yet reaching? Who are the hard-to-reach families? What might be done to communicate with and engage these families in their children's education? Are current partnership practices coordinated to include all families as a school community? Or are families whose children receive special services (e.g., Title I, special education, bilingual education) separated from other families?

- *Links to goals.* How are students faring on such measures of academic achievement as report card grades, on measures of attitudes and attendance, and on other indicators of success? How might family and community connections assist the school in helping more students reach higher goals and achieve greater success? Which practices of school, family, and community partnerships would directly connect to particular goals?

Step 4: Develop a Three-Year Outline and a One-Year Action Plan

From the ideas and goals for partnerships collected from teachers, parents, and students, the action team can develop a Three-Year Outline of the specific steps that will help the school progress from its starting point on each type of involvement to where it wants to be in three years. This plan outlines how each subcommittee will work over three years to make important, incremental advances to reach more families each year on each type of involvement. The Three-Year Outline also shows how all school, family, and community connections will be integrated into one coherent program of partnerships linked to school improvement goals.

In addition to the Three-Year Outline of goals for family and community involvement, a detailed One-Year Action Plan should be developed every year. It should include the specific activities that will be implemented, improved, or maintained for each type of involvement; a timeline of monthly actions needed for each activity; identification of the subcommittee chair who will be responsible either for each type of involvement or for involvement to promote specific goals for student success; identification of the teachers, parents, students, or others (not necessarily action team members) who will assist with the implementation of each activity; indicators of how the implementation and results of each major activity will be assessed; and other details of importance to the action team.

The Three-Year Outline and detailed One-Year Action Plan are shared with the school council and/or parent organization, with all teachers, and with the parents and students. Even if the action team makes only one good step forward each year on each of the six types of involvement, it will take 18 steps forward over three years to develop a more comprehensive, coordinated, and goal-oriented program of school, family, and community partnerships.

In short, based on the input from the parents, teachers, students, and others on the school's starting points and desired partnerships, the action team will address these issues:

- *Details.* What will be done each year, for three years, to implement a program of all six types of involvement? What, specifically, will be accomplished in the first year on each type of involvement? For which goals for student success?

- *Responsibilities.* Who will be responsible for developing and implementing practices of partnership for each type of involvement? Will staff development be needed? How will teachers, administrators, parents, and students be supported and recognized for their work?

- *Costs.* What costs are associated with the improvement and maintenance of the planned activities? What sources will provide the needed funds? Will small grants or other special budgets be needed?

- *Evaluation.* How well have the practices been implemented and what are the effects on students, teachers, and families? What indicators will we use that are closely linked to the practices implemented to determine their effects?

Step 5:   Continue Planning and Working

The action team should schedule an annual presentation and celebration of progress at the school so that all teachers, families, and students will know about the work that has been done each year to build partnerships. Or the district coordinator for school, family, and community partnerships might arrange an annual conference for all schools in the district. At the annual school or district meeting, the action team presents and displays its accomplishments on one or all six types of involvement and shares its best practices with other educators and parents. Problems are discussed and ideas are shared about improvements, additions, and continuations for the next year.

Each year, the action team updates the school's Three-Year Outline and develops a detailed One-Year Action Plan for the coming year's work. It is important for educators, families, students, and the community at large to be aware of annual progress, new plans, and how they can help.

In short, the action team addresses the following questions. How can it ensure that the program of school, family, and community partnerships will continue to improve its structure, processes, and practices to increase the number of families who are partners with the school in their children's education? What opportunities will teachers, parents, and students have to share information on successful practices and to strengthen and maintain their efforts?

Characteristics of Successful Programs

As schools have implemented partnership programs, their experience has helped to identify some important properties of successful partnerships.

Incremental Progress

Progress in partnerships is incremental, including more families each year in ways that benefit more students. Like reading or math programs, assessment programs, sports programs, or other school investments, partnership programs take time to develop, must be periodically reviewed, and should be continuously improved. Schools in our projects have shown that three years is the minimum time needed for an action team to complete a number of activities on each type of involvement and to establish its work as a productive and permanent structure in a school.

The development of a partnership program is a process, not a single event. All teachers, families, students, and community groups do not engage in all activities on all types of involvement all at once. Not all activities implemented will succeed with all families. But with good planning, thoughtful implementation, well-designed activities, and pointed improvements, more and more families and teachers can learn to work with one another on behalf of the children whose interests they share. Similarly, not all students instantly improve their attitudes or achievements when their families become involved in their education. After all, student learning depends mainly on good curricula and instruction and on the work completed by students. However, with a well-implemented program of partnerships, more students will receive support from their families, and more will be motivated to work harder.

Connection to Curricular and Instructional Reform

A program of school, family, and community partnerships that focuses on children's learning and development is an important component of curricular and instructional reform. Aspects of partnerships that aim to help more students succeed in school can be supported by federal, state, and local funds targeted for curricular and instructional reform. Helping families understand, monitor, and interact with students on homework, for example, can be a clear and important extension of classroom instruction, as can volunteer programs that bolster and broaden student skills, talents, and interests. Improving the content and conduct of parent-teacher-student conferences and goal-setting activities can be an important step in curricular reform; family support and family understanding of child and adolescent development and school curricula are necessary elements to assist students as learners.

The connection of partnerships to curriculum and instruction in schools and the location of leadership for these partnership programs in departments of curriculum and instruction in districts are important changes that move partnerships from being peripheral public relations activities about parents to being central programs about student learning and development.

Redefining Staff Development

The action team approach to partnerships guides the work of educators by restructuring staff development to mean colleagues working together and with parents to develop, implement, evaluate, and continue to improve practices of partnership. This is less a dose of inservice education than it is an active form of developing staff talents and capacities. The teachers, administrators, and others on the action team become the experts on this topic for their school. Their work in this area can be supported by various federal, state, and local funding programs as a clear investment in staff development for overall school reform. Indeed, the action team approach as outlined can be applied to any or all important topics on a school improvement agenda. It need not be restricted to the pursuit of successful partnerships.

It is important to note that the development of partnership programs would be easier if educators came to their schools prepared to work productively with families and communities. Courses or classes are needed in preservice teacher education and in advanced degree programs for teachers and administrators to help them define their professional work in terms of partnerships. Today, most educators enter schools without an understanding of family backgrounds, concepts of caring, the framework of partnerships, or the other basics that are discussed here. Thus, most principals and district leaders are not prepared to guide and lead their staffs in developing strong school and classroom practices that inform and involve families. Most teachers and administrators also are unprepared to understand, design, implement, or evaluate good practices of partnership with the families of their students. Colleges and universities that prepare educators and others who work with children and families should identify where in their curricula the theory, research, policy, and practical ideas about partnerships are presented or where in their programs these can be added (Ammon, 1990; Chavkin & Williams, 1988; Epstein, 2001; Hinz, Clark, & Nathan, 1992; see also Booth & Dunn, 1996; Christenson & Conoley, 1992; Fagnano & Werber, 1994; Fruchter, Galletta, & White, 1992; Rioux & Berla, 1993; Ryan, Adams, Gullotta, Weissberg, & Hampton, 1995; Swap, 1993).

Even with improved preservice and advanced coursework, however, each school's Action Team for Partnerships will have to tailor its selection of practices to the needs and goals of the teachers, families, and students in the school. The framework and guidelines offered in this chapter can be used by thoughtful educators to organize this work, school by school.

The Core of Caring

One school in Baltimore named its partnership program the I Care Program. It developed an I Care Parent Club that fostered fellowship and leadership of families, the *I Care Newsletter,* and many other events and activities. Other schools also gave catchy, positive names to their programs to indicate to families, students, teachers, and everyone else in the school community that important relationships and exchanges must be developed in order to assist students.

Interestingly, synonyms for "caring" match the six types of involvement:

Type 1—Parenting: supporting, nurturing, and child rearing

Type 2—Communicating: relating, reviewing, and overseeing

Type 3—Volunteering: supervising and fostering

Type 4—Learning at Home: managing, recognizing, and rewarding

Type 5—Decision Making: contributing, considering, and judging

Type 6—Collaborating With the Community: sharing and giving

Underlying all six types of involvement are two defining synonyms of caring: trusting and respecting. Of course, the varied meanings are interconnected, but it is striking that language permits us to call forth various elements of caring associated with activities for the six types of involvement. If all six types of involvement are operating well in a school's program of partnerships, then all these caring behaviors could be activated to assist children's learning and development.

Despite real progress in many states, districts, and schools over the past few years, there still are too many schools in which educators do not understand the families of their students, in which families do not understand their children's schools, and in which communities do not understand or assist the schools, families, or students. There are still too many states and districts without the policies, departments, leadership, staff, and fiscal support needed to help all schools develop good programs of partnership. Yet relatively small financial investments that support and assist the work of action teams could yield significant returns for all schools, teachers, families, and students. Educators who have led the way with trials, errors, and successes provide evidence that any state, district, or school can create similar programs (Lloyd, 1996; Wisconsin Department of Public Instruction, 1994).

Schools have choices. There are two common approaches to involving families in schools and in their children's education. One approach emphasizes conflict and views the school as a battleground. The conditions and relationships in this kind of environment guarantee power struggles and disharmony. The other approach emphasizes partnership and views the school as a homeland. The conditions and relationships in this kind of environment invite power sharing and mutual respect, and allow energies to be directed toward activities that foster student learning and development. Even when conflicts rage, however, peace must be restored sooner or later, and the partners in children's education must work together.

Next Steps: Strengthening Partnerships

Collaborative work and thoughtful give-and-take among researchers, policy leaders, educators, and parents are responsible for the progress that has been made over the past decade in understanding and developing school, family, and community partnerships. Similar collaborations will be important for future progress in this and other areas of school reform. To promote these approaches, the National Network of Partnership Schools at Johns Hopkins University was established. The National Network provides state, district, and other leaders with research-based tools and guidelines to help their elementary, middle, and high schools plan, implement, and maintain comprehensive programs of school, family, and community partnerships.

Partnership schools, districts, and states put the recommendations of this chapter into practice in ways that are appropriate to their locations. Implementation includes applying the theory of overlapping spheres of influence, the framework of six types of involvement, and the action team approach. Researchers and staff at Johns Hopkins University disseminate information, guidelines, and newsletters; offer e-mail and website assistance; and hold annual workshops to help state and district coordinators and school leaders learn new strategies and share successful ideas. Activities for leaders at the state and district levels are shared, along with school-level programs and successful partnership practices. With a strong research base, the National Network of Partnership Schools guides state and district leaders, educators, and parents to work together to establish and strengthen programs of family and community involvement that contribute to student success.

Note

An earlier version of this article appeared in *Phi Delta Kappan*, 1995, *76*(9), 701-712.

References

Ames, C., Khoju, M., & Watkins, T. (1993). *Parents and schools: The impact of school-to-home communications on parents' beliefs and perceptions* (Center Report 15). Baltimore: Johns Hopkins University, Center on Families, Communities, Schools and Children's Learning.

Ammon, M. S. (1990). University of California project on teacher preparation for parent involvement: Report 1, April 1989 Conference and initial follow-up (mimeo), University of California, Berkeley.

Baker, D. P., & Stevenson, D. L. (1986). Mothers' strategies for children's school achievement: Managing the transition to high school. *Sociology of Education, 59*, 156-166.

Bauch, P. A. (1988). Is parent involvement different in private schools? *Educational Horizons, 66*, 78-82.

Becker, H. J., & Epstein, J. L. (1982). Parent involvement: A study of teacher practices. *Elementary School Journal, 83*, 85-102.

Booth, A., & Dunn, J. F. (Eds.). (1996). *Family-school links: How do they affect educational outcomes?* Mahwah, NJ: Lawrence Erlbaum.

Boykin, A. W. (1994). Harvesting culture and talent: African American children and educational reform. In R. Rossi (Ed.), *Schools and students at risk* (pp. 116-139). New York: Teachers College Press.

Brandt, R. (1989). On parents and schools: A conversation with Joyce Epstein. *Educational Leadership, 47*(2), 24-27.

Burch, P., & Palanki, A. (1994). Action research on family-school-community partnerships. *Journal of Emotional and Behavioral Problems, 1*(4), 16-19.

Burch, P., Palanki, A., & Davies, D. (1995). *From clients to partners: Four case studies of collaboration and family involvement in the development of school-linked services* (Center Report 29). Baltimore: Johns Hopkins University, Center on Families, Communities, Schools and Children's Learning.

Chavkin, N., & Williams, D. (1988). Critical issues in teacher training for parent involvement. *Educational Horizons, 66*, 87-89.

Christenson, S. L., & Conoley, J. C. (Eds.). (1992). *Home-school collaboration: Enhancing children's academic competence.* Silver Spring, MD: National Association of School Psychologists.

Clark, R. M. (1983). *Family life and school achievement: Why poor Black children succeed or fail.* Chicago: University of Chicago Press.

Connors, L. J., & Epstein. J. L. (1994). *Taking stock: The views of teachers, parents, and students on school, family, and community partnerships in high schools* (Center Report 25). Baltimore: Johns Hopkins University, Center on Families, Communities, Schools and Children's Learning.

Dauber, S. L., & Epstein, J. L. (1993). Parents' attitudes and practices of involvement in inner-city elementary and middle schools. In N. Chavkin (Ed.), *Families and schools in a pluralistic society* (pp. 53-71). Albany: State University of New York Press.

Davies, D. (1991). Schools reaching out: Family, school and community partnerships for student success. *Phi Delta Kappan, 72*, 376-382.

Davies, D. (1993). A more distant mirror: Progress report on a cross-national project to study family-school-community partnerships. *Equity and Choice, 19*(1), 41-46.

Davies, D., Burch, P., & Johnson, V. (1992). *A portrait of schools reaching out: Report of a survey on practices and policies of family-community-school collaboration* (Center Report 1). Baltimore: Johns Hopkins University, Center on Families, Communities, Schools and Children's Learning.

Davies, D., Palanki, A., & Burch, P. (1993). *Getting started: Action research in family-school-community partnerships* (Center Report 17). Baltimore: Johns Hopkins University, Center on Families, Communities, Schools and Children's Learning.

Dornbusch, S. M., & Ritter, P. L. (1988). Parents of high school students: A neglected resource. *Educational Horizons, 66,* 75-77.

Eccles, J. S., & Harold, R. D. (1996). Family involvement in children's and adolescents' schooling. In A. Booth & J. F. Dunn (Eds.), *Family-school links: How do they affect educational outcomes?* (pp. 3-34). Mahwah, NJ: Lawrence Erlbaum.

Epstein, J. L. (1986). Parents' reactions to teacher practices of parent involvement. *Elementary School Journal, 86,* 277-294.

Epstein, J. L. (1987). Toward a theory of family-school connections: Teacher practices and parent involvement. In K. Hurrelmann, F. Kaufmann, & F. Losel (Eds.), *Social intervention: Potential and constraints* (pp. 121-136). New York: DeGruyter.

Epstein, J. L. (1990). Single parents and the schools: Effects of marital status on parent and teacher interactions. In M. Hallinan (Ed.), *Change in societal institutions* (pp. 91-121). New York: Plenum.

Epstein, J. L. (1991). Effects on student achievement of teacher practices of parent involvement. In S. Silvern (Ed.), *Literacy through family, community, and school interaction* (pp. 261-276). Greenwich, CT: JAI Press.

Epstein, J. L. (1992). School and family partnerships. In M. Alkin (Ed.), *Encyclopedia of educational research* (6th ed., pp. 1139-1151). New York: MacMillan.

Epstein, J. L. (1994). Theory to practice: School and family partnerships lead to school improvement and student success. In C. L. Fagnano & B. Z. Werber (Eds.), *School, family and community interaction: A view from the firing lines* (pp. 39-52). Boulder, CO: Westview Press.

Epstein, J. L. (1995). School/family/community partnerships: Caring for the children we share. *Phi Delta Kappan, 76,* 701-712.

Epstein, J. L. (1996). Perspectives and previews on research and policy for school, family, and community partnerships. In A. Booth & J. F. Dunn (Eds.), *Family-school links: How do they affect educational outcomes?* (pp. 209-246). Mahwah, NJ: Lawrence Erlbaum.

Epstein, J. L. (2001). *School, family, and community partnerships: Preparing educators and improving schools.* Boulder, CO: Westview Press.

Epstein, J. L., & Connors, L. J. (1994). *Trust fund: School, family, and community partnerships in high schools* (Center Report 24). Baltimore: Johns Hopkins University, Center on Families, Communities, Schools and Children's Learning.

Epstein, J. L., & Connors, L. J. (1995). School and family partnerships in the middle grades. In B. Rutherford (Ed.), *Creating family-school partnerships* (pp. 137-166). Columbus, OH: National Middle School Association.

Epstein, J. L., Connors, L J., & Salinas, K. C. (1993). *High school and family partnerships: Surveys and summaries (Questionnaires for teachers, parents, and students).* Baltimore: Johns Hopkins University, Center on School, Family, and Community Partnerships.

Epstein, J. L., & Dauber, S. L. (1991). School programs and teacher practices of parent involvement in inner-city elementary and middle schools. *Elementary School Journal, 91,* 289-303.

Epstein, J. L., & Dauber, S. L. (1995). Effects on students of an interdisciplinary program linking social studies, art, and family volunteers in the middle grades. *Journal of Early Adolescence, 15,* 237-266.

Epstein, J. L., Herrick, S. C., & Coates, L. (1996). Effects of summer home learning packets on student achievement in language arts in the middle grades. *School Effectiveness and School Improvement, 7*(3), 93-120.

Epstein, J. L., & Lee, S. (1995). National patterns of school and family connections in the middle grades. In B. A. Ryan, G. R. Adams, T. P. Gullotta, R. P. Weissberg, & R. L. Hampton (Eds.), *The family-school connection: Theory, research and practice* (pp. 108-154). Thousand Oaks, CA: Sage.

Epstein, J. L., & Salinas, K. C. (1993). *School and family partnerships: Surveys and summaries.* Baltimore: Johns Hopkins University, Center on School, Family, and Community Partnerships.

Epstein, J. L., & Sanders, M. G. (2000). School, family, and community connections: New directions for social research. In M. Hallinan (Ed.), *Handbook of sociology of education* (pp. 285-306). New York: Plenum Press.

Epstein, J. L., & Sanders, M. G. (2002). Family, school, and community partnerships. In M. Bornstein (Ed.), *Handbook of parenting* (2nd ed.). Mahwah, NJ: Lawrence Erlbaum.

Fagnano, C. L., & Werber, B. Z. (1994). *School, family, and community interaction: A view from the firing lines.* Boulder, CO: Westview Press.

Fruchter, N., Galletta, A., & White, J. L. (1992). *New directions in parent involvement.* Washington, DC: Academy for Educational Development.

Henderson, A. T., & Berla, N. (1994). *A new generation of evidence: The family is critical to student achievement.* Washington, DC: National Committee for Citizens in Education.

Hinz, L., Clarke, J., & Nathan, J. (1992). *A survey of parent involvement course offerings in Minnesota's undergraduate preparation programs.* Minneapolis: University of Minnesota, Humphrey Institute of Public Affairs, Center for School Change.

Johnson, V. R. (1994). *Parent centers in urban schools: Four case studies* (Center Report 23). Baltimore: Johns Hopkins University, Center on Families, Communities, Schools and Children's Learning.

Lareau, A. (1989). *Home advantage: Social class and parental intervention in elementary education.* Philadelphia: Falmer.

Lee, S. (1994). *Family-school connections and students' education: Continuity and change of family involvement from the middle grades to high school.* Unpublished doctoral dissertation, Johns Hopkins University.

Lewis, C. C., Schaps, E., & Watson, M. (1995). Beyond the pendulum: Creating challenging and caring schools. *Phi Delta Kappan, 76,* 547-554.

Lloyd, G. M. (1996). Research and practical application for school, family, and community partnerships. In A. Booth & J. F. Dunn (Eds.), *Family-school links: How do they affect educational outcomes?* (pp. 255-264). Mahwah, NJ: Lawrence Erlbaum.

Rioux, W., & Berla, N. (Eds.). (1993*). Innovations in parent and family involvement.* Princeton Junction, NJ: Eye on Education.

Ryan, B. A., Adams, G. R., Gullotta, T. P., Weissberg, R. P., & Hampton, R. L. (Eds.). (1995). *The family-school connection.* Thousand Oaks, CA: Sage.

Scott-Jones, D. (1995). Activities in the home that support school learning in the middle grades. In B. Rutherford (Ed.), *Creating family/school partnerships* (pp. 161-181). Columbus, OH: National Middle School Association.

Simon, B. S. (2001). Family involvement in high school: Predictors and effects. *NASSP Bulletin, 85*(627), 8-19.

Swap, S. M. (1993). *Developing home-school partnerships: From concepts to practice.* New York: Teachers College Press.

Viadero, D. (1994). Learning to care. *Education Week, 13,* 31-33.

Wisconsin Department of Public Instruction. (1994, August/September). *Sharesheet: The DPI family-community school partnership newsletter, 3,* 1-2.

1.2 Community Involvement in School Improvement: The Little Extra That Makes a Big Difference

Mavis G. Sanders

Rationale for School-Community Partnerships

Families and schools traditionally have been viewed as the institutions with the greatest effect on the development of children. Communities, however, have received increasing attention for their role in socializing youth and ensuring students' success in a variety of societal domains. Epstein's (1987, 1995) theory of overlapping spheres of influence, for example, identifies schools, families, and communities as major institutions that socialize and educate children. A central principle of the theory is that certain goals, such as student academic success, are of interest to each of these institutions and are best achieved through their cooperative action and support.

Similarly, Heath and McLaughlin (1987, p. 579) argued that community involvement is important because "the problems of educational achievement and academic success demand resources beyond the scope of the school and of most families." They identified changing family demographics, demands of the professional workplace, and growing diversity among students as some of the reasons that schools and families alone cannot provide sufficient resources to ensure that all children receive the experiences and support needed to succeed in the larger society.

When describing the importance of community involvement in educational reform, Shore (1994) focused on the mounting responsibilities placed on schools by a nation whose student population is increasingly placed "at risk." She stated, "Too many schools and school systems are failing to carry out their basic educational mission. Many of them—in urban and rural settings—are overwhelmed by the social and emotional needs of children who are growing up in poverty" (p. 2). She contended that schools need additional resources to successfully educate all students and that these resources, both human and material, are housed in students' communities.

Other authors also have emphasized the importance of schools, families, and communities working together to promote students' success. Toffler and Toffler (1995) asserted that school-family-community collaborations are one way to provide a caring component to today's often large, assembly-line schools. Benson (1997), Crowson and Boyd (1993), Dryfoos (1998), and others have suggested that schools must reach out into the community in an attempt to strengthen the social capital available to children. Similarly, Waddock (1995) agreed that schools alone cannot provide children and youth with the resources they need to be competent citizens in the 21st century. She explained that good schools are part of a total system of interactive forces, individuals, institutions, goals, and expectations that are linked together inextricably.

School-community partnerships, then, can be defined as the connections between schools and community individuals, organizations, and businesses that are forged to directly or indirectly promote students' social, emotional, physical, and intellectual development (Epstein, 1995). Within this definition of school-community partnerships, community is not constrained by the geographic boundaries of neighborhoods, but refers more to the "social interactions that can occur within or transcend local boundaries" (Nettles, 1991b, p. 380).

Forms of School-Community Partnerships

School-community partnerships can take a variety of forms, as shown in Table 1.2.1. The most common linkages are partnerships with businesses, which can differ significantly in focus, scope, and content. Other school-community linkages involve universities and educational institutions, government and military agencies, health care organizations, faith-based organizations, national service and volunteer organizations, senior citizen organizations, cultural and recreational institutions, other community-based organizations, and community volunteers that can provide resources and social support to youth and schools.

Partnership activities also may have multiple focuses. Activities may be student-, family-, school-, or community-centered, as shown in Table 1.2.2. Student-centered activities include those that provide direct services or goods to students, for example, mentoring and tutoring programs, contextual learning, and job-shadowing opportunities, as well as the provision of awards, incentives, and scholarships to students. Family-centered activities are those that have parents or entire families as their primary focus. This category includes activities such as parenting workshops, GED and other adult education classes, parent-family incentives and awards, family counseling, and family fun and learning nights. School-centered activities are those that benefit the school as a whole, such as beautification projects or the donation of school equipment and materials, or activities that benefit the faculty, such as staff development and classroom assistance. Community-centered activities have as their primary focus the community and its citizens, for example, charitable outreach, art and science exhibits, and community revitalization and beautification projects (Sanders, 2001).

TABLE 1.2.1   Examples of Community Partners

Businesses/Corporations: Local businesses, national corporations, and franchises

Universities and Educational Institutions: Colleges and universities, high schools, and other educational institutions

Health Care Organizations: Hospitals, health care centers, mental health facilities, health departments, health foundations, and associations

Government and Military Agencies: Fire departments, police departments, chambers of commerce, city councils, and other local and state government agencies and departments

National Service and Volunteer Organizations: Rotary Club, Lions Club, Kiwanis Club, VISTA, Concerned Black Men, Inc., Shriners, Boy Scouts, Girl Scouts, YMCA, United Way, Americorp, Urban League

Faith-Based Organizations: Churches, mosques, synagogues, other religious organizations, and charities

Senior Citizens Organizations: Nursing homes and senior volunteer and service organizations

Cultural and Recreational Institutions: Zoos, museums, libraries, and recreational centers

Other Community Organizations: Fraternities, sororities, foundations, neighborhood associations, and political, alumni, and local service organizations

Community Individuals: Individual volunteers from the surrounding school community

TABLE 1.2.2   Focuses of Partnership Activities and Examples of School-Community Partnership Activities

Student Centered	*Family Centered*	*School Centered*	*Community Centered*
Student awards, student incentives, scholarships, student trips, tutors, mentors, job shadowing, and other services and products for students	Parent workshops, family fun-nights, GED and other adult education classes, parent incentives and rewards, counseling, and other forms of assistance to parents	Equipment and materials, beautification and repair, teacher incentives and awards, funds for school events and programs, office and classroom assistance, and other school improvements	Community beautification, student exhibits and performances, charity, and other outreach

Role of Community Involvement in Partnership Programs

Community involvement activities are an important part of a school's comprehensive partnership program, which includes six major types of involvement: (1) parenting, (2) communicating, (3) volunteering, (4) learning at home, (5) decision making, and (6) collaborating with the community (Epstein, 1995).

Some community activities can support or strengthen the other types of involvement. For example, community partners might provide meeting space for parenting workshops (Type 1), interpreters for school meetings with families (Type 2), volunteer tutors (Type 3), information on books that families can read to and with their children at home (Type 4), and meals to increase parents' attendance at school meetings (Type 5).

Community collaborations also can be developed to enhance schools' curricula, identify and disseminate information about community resources, and further schools' community outreach (Type 6). One school in the National Network of Partnership Schools (NNPS), for example, worked with its state department of environmental protection to help science faculty integrate local resources and environmental concerns into the science curriculum. Another NNPS school developed a community resource handbook for its families. Other schools partnered with a local library to hold a community art exhibit of students' work and with local hospitals, dentists, nurses, and dieticians to develop a low-cost health care site to provide preventive and maintenance health care for students, families, and community members. These and other reported activities show how important community partnerships can be for students, schools, families, and communities (Sanders, 2001).

Outcomes of School-Community Partnerships

Community partnership activities can lead to measurable outcomes for students and schools. Mentoring programs have been found to have significant and positive effects on students' grades, school attendance, and exposure to career opportunities (McPartland & Nettles, 1991; Yonezawa, Thornton, & Stringfield, 1998). School-community collaborations focused on academic subjects have been shown to enhance students' attitudes toward these subjects, as well as the attitudes of teachers and parents (Beyerbach, Weber, Swift, & Gooding, 1996). Nettles (1991a) also reported positive effects of school-community collaborations with an instructional component on students' grades, attendance, and school persistence.

Documented benefits of school-linked service integration initiatives include behavioral and academic gains for students who receive intensive services (Newman, 1995; Wagner, 1995). Research also has shown improved student attendance, immunization rates, and student conduct at schools providing coordinated services (Amato, 1996). Finally, partnerships with businesses and other community organizations have provided schools with needed equipment, materials, and technical assistance and support for student instruction (Longoria, 1998; Mickelson, 1999; Sanders & Harvey, in press). School-community partnerships, then, are an important element in schools' programs of improvement and reform and an important part of a comprehensive program of school, family, and community partnerships.

Factors That Promote Community Involvement

Case study research identified four factors that support a school's ability to develop and maintain meaningful community partnerships (Sanders & Harvey, in press). These factors are (a) high commitment to learning, (b) principal support for community involvement, (c) a welcoming school climate, and (d) two-way communication with potential community partners about their level and kind of involvement.

High Commitment to Learning

Interviews with community partners representing faith-based organizations, nonprofit foundations, health care organizations, businesses, educational institutions, and senior citizen organizations revealed a common desire to support students' academic achievement. Community partners wanted to be a part of an effective school that was visibly focused on students' learning and to engage in activities that had demonstrable effects on student outcomes. Community partners identified schools that were well organized, student centered, family friendly, and academically rigorous as the most desirable partners for collaboration.

Principal Support for Community Involvement

Community partners also stated that a principal's support for community involvement was critical for successful collaboration. A school principal who not only allowed, but also created opportunities for community involvement was viewed as a necessary if not sufficient requirement for effective collaboration. Indeed, principal support largely explained the community partners' continued engagement in the case school. One community partner stated, "I don't want to pinpoint any schools, but I've gone into some and have been totally turned off by the administration. If I'm turned off, what's the interest in helping you . . . ?"

A Welcoming School Climate

Similarly, community partners expressed the importance of a school that is receptive to and appreciative of community involvement. Community partners stated that being greeted warmly at the school by staff, faculty, and students strengthened their commitment to the partnership and increased the enjoyment of their involvement. Although most community partners in the study agreed that formal acknowledgment was not necessary, they valued the school's expressions of gratitude. Several of the community partners reported that they received thank-you letters and notes from students, were thanked for their assistance over the intercom system, were stopped on the street by students and their parents and thanked for their service, were acknowledged in the school newsletter, and received certificates of appreciation at the school's annual awards ceremony.

Two-Way Communication

Community partners and school administrators interviewed for the case study also emphasized the importance of honest, two-way communication between schools and potential community partners so that each party is fully aware of the intent and expectations of the other. The school principal stated that initial honest and up-front conversations prevented both parties from "wasting each other's time." She used a simple measure to determine if a community partnership was "right" for the school. Her measure was whether the partnership would be positive for students.

These four factors that promote community partnerships were linked to the principal's actions as school leader. She created fertile ground in which school-community partnerships flourished by maintaining a school environment where teachers and parents focus on students' academic success, modeling for faculty and staff a genuine openness to community involvement and by establishing an expectation for partnerships, actively networking with individuals in the community to inform them of her school's needs and goals, and supporting others in developing leadership in the area of family and community involvement.

Factors That Improve School-Community Partnerships

In theory, then, community involvement in schools is an opportunity for a more democratic and participatory approach to school functioning that can revitalize communities, enhance students' achievement and well-being, assist families, and build stronger schools. In reality, however, community involvement is too often a reminder of the difficulty of implementing inclusive, collaborative strategies for school improvement. Evaluative studies of different forms of school-community collaboration underscore key challenges that, if addressed, may help to move the reality of community involvement in schools closer to theory (Sanders, 2002).

Professional Preparation

One issue that is highlighted in the community involvement literature is the importance of professional preparation for partnerships. Such preparation is especially important for educators at the state, district, and school levels, who arguably should be in the forefront of educational improvement. Ideally, professional preparation for collaboration would begin during the preservice stage of teacher and administrator training. It would include structured opportunities for future educators to develop the skills and capacity to work collaboratively with other educators and service providers and with adults in students' families and communities. It would be a theme present throughout educators' professional training so that they enter schools, classrooms, offices, and departments of education with a clear understanding of the rewards and benefits of collaboration and a working knowledge of strategies for successful collaboration. Collaboration also would be an ongoing theme in the inservice professional development of educators so that the day-to-day reality of teaching and managing schools and district and state departments and offices would not cloud educators' view of themselves as partners in the development of children and youth.

Schools that have successfully built a sense of community within their walls—that is, schools that are collaborative, communicative, and inclusive—appear to have the greatest success in developing strong connections with the community outside their walls (Crowson & Boyd, 1993; Merz & Furman, 1997; Sanders & Harvey, in press). This is no coincidence. When the capacity to collaborate becomes a part of educators' professional identity and knowledge base, community involvement becomes "business as usual" (Stroble & Luka, 1999). In complex school-community collaborations, challenges around turf, funding, roles, and responsibilities will surely arise (Crowson & Boyd, 1993; Epstein, 1995; Jehl & Kirst, 1992; Mawhinney, 1994). However, educators who have been prepared to collaborate will have the resources and skills to minimize and resolve these challenges (Epstein, 2001; Welch, 1998).

Partnership Selection

Professional development also will assist educators in selecting appropriate community partners and partnership opportunities. There are many community partners and opportunities available to schools. School districts and state departments of education also have choices of community partnership opportunities. The selection of partners should be based on shared goals and a common commitment to the basic tenets of successful collaboration—open communication, joint decision making, and respect for all stakeholders. Therefore, before a partnership begins, representatives from the partnering groups or organizations should meet to discuss the goals of the potential connection and how their work together will be organized.

When selecting community partners and partnership opportunities, educators also should consider the intensity and duration of collaborations. Community involvement in schools can range from very simple, short-term connections to very complex, long-term arrangements. For example, a school, a local health care agency, and community leaders may partner to hold a community health fair on the school grounds. This short-term partnership would require only basic collaborative skills, knowledge, and expertise. These same partners, however, may collaborate to open a school-based preventative health care clinic for students, families, and community members. This complex, long-term partnership would require more planning time to address issues related to funding, operational hours, program development and services, building security and maintenance, and other responsibilities and issues. Consequently, it also would require more sophisticated organizational processes and structures to ensure its successful implementation.

A school with little experience in community collaboration might elect to engage in some simple connections before venturing into more complex collaborations such as school-linked service integration initiatives. This purposeful, measured approach to the selection of community partners and community partnership opportunities would provide educators the necessary time to hone their collaborative skills, identify partnerships that are most important for achieving their schools' goals, and reflect on factors that influence their ability to successfully work with community partners.

Partnership Reflection and Evaluation

Finally, the literature on community involvement in schools highlights the importance of reflection and evaluation. Because school-community collaboration is a process and not an event, it is important that partners take the time to reflect on and evaluate the quality of their interactions and the implementation of their partnership activities. This exercise will assist in the refinement of collaborative efforts and the enhancement of collaborative skills. To engage in reflective action, partners need time to meet. Time is an increasingly rare commodity, especially among professional educators in schools. The challenge of finding time for professional educators to engage fully in collaborative efforts with the community is perhaps greatest in resource-poor urban schools that stand to benefit most from well-planned community partnerships.

This challenge has been successfully met in many schools (Sanders, 2001). One factor that is crucial to schools' planning and evaluation of partnerships is principal leadership. Many studies of community involvement cite the importance of effective principal leadership for successful school-community collaboration. An effective school leader is one who supports the faculty and staff in developing their professional skills as collaborators. This requires that the principal models such behavior, rewards such behavior, and provides teachers with the necessary time to plan partnerships and engage in collaborative action and evaluation (Sanders & Harvey, in press).

Research and practice clearly show that community involvement in schools can benefit students, schools, families, and communities. The success of such involvement requires that partners have collaborative skills, common goals, structures for inclusive decision making, and time for reflection and evaluation. For all its promise, community involvement is not a panacea for the ills of many of today's schools. It cannot replace sound educational policies, adequate funding, excellent teaching, and effective partnerships with families. It can, however, enhance the effect that these elements have on schools and on students. When properly executed, community involvement in schools can be the little extra that makes the big difference.

References

Amato, C. (1996). Freedom Elementary School and its community: An approach to school-linked service integration. *Remedial and Special Education, 17*(5), 303-309.

Benson, P. (1997). *All kids are our kids: What communities must do to raise caring and responsible children and adolescents.* San Francisco: Jossey-Bass.

Beyerbach, B. A., Weber, S., Swift, J. N., & Gooding, C. T. (1996). A school/business/university partnership for professional development. *School Community Journal, 6*(1), 101-112.

Crowson, R. L., & Boyd, W. (1993). Coordinated services for children: Designing arks for storms and seas unknown. *American Journal of Education, 101*, 140-179.

Dryfoos, J. (1998). The rise of the full-service community school. *High School Magazine, 6*(2), 38-42.

Epstein, J. L. (1987). Toward a theory of family-school connections: Teacher practices and parent involvement. In K. Hurrelmann, F. Kaufmann, & F. Losel (Eds.), *Social intervention: Potential and constraints* (pp. 121-136). New York: DeGruyter.

Epstein, J. L. (1995). School/family/community partnerships: Caring for the children we share. *Phi Delta Kappan, 76*(9), 701-712.

Epstein, J. L. (2001). *School, family, and community partnerships: Preparing educators and improving schools.* Boulder, CO: Westview Press.

Heath, S. B., & McLaughlin, M. W. (1987, April). A child resource policy: Moving beyond dependence on school and family. *Phi Delta Kappan, 68*, 576-580.

Jehl, J., & Kirst, M. (1992). Getting ready to provide school-linked services: What schools must do. *Future of Children, 2*, 95-106.

Longoria, T. Jr., (1998). School politics in Houston: The impact of business involvement. In C. Stone (Ed.), *Changing urban education* (pp. 184-198). Lawrence, KS: University Press of Kansas.

Mawhinney, H. B. (1994). The policy and practice of community enrichment of schools. *Proceedings of the Education and Community Conference, Department of Educational Administration.* Toronto: Ontario Institute for Studies in Educational Administration.

McPartland, J. M., & Nettles, S. M. (1991). Using community adults as advocates or mentors for at-risk middle school students: A two-year evaluation of project RAISE. *American Journal of Education, 99,* 568-586.

Merz, C., & Furman, G. (1997). *Community and schools: Promise and paradox.* New York: Teachers College Press.

Mickelson, R. (1999). International Business Machinations: A case study of corporate involvement in local educational reform. *Teachers College Record, 100*(3), 476-512.

Nettles, S. M. (1991a). Community contributions to school outcomes of African-American students. *Education and Urban Society, 24*(1), 132-147.

Nettles, S. M. (1991b). Community involvement and disadvantaged students: A review. *Review of Educational Research, 61*(3), 379-406.

Newman, L. (1995, April). *School-agency-community partnerships: What is the early impact on students school performance?* Paper presented at the annual meeting of the American Educational Research Association, San Francisco, CA.

Sanders, M. G. (2001). The role of "community" in comprehensive school, family, and community partnership programs. *The Elementary School Journal, 102*(1), 19-34.

Sanders, M. G. (2002). *Community involvement in schools: Factors influencing its viability as a school reform strategy* (working paper). Baltimore: Johns Hopkins University, Center for Research on the Education of Students Placed at Risk.

Sanders, M. G., & Harvey, A. (in press). Beyond the school walls: A case study of principal leadership for school-community collaboration. *Teachers College Record.*

Shore, R. (1994). *Moving the ladder: Toward a new community vision.* Aspen, CO: Aspen Institute.

Stroble, B., & Luka, H. (1999). It's my life, now: The impact of professional development school partnerships on university and school administrators. *Peabody Journal of Education, 74*(3-4), 123-135.

Toffler, A., & Toffler, H. (1995). Getting set for the coming millennium. *Futurist, 29*(2), 10-15.

Waddock, S. A. (1995). *Not by schools alone: Sharing responsibility for America's education reform.* Westport, CT: Praeger.

Wagner, M. (1995). What is the evidence of effectiveness of school-linked services? *The Evaluation Exchange: Emerging Strategies in Evaluating Child and Family Services, 1*(2).

Welch, M. (1998). Collaboration: Staying on the bandwagon. *Journal of Teacher Education, 49*(1), 5 26-37.

Yonezawa, S., Thornton, T., & Stringfield, S. (1998). *Dunbar-Hopkins Health Partnership Phase II evaluation: Preliminary report—year one.* Baltimore: Center for Social Organization of Schools.

Using the Framework in Practice

Stories From the Field

This chapter describes how the framework of six types of family and community involvement and the action team approach are implemented in practice. The reports are from leaders whose schools, districts, and states developed partnership programs as members of the National Network of Partnership Schools at Johns Hopkins University. Their ideas and experiences document the importance of planning, evaluating, and continually improving activities to sustain successful partnership programs.

School Stories: Examples of the Six Types of Involvement

Twelve examples from elementary, middle, and high schools describe activities that Action Teams for Partnerships (ATPs) might select or adapt for their schools' programs of school, family, and community partnerships. The examples include Type 1-Parenting activities to help elementary school parents obtain immunizations for children and to create parent-to-parent support groups in high school; Type 2-Communicating activities to increase two-way communications in elementary school and to target communications that increase attendance in high school; Type 3-Volunteering activities to organize volunteers to increase safety in middle schools and to create a directory of volunteers' talents and interests in middle and high schools; Type 4-Learning at Home activities to help parents read stories aloud and encourage young children's reading and to design homework that enables students to involve their family in science in the middle grades; Type 5-Decision Making activities to engage more families in Elementary School Improvement Team meetings and to organize officers for an Action Team for Partnerships; and Type 6-Collaborating With the Community activities to create productive connections between an elementary school and senior citizens and to help middle school students and families benefit from community learning opportunities.

District Stories: Leadership Activities That Help Schools Develop Programs of Partnership

Five examples from school districts in Baltimore, Maryland; Howard County, Maryland; Minneapolis, Minnesota; Los Angeles, California; and Grand Blanc, Michigan illustrate activities that other districts might use or adapt to organize leadership on school, family, and community partnerships. The examples represent two essential district leadership responsibilities: (1) implementing districtwide partnership activities and (2) facilitating the work of individual schools' teams to develop their partnership programs.

One role for district leaders of school, family, and community partnerships is to develop and conduct activities at the district level that may help the district and all schools. The examples are for district leaders for partnerships to coordinate interdepartmental communications among all district departments and programs that conduct family and community involvement activities, to design new approaches that all schools in the district can use to help parents support children's reading, and to produce a resource book of community services for use districtwide.

Another essential district responsibility is to facilitate and support the work of school-based ATPs and to help each school plan and implement its own program of family and community involvement. The examples are for district facilitators to motivate and guide the chairs of schools' ATPs and to develop a notebook of information that guides the work of each school's ATP so that plans for partnerships are well designed and implemented.

State Stories: Policies and Actions That Support Districts and Schools With Programs of Partnership

Three examples illustrate the actions by leaders in state departments of education that are working to improve programs of school, family, and community partnerships statewide. The reports from Ohio, Wisconsin, and Connecticut include ways for state leaders to influence and encourage districts and schools to build strong partnerships and ways for education leaders to connect with other state organizations and associations to strengthen leadership on partnerships. The examples describe state conferences for school teams to attend to learn how to develop their partnership programs, state grants to support partnership activities, and connections with the United Way to increase information and outreach on partnerships.

These are just a few of hundreds of activities and approaches that you may adopt or adapt in your schools, districts, and states. Many other examples are in the collections of *Promising Partnership Practices* (Salinas & Jansorn, 2001). See these collections on the National Network of Partnership Schools website at www.partnershipschools.org in the section "In the Spotlight."

Resource

Salinas, K. C., & Jansorn, N. (2001). *Promising partnership practices—2001.* Baltimore: Johns Hopkins University, Center on School, Family, and Community Partnerships.

SCHOOL STORIES
TYPE 1-PARENTING

Type 1-Parenting activities increase families' understanding of their children's growth and development. These activities may assist parents with information on children's health, safety, nutrition, other topics of child and adolescent development, and home conditions that support students' education at each grade level. Type 1 activities also increase schools' understanding of families with strategies that promote exchanges of information between educators, parents, and other caregivers about their concerns and goals for children.

Parents are responsible for children's health, including immunizations required by schools. Schools can work with families and the community to make it easier for all students to meet state and district health requirements. At Woodbury Elementary School in Shaker Heights, Ohio, educators, parents, and the city health department worked together to offer low-cost MMR (measles, mumps, and rubella) shots to students who were about to enter middle school.

A different kind of Type 1-Parenting activity is the parent support group organized by Shaker Heights High School in Shaker Heights, Ohio. Parents need good information from educators and from other parents in order to continue to influence their teens in positive ways. In this case, parents of ninth graders formed a discussion group to address important topics for parents of high school students.

These two examples are among hundreds of Type 1-Parenting activities that elementary and secondary schools may select or adapt for their programs of school, family, and community partnerships. Practices should be selected to meet the needs and interests of the families and students in each school and to help reach school improvement goals. As the Type 1 examples show, Action Teams for Partnerships must review the quality of implemented activities in order to decide how to improve them the next time they are conducted.

TYPE 1-PARENTING ACTIVITY

Providing Immunizations for Students Advancing to Middle School

Woodbury Elementary School
Shaker Heights, Ohio

One of the goals for our partnership program was to establish better communication among parents, the school system, and the community. As we brainstormed ways to assist families and include the community, members of the Action Team for Partnerships suggested that we look into providing immunization shots for sixth graders. The state of Ohio requires that all students entering seventh grade show proof of having received two MMR immunizations, one in infancy and one before starting middle school. We thought we might be able to offer the shots—possibly at a discount—at Woodbury Elementary School's open house.

The action team called the city health department and received authorization for Woodbury Elementary to offer MMR immunizations to rising seventh graders for the low cost of $5.00 per shot. On the night of the open house, we used the school nurse's office to administer the MMR shots. The school nurse assisted the Shaker Heights director of nursing in giving 33 shots in a two-hour period. Parents stayed with their children during the procedure. Volunteers assisted in organizing the crowd and gave juice to each child after he or she received the MMR immunization. Students who used Woodbury's service for their second MMR shot were entered into a drawing for a new bicycle, courtesy of the Shaker Heights Health Department.

The evening was very successful and benefited many of Woodbury's families. The service will be provided again, with the additional assistance of another nurse practitioner and more volunteers.

TYPE 1-PARENTING ACTIVITY

Support Group for Ninth Graders' Parents

Shaker Heights High School
Shaker Heights, Ohio

The Action Team for Partnerships at Shaker Heights High School developed a support group for ninth graders' parents to reach four main goals:

- To reconnect parents to one another

- To facilitate dialogue among parents

- To identify school and family concerns to the group and explore various options for addressing these issues

- To ease parental anxiety about their teens' development in high school

We invited freshmen students' parents to join a discussion group and asked for a four-week commitment to give the group time to bond. We chose an 8:00 p.m. meeting time to accommodate family schedules. The group met in the high school library. A teacher and two community members volunteered to act as group facilitators, and group members took turns bringing refreshments.

During the first session, the group established rules for discussion, such as maintaining group confidentiality and respecting others' right to participate. Members also identified the topics that they wanted to discuss, including balancing a teen's privacy with the parent's "right to know," opening dialogue when a teen refuses to share ideas, and handling anxiety when a teen is making bad choices.

At the beginning of each session, the group added other parenting concerns to the list and then chose which issues to discuss that evening. At first, we worried that people would be afraid to share their real parenting problems and solutions. Though they shared more as the meetings progressed, the group members said they felt comfortable from the outset and did not hesitate to express themselves.

All participants filled out an evaluation form. Most members believed that the group met its four goals. Most parents liked the 8:00 p.m. start time and meeting once a week for a set period. Most said they chose to return each week because they enjoyed the group, it offered a "release," they wanted to hear more about the topics, they wanted to discuss with the group issues that had occurred during the week with their own teens, and they liked meeting other freshman parents.

The ATP has planned several discussion groups for the next school year, and we may introduce a session to be held during the day. Our two biggest challenges are to increase the diversity of participants and to improve our communication about the groups. We are trying to explore avenues for attracting more males and more diverse families into the groups. We plan to increase and vary our advertising for the support group to reach all parents. We know that word-of-mouth publicity from group members is important, but takes time to spread and may not reach all interested parents.

SCHOOL STORIES
TYPE 2-COMMUNICATING

Type 2-Communicating activities include school-to-home and home-to-school communications about school and classroom programs and children's progress. Two-way communications by teachers and families increase understanding and cooperation between school and home. Thoughtful two-way communications also show students that their teachers and parents are working together to help students succeed in school.

Type 2 activities can be designed to increase two-way communications including parent-teacher conferences, phone calls, homework hotlines, newsletters with reaction sheets, report card pickups, e-mail, websites, and other creative strategies. Two-way communications encourage families to provide reactions, ideas, and preferences and to ask questions about school programs and children's progress.

One example of an effective Type 2 activity is a specially designed notepad at Fayetteville Elementary School in Fayetteville, New York. This simple but effective idea provides parents and teachers with a bright, easily identifiable pad of paper to encourage two-way communications.

An example from South St. Paul High School in South St. Paul, Minnesota, illustrates a comprehensive communications campaign to improve student attendance. Many different kinds of communications were designed and conducted with students, parents, teachers, and the community to get everyone's help in increasing high school students' attendance.

Type 2 activities can be designed for different purposes, such as making two-way communications easier and targeting communications to help reach specific goals for student success. Schools with students whose families do not speak or read English well must solve the challenge of adapting these and other Type 2 activities to communicate effectively with all students' families.

TYPE 2-COMMUNICATING ACTIVITY

Notepads for Two-Way Communications Between School and Home

Fayetteville Elementary School
Fayetteville, New York

The Fayetteville Elementary Site-Based Team (the school's Action Team for Partnerships) worked to develop more effective two-way communication between parents and teachers. Although the school's teachers and administrators sent plenty of notices and other information home to parents, we lacked a method for parents to communicate easily and consistently back to school. Daily, teachers received many kinds of notes from parents on all kinds of paper. There was no easy way for teachers to distinguish among notes about children's absences from questions about students' academic achievement or personal information about things going on in the children's lives.

The team decided to create an attractive notepad that would be given to all parents and teachers to encourage their communications. The design included a logo at the top of the page to show two-way communications between school and home. The bound notepad was a bright color making it easy to identify by both parents and teachers as it traveled back and forth. Each page included a box to check to alert the parent or teacher if the information in the note had been shared with the child. Once the design was chosen and reviewed by the staff, the school district's copying center produced the notepads.

The principal sent a letter home to introduce the use of the notepads. The school distributed the notepads to all parents after the first marking period along with a letter explaining the many different ways that parents and teachers might use them. Teachers also handed out the pads at parent-teacher conferences and described different kinds of communications that might strengthen connections of parents and teachers after the conference. In the future, we plan to distribute the notepads in a school packet created by the Home School Association at the beginning of the year, along with details about their use.

This two-way form of communication produced results almost immediately. One teacher said, "It makes it so easy for me to go through my notes quickly in the morning and determine which notes need to go to the office and which notes I need to set aside and take time to read and answer." One parent noted, "It's very easy to see when I go through my child's papers when there's a note from the teacher. I know this is something I need to read." Teachers and parents think the notepads provide an effective method for encouraging two-way communications from school to home and from home to school.

TYPE 2-COMMUNICATING ACTIVITY

Attendance Campaign:
"Be Cool . . . Pack the School!"

South St. Paul High School
South St. Paul, Minnesota

The purpose of our attendance campaign was to increase student attendance by educating students, parents, teachers, and the community about attendance issues. The Action Team for Partnerships developed the campaign to support South St. Paul High School's goal to improve student attendance. We also wanted to address results from a task force report that indicated parents did not understand attendance procedures. The campaign incorporated activities to educate and inform parents, students, teachers, and the community about the importance of good attendance and the school's attendance policies. Another goal was to recognize excellence and improvement in student attendance.

We mailed a packet to parents with a flyer that explained the importance of students attending school every day. The packet included simple steps for parents to follow when students are absent and when they return to school, an attendance magnet with a 24-hour call-in number, and easy-reference cards with phone numbers for parents to call when students are absent. The principal's monthly newsletter contained an attendance fact, and the student-parent handbook attendance page was revised to explain simple steps to follow when students are absent.

Students in the desktop publishing class created the campaign slogan, "Be Cool . . . Pack the School!" This was particularly appropriate because our athletic team is called the South St. Paul Packers. The students also designed posters to display throughout the school and classrooms. Morning announcements included an attendance fact or motivational quotation. Students received awards for perfect attendance. The student newspaper included an article about attendance.

Teachers read reminders about attendance in the weekly in-house staff memo. The high school held an instructional focus day on attendance. All teachers attended a half-hour presentation that included comments from teachers who have worked in the attendance office. To recognize effort and progress, teachers sent "Good News Notes" to parents when students had perfect or improved attendance.

The principal wrote an article about the importance of school attendance for the local newspaper. School attendance reminders and results were posted on the high school website. Local businesses received signs for posting that said, "If you're skipping school, skip this place."

Our district's printing and production departments designed and produced the parent flyer, magnet, and business card. Local businesses donated student rewards for perfect attendance.

As a result of the campaign, student attendance rates increased. We gave awards to 485 students for perfect attendance in the first term of the year. Parents and teachers gave positive feedback about the information, materials, and activities. We took a comprehensive approach to attendance that included students, families, teachers, district-level support, and community partners. Although attention to attendance is an ongoing focus, our attendance campaign has been most successful.

SCHOOL STORIES
TYPE 3-VOLUNTEERING

Type 3-Volunteering activities enable families to share their time and talents to support the school, teachers, and students. Volunteers may conduct activities at school, in classrooms, at home, or in the community. Family volunteers may assist individual teachers or help in the library, the family room, the computer room, the playground, the lunchroom, after-school programs, or other locations. Families also give their time to attend student performances, sports activities, assemblies, celebrations, and other events.

Various strategies may be used to recruit and train volunteers and to match their time and talents to the needs of teachers, students, and administrators. Schools also must decide how to schedule opportunities so that all families can volunteer and attend some events, even if they work during the school day.

Washington Junior High School in Naperville, Illinois, organized Washington Greeters, who help the school maintain a safe school environment. The volunteers welcome incoming visitors and deter anyone from entering the building who does not belong. Other schools may organize parent, grandparent, and neighborhood patrols to help students get to and from school safely each day. Ensuring a safe school is an important goal that can be assisted by well-organized volunteers.

The Williamston Middle and High Schools in Williamston, Michigan, designed the *Parent Resource Directory* to increase the number of parents who volunteer. The Action Team for Partnerships collects and organizes information on volunteers' talents, interests, and available time. Each school uses its directory to identify willing volunteers for many kinds of activities and events throughout the school year.

Parent volunteers who serve as assistants and contributors to school and classroom programs and as audiences at school activities and events help strengthen school programs. Their presence tells students, faculty, and the community that parents care about the quality of the school and the success of all students. By organizing and training volunteers to assist in many ways and in many locations, educators convey that parents and others are welcome and that their time and talents are valued.

TYPE 3-VOLUNTEERING ACTIVITY

Washington Greeters Contribute to a Safer School

Washington Junior High School
Naperville, Illinois

The Parent Involvement Team of Washington Junior High School met to talk about the violence that had occurred in schools around the United States. The discussion led to the idea of the Washington Greeters, a school safety initiative. The program created a friendly way to welcome visitors who enter the school and deter anyone from entering the building that did not belong there.

A core group of volunteers met several times over the summer to plan how the program would run for the upcoming school year. We put together a short manual that contained important information for the Greeters. This information included a map of the school, emergency procedures, and sample daily announcements and school events. We also communicated at length with the principal and staff in the main office so that procedures established for the Greeters blended well with what was already happening in the school.

Communicating the new program to parents, staff, and students was the next big step for the coordinators of the program. Parents heard about the Washington Greeters several times in August and September at school meetings and read about the program in the parent newsletter. Interested parents could volunteer a morning or afternoon to greet visitors who came to the school. Staff and students learned about the program when they returned to school.

Custodians were critical when the program started because they wanted to be available to adjust some procedures such as determining which school doors to lock and when. Most procedural adjustments were made during the first few weeks of the school year.

The Washington Greeters program has been a positive experience for the school community. More parents volunteered, the staff interacted with parents more often, and visitors to Washington Junior High School received a warm welcome and assistance in a safe school environment.

TYPE 3-VOLUNTEERING ACTIVITY

Parent Resource Directory to Organize Volunteers

Williamston Middle School and Williamston High School
Williamston, Michigan

Our middle and high schools faced an interesting challenge: How could we tap into the tremendous resources that our schools' parents had to offer? To meet this challenge, we decided to create the *Parent Resource Directory*. Our goal was to more effectively recognize and use the talents, skills, and expertise of as many parents as possible.

We began by creating a short survey asking parents about the resources they might offer to our students. The survey included opportunities for volunteers at the school as well as at home. The survey also explained that by filling it out, parents were giving us information about their interests in ways they might help the school during the school year; they were not committing to volunteer.

We presented the survey at the fall open house to parents gathered in the audience. We expressed our appreciation for their talents and abilities, and stressed that the survey would allow us to set up a database for future volunteering opportunities. The principal asked parents to fill out the survey at the end of our presentation. At our high school, we gathered 230 surveys at two events (orientation and open house). At our middle school, we collected 125 surveys at our open house.

Once we had the completed surveys, we set up a simple database with all the information that was collected. From this database, we generated separate lists of the names and phone numbers of parents willing to help with staff appreciation, make phone calls to other parents, talk about a hobby or interest with a class, provide snacks, or help in a classroom, in the office, or in other ways. We bound the lists together in the *Parent Resource Directory*. Then, we distributed the directory to all staff members, showing them how to use it and explaining the need to call on as many different parents as possible.

Next, we recruited a parent at each grade level to serve as volunteer coordinator for that grade level. We explained to the coordinators how to use the *Parent Resource Directory* and again stressed the need to "spread the wealth" by involving as many different parents as possible. We also added lists of parents' addresses so that teachers and volunteer coordinators could easily find addresses when writing thank-you notes to parents who helped in different ways.

The front of the directory includes a Parent Volunteer Request Form. This reproducible form contains all the information a volunteer coordinator needs to line up parent help: a description of the activity, type of help needed, number of parents, date and times needed, other instructions, and contact person. The teacher or other staff person could simply photocopy the form, fill out the information, and turn it in to the appropriate volunteer coordinator. The coordinator, in turn, would go to the *Parent Resource Directory* to find parents who might be suited for or interested in helping with that particular project. After contacting the parents, the coordinator would then record on the bottom of the form the names and phone numbers of the volunteers who agreed to help and return the form to the teacher, administrator, or parent leader who made the request. The initiator would then have a list of parent helpers and their phone numbers in case of last-minute changes or instructions.

Since we produced and distributed the directory, we have seen an *explosion* of parent help and involvement in our secondary schools, where parents were formerly infrequently involved as volunteers. In the middle school, over 70 different parents chaperoned parties and field trips, helped with a sixth-grade cookout, helped in seventh-grade classrooms with special projects, came in to work with students on a regular basis, helped in the computer lab, graded papers at home, agreed to make phone calls to other parents, and came in to speak to students about their careers, their ethnic backgrounds, and their travels.

At the high school level, parents participated in a career fair and conducted mock interviews for 11th graders, served bagels and juice to students during exam week, helped evaluate student presentations in physics classes, organized a committee to host an all-night after-prom party, and helped evaluate book talks presented by 10th graders.

The faculty and staff regularly refer to the directory to find parent help for the middle and high schools. Parents often express their appreciation at getting the chance to participate in their teens' education in more meaningful ways. The *Parent Resource Directory* has been a useful tool and a great success!

SCHOOL STORIES
TYPE 4-LEARNING AT HOME

Type 4-Learning at Home activities provide information and ideas to families about the academic work that their children do in class, how to help their children with homework, and other curriculum-related activities and decisions. Type 4 activities increase teacher-parent communications and parent-child discussions at home through reviewing student work, practicing skills to pass a course, monitoring and discussing homework, choosing courses, and conducting other academic and curricular activities.

At Woodridge Primary School, in Cuyahoga Falls, Ohio, the Action Team for Partnerships implemented storytelling time for parents and students to enjoy reading together. The activity helps parents of kindergarten students learn effective read-aloud techniques and ways to strengthen students' language skills at home.

The second Type 4 example features Pikesville Middle School in Baltimore County, Maryland, for its work on Teachers Involve Parents in Schoolwork (TIPS) interactive science homework. Teachers developed interactive science homework assignments that enable students in Grades 6, 7, and 8 to share and discuss interesting science skills and information with their families. The assignments also help parents link their real-world experiences to students' work. Used on a regular schedule, interactive homework helps parents remain aware of what their children are learning in school. The school collaborated in a study which revealed positive effects of TIPS for students' science skills and family involvement.

In Type 4 activities, students are key participants because learning and homework are their responsibilities. There are many ways to involve families with students on curriculum-related assignments and decisions through high school. The two examples illustrate activities that encourage parent-student interactions about schoolwork in age-appropriate ways.

TYPE 4-LEARNING AT HOME ACTIVITY

Storytelling Time Promotes Reading at Home

Woodridge Primary School
Cuyahoga Falls, Ohio

Woodridge Primary School invited families to Storytelling Time to inform families about the importance of reading for students' school success. Teachers and a professional storyteller provided information and demonstrated techniques that parents could use to help encourage students to become more active and effective readers.

Children dressed in their pajamas, armed with blankets and teddy bears, enjoyed hot chocolate and cookies and listened to many stories with their families. Despite blizzard conditions, 130 people attended.

The professional storyteller demonstrated a variety of read-aloud techniques, including felt-board storytelling with manipulatives. Our kindergarten teacher talked about the benefits of reading and modeled for parents how to present a story to their children at home.

At a reading table, families browsed through a selection of books for kindergarten readers, including wordless books, picture books, easy readers, multicultural books, and homemade books. Families were offered additional information from reading journals and literacy materials to take home.

This activity

- Highlighted the importance of parents reading to their children

- Demonstrated a variety of ways for parents to tell stories and build children's language skills

- Encouraged intergenerational language activity time at home

- Stressed the importance of restricting television time

- Gave families an opportunity to socialize and meet other kindergarten families, building stronger school connections

- Provided additional materials on reading to help parents understand and conduct reading activities with children at home

TYPE 4-LEARNING AT HOME ACTIVITY

Involving Families in Science Homework

Pikesville Middle School
Baltimore, Maryland

A group of teachers and the principal at Pikesville Middle School wanted to increase students' science skills and promote family involvement in student learning. To reach these goals, we decided to use Teachers Involve Parents in Schoolwork (TIPS) interactive homework in selected science classes. TIPS assignments differ from standard homework in that (a) the activities include some sections for students to complete with a family partner; (b) the activities are assigned over several days to give students and families time to complete them; and (c) the activities include a section that asks family partners to evaluate the content, enjoyment, and usefulness of the activity and to provide comments or other feedback to the teacher.

A team of four science teachers (Grades 6 and 8) assigned TIPS activities weekly over the course of the school year. Teachers were paid to work in teams of two for three weeks during the summer to write, edit, and type assignments into a computer to prepare the assignments for use during the school year. Each grade level team of teachers wrote 40 activities linked to their curriculum and lesson plans. Units included topics such as astronomy, chemistry, genetics, geology, light and sound, machines, and oceanography.

To orient students and families to TIPS interactive homework, the teachers and principal wrote a letter to families and also described the process at Open House Night. The letter explained that TIPS science activities would be assigned on a Wednesday and due the following Tuesday. Teachers copied assignments on green paper so students could easily find the assignments.

Teachers worked with a researcher to evaluate the results of the TIPS assignments on students' attitudes and achievement and on parents' attitudes and involvement. The researcher and teachers found that students who more regularly involved family partners and who reported liking the assignments completed more homework activities. Both parents and students indicated that they found the TIPS assignments enjoyable and helpful in developing new skills. Two typical comments from parents were

> "They are a great way for us to work together and keep me informed of what is going on in school."

> "These experiments are more fun to do than when I was in school; I may change careers."

Teachers at the school continued to expand the program. A new team developed TIPS science activities for the seventh grade. Now the school has a full set of weekly TIPS science assignments for Grades 6, 7, and 8. Several teachers revised activities based on student and family feedback, others set higher standards for homework return rates, and several teachers expanded the use of TIPS to more classes.

See Chapter 8 for more information about TIPS.

SCHOOL STORIES
TYPE 5-DECISION MAKING

Type 5-Decision Making activities enable families to participate in decisions about school programs that affect their own and other children. Family representatives on School Councils, school improvement teams, and various committees and in PTA, PTO, or other parent organizations ensure that parents' voices are heard on important school decisions.

At Aniwa Elementary School in Aniwa, Wisconsin, educators and parents wanted to engage more families in the work and decisions of the School Effectiveness Team (SET)—the equivalent of a School Council or school improvement team. The school conducts some SET meetings in conjunction with PTO potluck dinner meetings, which tend to attract many parents. In this way, more parents can learn about and contribute to school discussions and decisions.

An Action Team for Partnerships (ATP) is the basic structure that ensures strong programs of school, family, and community partnerships. At Harbor View Elementary School in Baltimore, Maryland, the ATP found it helpful to delegate roles and responsibilities to team members. A chair and co-chair were chosen to lead the team. These leaders also make presentations about their program of partnerships to other school and community groups. The ATP also organized co-chairs for specific committees on the six types of involvement. Other schools may choose to organize ATP committees to focus partnerships on school improvement goals. The leaders and members of the ATP become the experts for the school in understanding and organizing activities in family and community involvement.

Some parents serve in leadership roles on School Councils, action teams, and other committees. However, all families need good information about school policies and opportunities to offer ideas and reactions to improve their schools. When parent representatives do their jobs well, they gather ideas from and return information to the families they represent. Well-implemented Type 5-Decision Making activities increase all parents' awareness of and input to the workings of the school and school system, and feelings of ownership of the school.

TYPE 5-DECISION MAKING ACTIVITY

Potluck Dinner Meetings
for the School Effectiveness Team and PTO

Aniwa Elementary School
Aniwa, Wisconsin

Aniwa Elementary School and all schools in the Antigo School District were required to establish a School Effectiveness Team to address school improvement goals and decisions. Each school's team was connected to a districtwide team with representative parents, teachers, administrators, and other school staff.

At Aniwa Elementary School, we faced a challenge: How could we get large numbers of parents to come to the School Effectiveness Team meetings to participate in school decision making? Although we knew that most of our PTO meetings attracted only the PTO officers and a few school staff members, we also recognized that the PTO meetings that had the greatest attendance were the occasional potluck dinners.

The three to four annual PTO potlucks have been a great way to motivate parents to come to meetings, talk with teachers and other parents in a relaxed setting, and help all parents—especially those new to our school—feel that they belong. We publicize the potluck dinners in our monthly school newsletter and in the school calendar. The children really love to come and make sure their parents know it!

We decided to connect the new School Effectiveness Team goals and meetings to the PTO potlucks and invite the whole family to come along. The school staff and families eat together from 6 to 7 p.m. At 7 p.m., the children play in the gym under the supervision of a volunteer who receives a small stipend from the PTO. Parents meet in the school library for the night's program and discussion. We wrap up the meeting no later than 8:30 p.m. Some of the topics we discussed include school and district goals, ideas for age-appropriate learning activities at home, good approaches to child discipline, and what families and teachers could do together to improve students' reading and writing skills and scores on state tests.

We also try to make the meetings fun. Each spring, students receive a packet of seeds to plant at home. We kick off the first potluck dinner and meeting of the school year by inviting students to bring their produce grown with the seeds back to school and show off their gardening efforts. We award prizes for the most creative, biggest, roundest, and so on. We also used one potluck dinner and meeting to have students exhibit and demonstrate their science fair projects for parents—a learning experience for everyone.

The potluck dinners cost very little because everyone brings a dish based on the food theme for the meeting. Occasionally, the PTO contributes funds for a special menu item. A local fast-food restaurant donated juice for some potlucks.

By combining School Effectiveness Team and PTO decision-making meetings and topics, more families at Aniwa Elementary have been involved in school decisions.

TYPE 5-DECISION MAKING ACTIVITY

Organizing an Action Team for Partnerships

Harbor View School
Baltimore, Maryland

The School/Family/Community/Partnership Action Team for Harbor View School decided that an organizational chart would help the members of the Action Team for Partnerships (ATP) manage their responsibilities and workload.[1] Our chart identifies the following four positions on the Action Team:

1.   The chairperson of the ATP oversees the school, family, and community partnership program in the school. This person brings together the full ATP and makes sure that each committee understands its goals and has a meeting schedule. The key contact chairperson works with the ATP's committees to discuss ideas, concerns, complaints, and opinions. This person represents the school's ATP in meetings with the School Improvement Team and with the district facilitator for partnerships. The chairperson helps coordinate meetings on school, family, and community partnerships with other schools and with the broader community. The chairperson also makes sure that all information for the district facilitator and for the National Network of Partnership Schools is turned in on time.

2.   The co-chairperson of the ATP serves as the team's vice-president and is designated to take over meetings and other responsibilities if the chairperson is unable to do so. The co-chairperson should have as much knowledge about school-family-community partnerships as the chairperson. The two team leaders may report to the School Improvement Team and make presentations to other groups about the school's program of partnerships.

3.   Committee co-chairs are responsible for overseeing committees on each of the six types of involvement. These co-chairs serve as leaders and

---

[1] Harbor View School adapted the organization of Action Team committees from Action Team Structure T, page 89 of this *Handbook,* and pages 87-90 on organizing commitees.

sources of knowledge to organize their committees and implement activities for each type of involvement that link to specific school goals for student success. It is the committee co-chair's responsibility to make sure that all committee members follow through with their responsibilities so that planned activities are implemented effectively and include a large number of families. The committee leaders report directly to the chairperson.

4.   Committee members work together with the committee co-chairs to implement the activities for each type of involvement in the One-Year Action Plan. They become the school's experts in each type of involvement. The chair of the ATP may delegate new work that arises during the school year to the appropriate committee. With committees, we have been able to conduct activities to inform and involve all families of students in our school. All team members share leadership and work together to plan and implement partnership activities. Other teachers, parents, and community partners help with specific activities.

SCHOOL STORIES
TYPE 6-COLLABORATING WITH THE COMMUNITY

Type 6-Collaborating With the Community activities encourage the cooperation of schools, families, and community groups, organizations, agencies, and individuals. The connections can be mutually beneficial:

- Community resources may help schools, families, and students.

- Educators, parents, and students may help their communities.

Like families and schools, communities have significant roles to play in the education, development, and well-being of students. Within communities, there are many resources—human, economic, material, and social— that may support and enhance home and school activities. Type 6 activities identify and integrate community resources in many different ways to improve schools, strengthen families, and assist students to succeed in school and in life.

An activity from Highlands Elementary School in Naperville, Illinois, illustrates how students contribute skills and talents to enliven and assist a community organization—here, a senior citizens' housing facility. In so doing, the students, teachers, and families gained new knowledge about their neighbors and applied school skills to real-world situations.

Lombard Middle School in Baltimore, Maryland, arranged a partnership with a community organization to provide hands-on active learning experiences to help students increase their reading and math skills. In this program, the community organization helps the school, students, and families by providing out-of-school experiences that stress the importance of school skills.

There are hundreds of Type 6 activities to connect schools, students, and families with their communities. Some schools begin by creating a community portrait to identify the programs and services in their communities that schools, families, and students may use. Some tap business and community partners to design and implement big programs (e.g., afterschool programs) or projects (e.g., creating a new playground). Other schools work, as the examples illustrate, with specific organizations to help reach school goals, including improving student achievement or increasing student service to others.

TYPE 6-COLLABORATING WITH THE COMMUNITY ACTIVITY

A Community Partnership With Sunrise Assisted Living

Highlands Elementary School
Naperville, Illinois

One school improvement goal for Highlands Elementary School encouraged intergenerational understanding and provided opportunities for students and senior citizens to learn about each other's unique life experiences, skills, needs, and responsibilities. To achieve our goal, a team of teachers, parents, and Sunrise Assisted Living staff brainstormed ideas that would (a) give seniors the chance to share their knowledge and experiences with students and become more active in the community, and (b) offer students a unique educational experience and demonstrate the importance of community service.

Prior to the summer break, the Action Team for Partnerships sent all teachers a preliminary list of more than 15 possible purposeful connections between students and senior citizens. In the fall, we held a school staff meeting at Sunrise Assisted Living to give teachers a chance to tour the home, meet the staff and residents, and then sign up for specific projects they wanted to sponsor in their classes. The action team also provided an overview of the partnership to the school's Home and School Association and to the Highlands Cub Scout and Brownie troops so they could look for possible tie-in activities. Articles in the school newsletter shared information with all Highlands parents about the activities and goals of partnerships.

In its first year, this partnership grew into a very special relationship between Highlands and Sunrise. Every grade level interacted with the senior citizens. Sample activities included the following:

- A fifth grade class visited Sunrise each month for a preplanned "knowledge share." For example, one month, for their history reports, students interviewed some seniors about their experiences during World War II.

- Several grades created "Happy Notes" and "Class Books" for the residents that were related to topics of the classroom curriculum.

- Seniors attended several school assemblies and musical performances.

- Home and School held one of its monthly meetings for parents at the Sunrise Assisted Living facility.

- The art department displayed student projects on a special bulletin board at Sunrise.

- The Sunrise program coordinator volunteered at the school once a month at Highlands Pennysaver Bank, and one of the senior residents volunteered twice a month in the school's Learning Resource Center.

- Brownie troops and Cub packs completed community service projects for Sunrise.

Collaborating with the community is proving beneficial for seniors, families, school staff, community members, and, most important, the students at Highlands Elementary School.

TYPE 6-COLLABORATING WITH THE COMMUNITY ACTIVITY

Hands-On Learning to Increase Math and Reading Skills

Lombard Middle School
Baltimore, Maryland

Lombard Middle School's Action Team for Partnerships (ATP) decided to use community resources to reinforce students' learning skills. The ATP members turned for help to the Living Classroom Foundation, located a few blocks from the school.

Students in science classes often went to that center to do projects after school. On several occasions, the ATP chairperson visited the Foundation with the students. Impressed with what she saw, the chairperson suggested that the ATP develop a partnership with the Foundation to improve students' math and reading scores.

The principal attended a board meeting with the founders and staff of the Living Classroom Foundation and learned how to obtain funding so that more students from Lombard could participate in the Foundation's activities. The ATP set out to design a program for the students and obtained funding.

The ATP believed that if students understood how they would use math and reading every day in the real world, the purpose of going to school and learning would be more meaningful. Therefore, the ATP planned a program with the Living Classroom that would engage students in hands-on activities to strengthen math and reading skills.

Each day a group of 10 students went to the Living Classroom. Students learned how to read a set of directions to build a model boat, set a measured course up the river, and measure wood to design a chair. They visited a school for students with special needs, visited the city mayor's office, and observed the types of jobs available to people with a good education. To participate in the program, students needed good attendance, a positive attitude, average or better grades, a teacher's recommendation, and a parent willing to visit the Living Classroom once during the six-week session.

The school's collaboration with the Living Classroom Foundation started in 1996 and has continued to the present. Many students and parents have attended various programs and activities at the center.

This partnership has increased family involvement at our school with students in the program at the Living Classroom Foundation. The activities have helped improve attendance and motivate students to work hard to achieve academic progress. Students in the program also have developed very positive attitudes about school.

DISTRICT LEADERSHIP ACTIVITIES

District leaders for school, family, and community partnerships conduct two kinds of leadership activities to increase and improve family and community involvement. District leaders

- Develop leadership and districtwide partnership activities
- Facilitate each elementary, middle, and high school in developing an effective program of partnerships

A district's program is based on a leadership plan for partnerships that identifies goals and schedules for specific activities to improve family and community involvement. The plan may include professional development on partnerships, grants to schools, services to families, activities with businesses and community groups, rewards and recognition for excellent practices, and other districtwide activities to strengthen school, family, and community partnerships.

A district's annual leadership plan also specifies how district leaders will facilitate the work of each school in developing its partnership program. This includes helping each elementary, middle, and high school assemble a well-functioning Action Team for Partnerships, write a One-Year Action Plan for partnerships, evaluate progress, share best practices with other schools, and continue annual plans to improve partnership practices.

The examples in this section illustrate how district leaders are working to fulfill these two major responsibilities. One activity, An "Egg-citing" Beginning, enabled a district facilitator in Baltimore, Maryland, to meet with the chairpersons of Action Teams for Partnerships from over 20 schools. With a good breakfast, clear guidelines, important examples, and other useful information, the school team leaders start the school year in good spirits and with the knowledge that the district leaders support their work on school, family, and community partnerships.

In Howard County, Maryland, the coordinator for partnerships established an interdepartmental leadership committee, the Family Involvement Coordinating Committee (FICC), to encourage leaders from many departments to communicate periodically about their work on family and community involvement. All leaders need to know about the services that are offered by their colleagues in order to help the schools and families they contact. The FICC meeting agendas stress the development of plans for better partnership activities, not just social exchanges.

In Minneapolis, the Leadership Team for Partnerships developed a notebook including guidelines and other materials to supplement the *Handbook for Action* used by members of the National Network of Partnership Schools. The Minneapolis notebook includes information on local policies and standards, district information for parents, examples of the six types of involvement, strategies for evaluating partnership activities, and other topics of importance in Minneapolis. The notebook is noteworthy because it was a collaborative activity of the family involvement and Title I offices. These leaders share a common goal to help every school in the district establish a partnership program that involves all families in children's learning and success.

In Local District B of the Los Angeles Unified School District, leaders help all schools develop their partnership programs. They also designed some activities that many schools could implement or adapt. For example, the Parent Library on Wheels is an innovative approach that can be used by schools with parent centers. The Parent Library on Wheels brings books for parents to read with children at home out to the sidewalk near the school building. It attracts many parents who were initially shy about going inside the parent center to obtain books and materials. The district leaders found that schools with this approach, along with other reading involvement activities, had students with better reading scores.

In Grand Blanc, Michigan, district leaders helped all schools strengthen their Type 6-Collaborating With the Community activities by creating a districtwide *Resource and Referral Booklet* that identifies social, psychological, and education programs, family counseling, legal services, tutoring, food and clothing assistance, and other programs and services for family and student support. By producing a districtwide directory that all schools can distribute to all families, the district leaders saved individual schools the time and effort of compiling similar directories.

These examples illustrate a few of the many ways that district leaders may encourage and assist all principals, teachers, and parents to develop strong programs of partnership at their schools.

DISTRICT LEADERSHIP ACTIVITY

An "Egg-citing" Beginning

Baltimore City Public Schools
Baltimore, Maryland

The district-level facilitator for school, family, and community partnerships and the area executive officer (area superintendent) in the Southwest area of Baltimore knew how important it was for the chairpersons of the Action Teams for Partnerships in all schools to be ready, able, and enthusiastic about leading their teams. As district leaders, we planned a special event to help the chairs of all Action Teams for Partnerships start the school year off right.

The event was a breakfast meeting for the chairs of more than 20 schools' Action Teams for Partnerships. We chose a comfortable setting outside of a school so that there would not be conflicts with cafeteria schedules or other distractions. "The Omelet Man," a local caterer, prepared omelets-to-order for all attendees.

A few speakers from various parts of the school system came to discuss the strengths of the National Network of Partnership Schools, the six types of involvement, organizing an effective action team, and implementing a One-Year Action Plan for partnerships. One presenter was an experienced ATP chair. She shared her ideas and successes and assured the new and returning chairs that progress comes in small, incremental steps. She did an excellent job mapping out an effective path that all ATPs could follow. After the speakers' presentations, the new chairs asked questions. The questions alerted us, as district leaders, to other ways that we needed to help the schools.

At the meeting, we supplied useful materials to help all ATP chairs with their work. Many of the handouts came from the first edition of *School, Family, and Community Partnerships: Your Handbook for Action*, including "Who Are the Members of Your Action Team?," "Action Team Structures," and "Are You Ready?" A brochure also was included which described the Southwest area's school, family, and community partnership program and listed the names and phone numbers of all the chairs of the school ATPs in our area. A great deal of information was provided in an efficient manner.

As a result of the meeting, the chairs of the ATPs were encouraged and felt more confident that they could lead their schools' teams in implementing their programs of partnership for the new school year. They left with a stronger vision of their responsibilities at their schools. The success of this activity was well worth the price of $6.99 per person for The Omelet Man. This activity helped the district leaders and the ATP chairs renew and strengthen relationships, and begin the year in a positive and motivating way.

DISTRICT LEADERSHIP ACTIVITY

Family Involvement Coordinating Committee

Howard County Public School System
Ellicott City, Maryland

The Howard County Public School System (HCPSS) developed an action team approach at the district level. The objectives of the Family Involvement Coordinating Committee (FICC) were to (a) gain an awareness of all family-linked services and involvement activities across departments, (b) identify and solve problems to better align family services, and (c) evaluate the effectiveness of school, family, and community partnerships in HCPSS.

We invited representatives from all central office programs to the first meeting of FICC. District administrators helped create the list of invitees from A to Z—or in this case, from Buses to Testing and all departments in between. Invitees were sent a questionnaire about each department's family and community involvement practices to be returned before the meeting.

Of the 30 people invited, 23 attended the first meeting and five more returned completed questionnaires for their departments. Many attendees did not know each other, even if they had heard their colleagues' names or seen their faces at the district office. After the objectives of FICC were discussed, an activity called "A Fascinating Family Service Fact!" helped participants introduce themselves and their department's work on family and community involvement. Results were presented from a districtwide survey that included questions about county residents' satisfaction with the local schools, along with results of focus group meetings with members of the Korean, Latino, Haitian, African American, and White communities.

In small groups, FICC members identified their concerns about gaps in the delivery of services to all families. Next, the concerns were prioritized by the whole group. The top concerns included the need to improve communications about education and children's development with all families and to provide more coordinated education, health, and social services to families of students in kindergarten through high school.

At the next meeting, we distributed a notebook that included a directory of FICC members and the services provided by their departments, family involvement resource materials, promising partnership practices from the National Network of Partnership Schools, and other useful materials. We developed strategies to address the district, school, and family communication concerns that were raised by the group in its earlier meeting. We also created task groups to focus on the remaining concerns and questions about district-level family services and involvement.

FICC planned to meet quarterly, with the task groups meeting more frequently, as needed, on their special projects. For example, one task group planned to play a large role in organizing a countywide family involvement conference. Over time, the task groups will develop district-level leadership activities to involve all Howard County families in their children's education. At the same time, the district will work to help each school plan and implement its program of family and community involvement.

DISTRICT LEADERSHIP ACTIVITY

Family Involvement Notebook

Minneapolis Public Schools
Minneapolis, Minnesota

Minneapolis Public Schools (MPS) is working to increase the level and quality of family involvement in the education of students in all schools. Many phone calls came to the district's family involvement and Title I specialists from educators in schools who were seeking additional information and help in developing productive partnership programs. As a result, leaders from the two offices jointly developed the *Family Involvement Notebook* to serve as a resource for all schools seeking to form more effective partnerships with their students' families.

Designed as a three-ring binder that can be expanded and updated, the notebook addresses policies, standards, strategies, and services focused on partnerships. It contains information for staff and materials that can be reproduced and sent to parents. It also includes a copy of the MPS Family Involvement Standards and copies of *Bright Ideas for Family Involvement*, Vols. I and II. These booklets contain examples of some of the best practices in Minneapolis schools and classrooms for building partnerships with families.

Developed for use in all elementary, middle, and high schools, the notebooks were given to principals, Title I contact teachers, and family liaisons at all 97 Minneapolis school sites. Leaders distributed the *Family Involvement Notebooks* and demonstrated their use at principal, Title I contact teacher, and family liaison meetings. Specialists for school, family, and community partnerships met personally with and delivered notebooks to people who did not attend these meetings. Other district administrators received copies, including the superintendent, area superintendents, and directors of teaching and instructional strategies, Title I, communications, and special education.

In addition to being a resource, the notebook also serves as a place for schools to keep records of their family involvement efforts. There are sections for each of the six types of involvement, evaluations, budget information, newsletters, and computer disks and two blank sections in the notebook for the school's use.

Schools are using the information in the notebooks to answer their basic questions about partnerships. Calls to the district's family involvement specialists now are usually about more challenging questions or for additional materials or assistance. For example, in response to new requests from schools, we plan to provide templates on computer disks for frequent fliers and announcements in the major languages used by Minneapolis families.

The *Family Involvement Notebook* is one of several successful collaborations between family involvement and Title I leaders in Minneapolis to help all schools build better programs of school, family, and community partnerships.

DISTRICT LEADERSHIP ACTIVITY

Parent Libraries on Wheels

Local School District B
Los Angeles Unified School District
Sun Valley, California

Local School District B (a district-area of the Los Angeles Unified School District—LAUSD) established Parent Libraries in all family centers in the district to help parents meet the challenges of child rearing and to improve student reading achievement. Previously, families may have looked for information, but often did not know what resources were available or how to access them.

The Parent Libraries helped the district support families by making available accurate and relevant parenting information and children's literature. Materials that could be checked out included books, leaflets, audiotapes, videos, and other resources for parents in both English and Spanish.

In order to increase the number of parents using the library services, the family centers displayed an assortment of books on rolling carts twice a week at each school's front gate or curb, where parents could easily make their selections. Borrowed books were returned inside the family centers to ensure that new parents saw they were welcome at the school and that they discovered the centers and services.

When parents checked out materials, they received fliers listing upcoming workshops on how to share books with their children and other events sponsored by the centers. Leaders were trained to conduct a variety of bilingual workshops on family reading, high frequency words, Latino family literacy, and other reading-related topics to help parents reinforce students' reading skills.

Records were kept of the number of parents using the curbside libraries, the number of workshop series presented, and how many parents attended. In addition, Los Angeles Compact on Evaluation studied a group of comparison schools to measure the effects of the district's parent involvement efforts on student achievement. Data for the 1998-1999 school year showed a 5.7% increase in students' reading scores and a 4.7% increase in students' language scores for the schools in the program.

District leaders can work with many schools to help organize and improve goal-oriented family and community partnerships. Parent Libraries on Wheels is just one of many ways to help parents in every school help children focus on reading.

DISTRICT LEADERSHIP ACTIVITY

R and R—Resource and Referral Booklet

Grand Blanc Community Schools
Grand Blanc, Michigan

When families in Grand Blanc schools tried to obtain information about community services and resources, they often did not know what those resources were or how to access them. To support families with current, accurate, and relevant resource information for referrals, the district's leadership team for partnerships created our own *Resource and Referral Booklet*.

We purchased the county's *Resource Book* that had just been reprinted and updated. Meetings were held with district social workers and psychologists to determine the most common needs and requests for referrals of families they worked with in our district. We asked the social workers and psychologists to identify the professionals and agencies from the county's *Resource Book* that they would recommend based on past experience. The mental health professionals also identified other helpful resources that were not listed in the county's book. Similar meetings were held with directors of other programs in the district such as Parents as Partners, Children's Garden, and Family Service Center.

Based on the information gained from these professionals, our *Resource and Referral Booklet* contains information on how families can access and obtain the following resources: clothing assistance, counseling assistance, education support services, food assistance, hotlines, legal assistance, parenting information and services, support groups, and other sources of support. We made a strong effort to list resources that were geographically close to the families in our district.

The booklet lists the names of the professionals and agencies, their addresses and phone numbers, and brief descriptions of the services provided. A final phone call was made to each of the contact people to check for accuracy before the booklet was printed.

The district's print shop produced 750 copies of the booklet, which were distributed to the home-school liaisons in all elementary schools, the counselors in the middle and high schools, and the social workers and directors of programs within the district. All these leaders will make the *Resource and Referral Booklet* available to families as needed.

Feedback about the booklet has been very positive from both staff and families. The plan is to evaluate the *Resource and Referral Booklet* annually to improve and update its listings.

STATE LEADERSHIP ACTIVITIES

State departments of education need a clear, written policy on school, family, and community partnerships; enactments to support the implementation of the policy; and an office or department responsible for providing that assistance to districts and schools statewide. These activities show that the state officially supports the development of partnership programs.

An annual state leadership plan identifies goals and activities to support the state policy on partnerships. A good plan specifies how leaders will assist districts and schools to enact the state policy and meet special conditions in each location. State leaders for partnerships may conduct awareness sessions, team-training workshops, and annual conferences to share best practices and to advance skills and knowledge on partnerships. State leaders also may establish business collaborations; offer grants to districts and schools to improve practices; produce and disseminate publications and provide services for families, schools, and districts; recognize and reward excellent practices; and conduct other statewide family and community involvement activities.

The designated state leader for partnerships should form a leadership team with representatives from other programs in the state department of education and other state organizations (e.g., regional staff development offices, state PTA, teacher and administrator unions) who work to improve school, family, and community partnerships. Periodic meetings of the leadership team ensure that everyone will know how their projects are contributing to the overall goals of improving partnership programs in districts and schools statewide.

The examples in this section illustrate different ways that state leaders are applying budgets and maximizing resources to encourage, support, and guide districts and schools to improve their leadership, knowledge, and programs of partnership.

In Ohio, leaders created an interagency leadership team. The leaders not only informed one another about their own projects, but also collaborated to provide training to school teams and district leaders at state conferences and regional workshops. The state awarded small grants to hundreds of schools to initiate their work on partnerships. These activities increased awareness about school, family, and community partnerships and helped many schools develop new knowledge, skills, and programs in many schools and districts.

Wisconsin's state coordinators describe the comprehensive approach that they have taken over several years to help schools and districts strengthen programs of school, family, and community partnerships. The state coordinators offer awareness sessions, team training, seed money and small grants, opportunities to share best practices, and other activities that help schools and districts continue to work on partnerships from one year to the next. Their efforts have increasingly focused on linking school, family, and community partnerships with school improvement goals for student success.

Connecticut's example illustrates how leaders in the state department of education work with other state organizations—here, the United Way of Connecticut—to increase support for school, family, and community partnerships statewide. The United Way uses its connections with many local programs to increase awareness of the importance of partnerships and to encourage local United Way chapters to use resources for building partnerships. The state's Bureau of School-Family-Community Partnerships provides in-depth training for school teams that are ready to implement strong partnership programs.

Every state department of education is different due to the size and geography of the state, the number of school districts and schools, demographics of students, families, and communities, and other features. Nevertheless, all states recognize the importance of family and community involvement and must develop a leadership policy, plan, and program for this component of school improvement.

STATE LEADERSHIP ACTIVITY

Spring Partnership Rally

Ohio Department of Education
Columbus, Ohio

Work on school, family, and community partnerships at the state level is conducted by an interagency team from the Ohio Department of Education, including Title I, Special Education, Ohio's PTA, the Parent Information and Resource Center (OhioPIRC), and Ohio Family and Children First, the governor's family support initiative. One strong example of the collaborative work of this leadership team is the Spring Partnership Rally.

The team wanted to host an event that would increase awareness of Ohio's school, family, and community partnership initiative. The team obtained funding for the rally through a grant from the Martha Holden Jennings Foundation, which supports Ohio initiatives. With funding secured, the leadership team began plans for the rally.

Leadership team members led sessions on the six types of involvement and on Ohio's opportunities for grants on partnerships. Other speakers led small group sessions about how educators, parents, and community partners can work together successfully. The Ohio Department of Education's interagency leadership team spent many hours developing the special session on what it means to work in partnership. By attending all the sessions, attendees could leave the rally not only with information about the six types of involvement, but also with a sense of how to work collaboratively.

The OhioPIRC took major responsibility for compiling and distributing a *Bright Ideas* booklet of promising partnership activities that were shared by Ohio Partnership Schools in their midyear progress reports. Later, the interagency team led four regional workshops across the state, two of which were held on Saturdays, to provide the same information to teams that were not able to come to Columbus on the day of the rally.

The leadership team publicized the upcoming rally in its statewide publications to schools and districts. We recommended that participants attend the rally in teams of parents, teachers, and community partners.

The overall effect of this event and follow-up activities was to greatly increase educators' and parents' awareness of the state's partnership initiative. The member of the state board of education who welcomed rally participants returned to the next board meeting declaring that the effort to help districts and schools develop their partnership programs was the best-kept secret in the department.

By consistently building on the framework of the six types of involvement and by inviting schools to join Ohio's Network and the National Network of Partnership Schools, we have begun to develop a statewide focus on school, family, and community partnerships. This was reinforced by the establishment of the Center for Students, Families, and Communities as one division of the Ohio Department of Education, by collaborating with the Title I office, and by making annual Ohio Family Partnership Awards for schools and districts that conduct outstanding parental involvement practices.

STATE LEADERSHIP ACTIVITY

Sowing Seeds, Planting Partnerships, and Harvesting Relationships

Wisconsin Department of Public Instruction
Madison, Wisconsin

Historically, Wisconsin has been a state of strong local control. The partnership practices of the Wisconsin Department of Public Instruction (DPI) reflect this faith in that which is "homegrown." Our state leadership efforts can be divided into three strands: sowing seeds, planting partnerships, and harvesting relationships.

"Sowing seeds" informs schools and districts about how to develop and continually improve their partnership programs and practices at an annual DPI Family-School-Community Partnership Conference. The school action teams that attend this conference include at least one parent, teacher, school administrator, and school board or community member.

The conference provides teams with the guidelines and time to think about, talk about, and plan their partnership programs. The emphasis for the estimated 250 teams who have participated in conferences over the past few years is on asking parents and teachers about their school goals and the kinds of partnerships they need at their schools. Then, through reflection and group consensus, the teams decide which actions will help meet their goals and needs. They write a One-Year Action Plan, which clearly outlines the schedule for implementing activities and who will be responsible for each task. To ensure that no team goes home without a little "fertilizer" to help their partnership plans take root, we offer $300 to $500 seed grants to all teams attending the workshop.

To help "plant partnerships," or gently fold them into the operating structure of the school or district, DPI also offers teams who join the National Network of Partnership Schools the opportunity to apply for a $2,000 Wisconsin Partnership Schools grant. These grants must be used to pay a partnership coordinator, usually a parent, to chair the school team for partnership planning and activities and to support the school's connections with other schools and districts engaged in partnerships. Recipients report that the Wisconsin Partnership Schools grant allowed them to complete partnership plans and activities at a higher level by connecting them to student learning objectives.

At the state level, we "harvest relationships" by helping our partnership practitioners get to know one another. We cultivate their willingness to call upon our office and each other for advice and to celebrate progress and best practices. Many partnership teams return each year to the state's partnership conferences to learn and share strategies with the other teams. We call upon school and district leaders to present at the conferences and invite them to share experiences during two statewide videoconferences that DPI hosts for partnership schools during the year. The districts' and schools' stories are also told in two *Learning Together* packets DPI publishes annually and sends to all Wisconsin schools, districts, PTA leaders, and teachers statewide.

A "must" for any state attempting to implement and spread partnerships is strong and active support and encouragement from the state superintendent and state board of education. It also is imperative to cultivate communications about school-family-community partnerships across the educational programs and initiatives in all departments.

STATE LEADERSHIP ACTIVITY

Partnering With the United Way of Connecticut

Connecticut State Department of Education
Hartford, Connecticut

The United Way of Connecticut and the Connecticut State Department of Education signed an agreement to work together to build linkages between schools, families, and their communities. The purpose of this joint agreement is to

- Support and extend the standards for partnerships identified in the *Position Statement on School-Family-Community Partnerships* adopted by the state board of education on August 7, 1997

- Increase public and private stakeholders' awareness of the purpose and benefit of school-family-community partnerships

- Encourage active partnerships between Connecticut's local affiliates of the United Way, schools, and other community organizations to support students' optimal development and academic success

The chairman of the board of directors of the United Way of Connecticut encourages the local chapters of the United Way to support their schools. In a column in the United Way's newsletter, he implored local chapters to help by

- Increasing the awareness and participation of businesses in setting local priorities and supporting solutions that address the identified needs of children, youth, and families

- Developing and supporting effective local planning that uses resources to

  - Fund unmet service needs

  - Increase local leadership capacity

  - Engage local stakeholders, including families, to improve educational opportunities and reduce health, safety, and social risks to children in communities

- Supporting community collaboration to provide out-of-school and extended-school services for students and families

The Connecticut Sate Department of Education is making important advances in developing school, family, and community partnerships in elementary, middle, and high schools statewide. The commissioner supported the establishment of a Bureau of School-Family-Community Partnerships in the Division of School Improvement. The staff conducts many important activities to prepare and support schools to plan and implement strong partnership programs. By partnering with an important statewide organization that has strong ties to local community agencies, our team seeks to strengthen the community part of our school-family-community partnerships.

3

Taking an Action Team Approach

This chapter presents information and tools to help schools' Action Teams for Partnerships (ATPs) organize their work and succeed as teams. Teachers, parents, administrators, other family members, and community partners must talk and work together to support students. Teamwork is essential for implementing excellent programs of school, family, and community partnerships.

School leaders, district facilitators, and others need to know the steps that ATPs must take to write good plans for family and community involvement, conduct effective team meetings, organize committees, and implement activities that contribute to student learning and success in school. ATP members need to understand how principals, teachers, counselors, parents, community groups, and students can share leadership and conduct activities that involve all families in their children's education.

The introductory article in this chapter addresses 12 common questions about the purposes, members, committees, and responsibilities of an ATP. The article also explains how an ATP differs from and enhances the work of a School Council and PTA or PTO.

Several summaries, checklists, and guidelines are provided to assist a school's ATP with its work. These tools may be used as handouts in workshops or meetings to explain what an ATP does, to check progress, and to improve the quality of teamwork over time.

Ten Steps to Success in School, Family, and Community Partnerships

Review 10 basic steps for creating a successful program of school, family, and community partnerships in any elementary, middle, or high school. Success starts with an ATP. The team must set goals for partnerships, write and implement annual plans, conduct thoughtful evaluations, celebrate progress, and continue to work on partnerships from year to year. District leaders should facilitate the 10 steps in all schools.

Checklist: Are You Ready?

Use this checklist to help an Action Team for Partnerships keep track of its progress in initiating a program of school, family, and community partnerships.

Who Are the Members of the Action Team for Partnerships?

Compile a directory of team members and the skills and talents that they bring to the team. Also, list the ATP committees and committee leaders for the school year. Provide copies to all team members to facilitate communication.

First ATP Meeting of the School Year

Start the year with a well-planned agenda for the first meeting of the full ATP. This guide for chairs or co-chairs suggests that, at the first meeting each year, the ATP should review how leadership will be shared, how committees are organized, how team members will communicate, what the One-Year Action Plan includes, and what the team and its committee will do to implement the activities scheduled for the first month of the new school year.

Communication Ground Rules

Decide how the members of the ATP will communicate with one another. Identify rules for interactions at meetings and at other times that will foster teamwork and team spirit.

What Do Successful Action Teams for Partnership Do?

Discuss the qualities that help ATPs succeed in leading their schools' partnership programs. Good teams help members communicate with each other and with other groups, conduct well-organized team meetings, solve problems, and improve plans for partnerships from year to year.

Annual Review of Team Processes

Assess the quality of teamwork at the end of each year. This evaluation focuses on 18 team processes. Team members can discuss how they can be even more effective in the future. Also see Chapter 9 for tools to evaluate the quality of the school's partnership program and practices.

The ABCs of Action Team Leadership

Help the chair or co-chairs of the ATP and its committees develop strong leadership qualities. The ABCs guide team leaders to *Accept* leadership, *Be* ready to share leadership, *Communicate* with all partners, *Develop* good plans, *Evaluate* progress, and *Foster* team spirit. ATP leaders need these skills to help all team members work well together and accomplish their plans for partnership.

Action Team Discussion on Meeting Key Challenges to Excellent Partnerships

Discuss ways that the ATP may involve families who are presently hard to reach and ways to meet key challenges for the six types of involvement.

Sample Pledges, Compacts, or Contracts

Establish agreements with parents, teachers, students, and administrators to work together for student success. These parallel pledges list a few basic responsibilities to help all partners identify their common goals, shared responsibilities, and personal commitments.

Organizing an Effective Action Team for Partnerships: Questions and Answers

Joyce L. Epstein

Who is responsible for developing and sustaining school, family, and community partnerships? The answer, of course, is that everyone with an interest in students' success has a role to play in conducting productive partnership activities. We have learned from many schools that one principal, one teacher, or one parent working alone cannot create a comprehensive and lasting program of partnerships. Rather, an Action Team for Partnerships (ATP) is needed to plan, implement, evaluate, and continually improve family and community involvement activities to create a welcoming school climate and to help all students succeed. Also, state and district leaders can and should help facilitate good partnership programs in all schools. See Chapter 7 in this *Handbook*.

This chapter addresses several key questions about the Action Team for Partnerships:[1]

- What is an Action Team for Partnerships?

- Who are the members of the Action Team for Partnerships?

- What does an Action Team for Partnerships do?

- How should an Action Team for Partnerships organize its work?

- How do members of the Action Team for Partnerships share leadership?

- How do members become an effective team?

- How often should an Action Team for Partnerships meet?

- What planning and evaluation tools help an Action Team for Partnerships?

- What will the Action Team for Partnerships be named?

- How does an Action Team for Partnerships differ from the School Council or School Improvement Team?

- How does an Action Team for Partnerships differ from the PTA, PTO, or Home-School Association?

- How may the action team approach be used to organize comprehensive school reform (CSR)?

The answers to these questions will help every elementary, middle, and high school create an effective ATP and conduct a successful program of school, family, and community partnerships.

What Is an Action Team for Partnerships?

The ATP is an action arm or work group of a School Council or School Improvement Team. The ATP writes and implements plans for partnerships to produce desired results for students, for families, and for the school as a whole. The ATP includes teachers, administrators, parents and other family members, business and community partners, and, at the high school level, students. The members of the ATP work together to review school goals; select, design, implement, and evaluate partnership activities; and improve partnership practices. The work that the members of the ATP do together helps create and sustain a climate of good partnerships at the school. The ATP's primary goal is to involve families and the community in productive ways so that more students reach important educational goals for learning and success.

Who Are the Members of the Action Team for Partnerships?

A well-functioning ATP has 6 to 12 members. Members include at least two teachers, at least two parents, an administrator, and other school and family leaders who have important connections with families and students (e.g., the school nurse, social worker, Title I parent liaison, a PTA/PTO officer or representative, instructional aide, secretary, custodian, grandparent who is raising a student, or others). The ATP also may include representatives from the community (e.g., business partners, interfaith leaders, representatives from literary, cultural, or civic organizations, and others). High school ATPs must include one or two students. The diverse members contribute many points of view, connections, talents, and resources for planning, implementing, and evaluating school, family, and community partnership activities.

Very small schools may adapt these guidelines to create smaller ATPs. Very large middle and high schools may create multiple ATPs for schools-within-the-school, grade levels, houses, career academies, or other large subdivisions. Other appropriate structural and procedural adaptations may be needed to accommodate the characteristics and constraints in diverse schools.

The ATP serves as a stable structure linked directly to the School Council or School Improvement Team and accountable to the principal.

The ATP continues from year to year, even when some team members leave. New team members representing the same positions replace those who leave. That is, teachers who leave the team are replaced by teachers, parents are replaced by parents, and so on. New team members must be oriented to the plans and work of the ATP and to their roles and responsibilities. See pages 106-107 to account for the members of the ATP each year and to provide a directory with contact information to foster communication among team members.

What Does an Action Team for Partnerships Do?

In elementary, middle, and high schools, the ATP writes a plan, implements and coordinates activities, monitors progress, solves problems, publicizes activities, and reports on the school's program of partnerships to the School Council or similar body and to other groups at the school and in the community. Members of the ATP do not work alone. They recruit other teachers, students, administrators, parents, and community members, the parent association, the parent liaison, the nurse or counselors, district leaders, and others to lead and participate in family and community involvement activities. The ATP also recognizes the family and community involvement activities conducted by individual teachers and other groups (e.g., PTA/PTO, an after-school program, or business partners). The school's partnership program includes all family and community involvement activities that are conducted for the school as a whole, in specific grade levels, and by individual teachers each year. Specifically, in each elementary, middle, and high school, the ATP will do the following:

- Select a committee structure to organize its work by focusing on the six types of involvement or specific school improvement goals (see the next section)

- Select or elect the ATP chair or co-chairs and committee chairs or co-chairs

- Develop a detailed annual One-Year Action Plan for improving partnerships linked to school improvement plans, including activities for all six types of involvement that involve families in ways that help students reach school goals

- Identify the budget(s) that will support the activities in the One-Year Action Plan

- Meet monthly as a whole team to ensure continuous progress in plans and activities, and meet in smaller committees, as needed, to implement activities in the One-Year Action Plan

- Conduct or delegate leadership to implement planned activities as scheduled

- Establish goals and guidelines for teamwork, including how team members will communicate, discuss ideas, solve problems, and make decisions

- Report progress semiannually or more often to the School Council or School Improvement Team, faculty, and parent organization

- Publicize activities to all parents, students, and teachers, and, as appropriate, the broader community

- Recognize and celebrate excellent participation from parents, other family members, students, and others in the community who contribute to the success of planned partnership activities

- Evaluate progress to improve the quality of implementations and the strength of results of various involvement activities

- Gather ideas for new activities

- Solve problems that impede progress on partnership activities

- Write a new One-Year Action Plan each year to ensure an ongoing program of partnerships in the life and work of the school

- Replace teachers, parents, administrators, or other members who leave the ATP with new members from the same positions so that a full team is always ready to conduct a planned program of partnerships at the school

These steps must be followed and improved each year to sustain an excellent program of school, family, and community partnerships. By conducting these activities, the ATP helps everyone in the school know that the school has an active partnership program. All teachers, parents, school staff, community members, and students should know about the many ways that they may help select, design, conduct, enjoy, benefit from, and evaluate partnership activities. From year to year, the number and quality of activities in a school's One-Year Action Plan for partnerships should improve, along with positive results of the activities.

How Should an Action Team for Partnerships Organize Its Work?

An ATP may organize its work by focusing on the six types of involvement *or* on specific school improvement goals. This choice determines the structure of the ATP's committees, how One-Year Action Plans are written, and how the program is evaluated.

Organize committees to strengthen the six types of involvement. One way to organize ATP committees, plans, and evaluations is to focus on the six types of involvement: *parenting, communicating, volunteering, learning at home, decision making, and collaborating with the community.* In this approach, the ATP creates committees with a chair or co-chairs and members who become the school's experts on each of the six types of involvement, as shown in Figure 3.1a. Each committee writes one section of the One-Year Action Plan for partnerships, obtains input from the rest of the team, and is responsible for implementing and evaluating the activities for the specific type of involvement.

For example, one or two members of the ATP will chair or co-chair the Type 1-Parenting committee. They will call upon and work with other members of the ATP or other educators, parents, students, and community partners who are not members of the ATP. The Type 1-Parenting committee of leaders and helpers will plan, organize, monitor, and delegate leadership for parent workshops on child development, parent-to-parent connections, activities for families to inform the school about their children's needs or family goals, or other Type 1 activities.

Other members of the ATP will co-chair the Type 2-Communicating committee. They will call upon and work with other members of the ATP or other educators, parents, students, and community partners who are not members of the ATP. The Type 2-Communicating committee of leaders and helpers will plan, organize, monitor, and delegate leadership for activities that create two-way channels of communication, secure translators needed at parent-teacher conferences, develop new technologies for communicating, or perform other Type 2 activities. Thus, each type of involvement is directed by at least one ATP member and many other helpers so that the planned activities are successfully implemented and reach all families.

From year to year, the quality and results of activities for all six types of involvement should improve, along with the ATP members' expertise and teamwork. (See pp. 326-329 in this *Handbook* for the planning and evaluation tools that are organized by the six types of involvement.)

Organize committees to focus family and community involvement on helping to reach school improvement goals. Another way to organize ATP committees, plans, and evaluations is to focus family and community involvement on helping the school and students reach specific improvement goals. In this approach, the ATP creates committees with a chair or co-chairs and members who become the school's experts on how family and community involvement can help students reach selected academic and nonacademic goals such as improving reading, math, or science skills, attendance, behavior, or other goals for students and improving home-school-community connections overall. See Figure 3.1b.

Figure 3.1. Team Structures

3.1a. Action Team for Partnerships Structure T (Focus on Types)

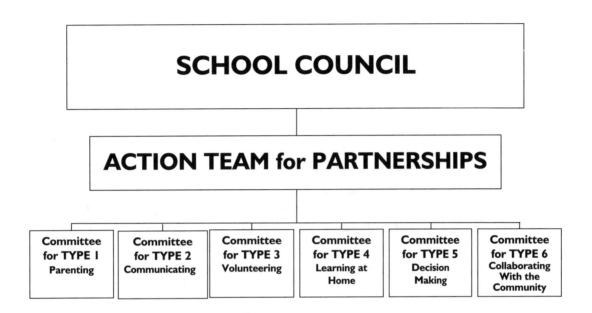

3.1b. Action Team for Partnerships Structure G (Focus on Goals)

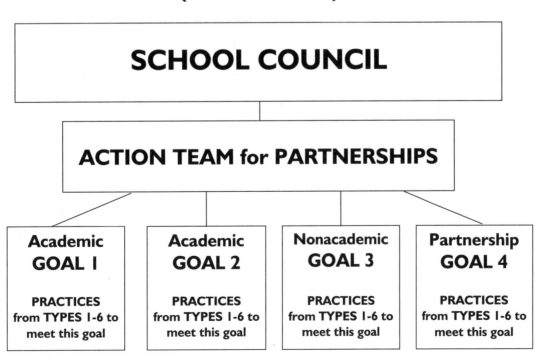

For example, if one goal is to improve student attendance, then the ATP's attendance committee would select activities for some or all six types of involvement to engage family and community members in ways that ensure that healthy students attend school every day and that they arrive on time. The ATP's attendance committee may select activities to increase families' understanding of school policies about attendance, clarify report card statistics on attendance, train volunteers to telephone absent students' families, have families pick up and monitor homework for students who are absent, and address other ways to improve student attendance and reduce lateness (Epstein & Sheldon, 2002). Field tests indicate that ATPs can effectively address four school goals each year with committees that focus on two academic goals, one behavioral goal, and one goal to conduct all other partnership activities that create a welcoming school climate. The ATP evaluates its progress and plans improvements based on the quality of implementation of each committee's family and community involvement activities and how well the activities contribute to the attainment of the selected school improvement goals. (See pp. 326-329 in this *Handbook* for the planning and evaluation tools that are organized to address selected school improvement goals.)

The two approaches for organizing ATP committees are not mutually exclusive. Plans for partnerships based on the six types of involvement must include activities that help reach important school goals. Plans for partnerships based on school improvement goals must include activities for all six types of involvement. The differences in the two approaches are in how ATP members organize committees, explain their roles and responsibilities, and write their One-Year Action Plans and End-of-Year Evaluations (see pp. 215-216 for an activity to help organize an ATP).

How Do Members of the Action Team for Partnerships Share Leadership?

Many people play important leadership roles on an ATP. All members of the team contribute ideas to the One-Year Action Plan, lead or colead committees or activities, delegate leadership and mobilize support for other activities, and evaluate the results of their efforts.

Each ATP has a chairperson or, optimally, co-chairs. Co-chairs should be educators and parents who are recognized and accepted as leaders by all team members. Each ATP committee also has a chair or co-chairs (or coleaders). The co-chair structure gives greater stability to the ATP and to its committees in case some members leave the school. (Also see the ABCs of Action Team Leadership, pp. 112-117.)

The following sections discuss some of the roles and responsibilities of various members of an ATP including school principals, guidance counselors and specialists, teachers, paraprofessional and other staff, parents, community partners, and students.

Principals

School principals are essential members of the ATP. They support and guide the ATP's connections to the School Council or a similar body. At the middle and high school levels, assistant principals may serve on the ATP in the principal's place. Most principals do not serve as the overall chair of the ATP, leaving that leadership role to a teacher or to teacher-parent co-chairs. Some principals serve as chair or co-chair of an ATP committee for one of the six types of involvement or for one of the targeted school goals.

Principals' leadership includes the following:

- Call all teachers' attention to the importance of planning and conducting school, family, and community partnerships with their students' families

- Allocate funds for the planned program of school, family, and community partnerships, and include the funds as a line item in the annual school budget

- Provide time and space for ATP meetings, including arrangements for teachers on the ATP to meet at the same time or provisions for the school to be open for meetings before or after school hours

- Encourage all educators and families to participate in involvement activities to develop a welcoming school climate and sense of community

- Publicize scheduled involvement activities throughout the school year

- Evaluate each teacher's activities to involve families as part of an annual or periodic professional review

- Guide the ATP in making periodic reports to the School Council or School Improvement Team on plans and accomplishments

- Work with community groups and leaders to locate resources that will enrich the curriculum and help students, teachers, and parents in important ways

- Recognize and thank ATP leaders and team members, active family volunteers, and other participants in involvement activities

- Work with school district facilitators, district administrators, and principals from other schools to understand and improve school, family, and community partnerships

Guidance Counselors and Specialists

Guidance counselors, school psychologists, school social workers, and other social service professionals may be members of an ATP and may serve as ATP chair or co-chairs and as leaders of an ATP committee. Assistant principals and guidance counselors are particularly helpful team leaders or co-chairs in middle and high schools because their professional agendas link directly to students, families, and communities. These school professionals tend to have more time, training, and experience to plan and conduct meetings and to guide teachers, parents, students, and community members to work effectively together.

Teachers

At least two or three *teachers* must be members of the ATP and may serve as team or committee chairs or co-chairs. These may include master teachers, lead teachers, and department chairs, along with classroom teachers from different grade levels. Teachers on the ATP contribute ideas for family and community involvement activities linked to academic goals for students. Teachers also work with the other teachers in the school to reinforce the importance of connections with students' families, help teachers share their own best practices to involve families and the community, and encourage teachers to participate in schoolwide partnership events. Some schools increase the number of ATP members to include one teacher from each grade level to ensure that family involvement activities are planned, implemented, and shared across the grades and with all families.

The ATP should collect information from all teachers in the school on their family and community involvement activities. In this way, individual teachers' efforts contribute to the school's overall partnership program, along with schoolwide or grade-level activities. Teachers may help each other become more effective in communicating with parents about homework, schoolwork, grades, and test scores and in parent-teacher-student conferences.

Paraprofessionals

Parent liaisons are paid aides who help educators connect and communicate with parents and other family members. They should be part of the Action Team for Partnerships, not solely in charge of all family involvement activities. Parent liaisons may serve as co-chairs with an educator of the ATP or as chairs or co-chairs of ATP committees. They may be particularly appropriate leaders of activities that directly assist families, such as Type 1-Parenting activities or Type 6-Collaborating With the Community activities. They also may help train parent volunteers (Type 3-Volunteering) or serve as translators for parents (Type 2-Communicating). Other paraprofessionals (e.g., instructional aides or assistants in libraries, computer labs, and other locations) and other school staff (e.g., secretarial, cafeteria, custodial, and transportation staff) also may serve as members of the Action Team for Partnerships.

Families

Parents or other family members are essential members of the ATP and, along with a school faculty or staff member, may serve as co-chairs of the team. Parents also may serve as chairs or co-chairs of ATP committees on the six types of involvement or on specific school goals. Parent leaders should come from various neighborhoods or family groups that are served by the school. A PTA or PTO representative may be one of the parents on the Action Team for Partnerships. Parents and other family members on the ATP contribute ideas on topics that will be important for families, design ways to involve all families, conduct activities on family-friendly schedules, recruit families to lead and implement activities, and encourage families to participate in activities. Some schools recruit a family representative from each grade level to serve on the team. With such representation, all parents in the school will see that they have a voice on the ATP and a contact with whom to share ideas and information.

Community Partners

Business and other community partners also may serve on an ATP and take appropriate leadership roles. For example, a business partner may co-chair a committee for Type 6-Collaborating With the Community activities. Some ATPs include a community partner (e.g., business partner, librarian, police officer, city council official, scientist, medical expert, faith-based leader) to serve on the team. Community partners may bring expert knowledge, useful connections, and various resources to ATP committees on the six types of involvement or to committees on particular school improvement goals such as improving reading, safety, behavior, or student and family health.

Students

Students must serve on the ATP in high schools. They may not serve as ATP chairs or co-chairs, but may serve as co-chairs with educators or parents of an ATP committee on the six types of involvement or on specific school goals. Other members on high school ATPs value the students' ideas for and reactions to plans for partnerships. The student members communicate with other high school students in various ways to gather ideas about which school, family, and community partnerships will be important and acceptable to students and their families.

In elementary, middle, and high schools, students are the main actors in their own education. Even if they are not members of the Action Team for Partnerships, students play key roles in conducting family and community involvement activities. Students deliver messages from school to home and from home to school. Students often interpret and explain notes and memos to parents. Students are leaders in discussions with parents about homework, report cards, school events, and problems they may have at school. Therefore, students at all grade levels should be well informed about the goals of the ATP and have input to each year's activities to involve their families. Only with student involvement and support will programs of school, family, and community partnerships succeed.

All members of the ATP are expected to be able to speak knowledgeably about the school's One-Year Action Plan for partnerships, provide leadership for implementing some family and community involvement activities, and work with others to sustain an effective team and productive partnership program.

How Do Members Become an Effective Team?

Teachers, administrators, parents, community partners, and others on an ATP must learn to function well as a team. They meet each other, learn each other's strengths and talents, set ground rules for communicating, plan and implement activities, produce results, share successes, solve problems, replace members who leave, and improve plans and processes over time to sustain their work as a team. The team itself is a message that educators, parents, and community partners will work together to help more students succeed in school. Only a well-functioning team, however, will produce the desired results.

Over time, most groups progress through four developmental steps to become an effective team: *forming, storming, norming,* and *performing* (see Hirsh & Valentine, 1998, for the derivation and descriptions of these stages). That is, teams need to get a good start, minimize conflict, establish rules and procedures, and take action. Some Action Teams for Partnerships move quickly through these stages to become productive and successful. Other ATPs move slowly but steadily, and still other teams fail to function. As new members are added, some ATPs remain strong and productive, whereas others must redevelop their team qualities before they can move ahead with their work on partnerships.

Get a good start. When teams are *forming,* members have high expectations for success and many questions about the charge to the team and their own roles and responsibilities. Members must learn about each other's strengths and talents and establish basic ground rules for communicating with one another (see pp. 106-110 of this *Handbook*). Each year, some new members may join the Action Team for Partnerships. Thus, each year it is necessary to reintroduce the team's charge, review the team's goals and plans, and reassign members' roles and responsibilities.

It is important to select teachers, parents, administrators, and other members of the team who believe that families and the community can support students and the school. Then, the team should elect effective leaders, provide copies of action plans for partnerships to all members, and share contact information so that all members can communicate easily with each other.

When teams convene at the start of the school year, the principal, chair of the School Improvement Team, or a district leader should review the team's charge, express support, and discuss the resources available for the team's work. The chair or co-chairs of the ATP may conduct a team-building activity to help members get to know one another.

Minimize conflict. Some teams enter short periods when individuals or subgroups seem to be *storming* with each other. If the ATP's charge is unclear or if the One-Year Action Plan is not addressing important goals, members may be uncertain why they are on the team. If meetings are irregular or poorly planned, members may become critical of the team leaders and question the need for their own participation.

These concerns and confusions can be minimized or eliminated by writing good plans and by establishing thoughtful team processes. An action plan for partnerships should be written each spring for the next school year and reviewed and refreshed by the team that reassembles each fall (see pp. 343-352 of this *Handbook)*. Leaders and members must set realistic schedules and important agendas for team and committee meetings, and start and end meetings on time. Team-building activities can be conducted as needed, to draw attention to particularly important norms, rules, and skills for good teamwork, such as listening to each other, discussing disagreements, and respecting differences in opinions.

Establish rules and procedures. The process of *norming* occurs when all team members contribute ideas for rules on how the ATP will conduct its meetings and its work. Members may create specific roles to ensure more effective team meetings. A *recorder* or *secretary* may take notes and distribute summaries of team meetings to those who could not attend. A *timekeeper* may help keep the meeting moving on schedule. *Liaisons* to the School Improvement Team and PTA or PTO may help alert and recruit participants for activities for family and community involvement.

Members may agree to procedures and rules for how team members will listen to each other, solicit ideas, express disagreements, discuss solutions to problems, agree to compromises, and make decisions. The norms for teamwork help members build trust and respect for one another and strengthen the spirit of cooperation for work that must be done.

Take action. When members understand the team's goals, know their own and others' responsibilities and talents, and agree on the rules for interaction and cooperation, then Action Teams for Partnerships can become high-performing leadership units in any elementary, middle, or high school. High-performing teams cooperate and communicate to implement planned activities, evaluate the quality and results of activities, and celebrate successes. Each year, good teams review their meeting schedules, procedures, responsibilities, and activities and write new annual plans to continually improve their partnership programs, practices, and results.

Every Action Team for Partnerships, with parents, teachers, administrators, community partners, school staff, and others as members, has a responsibility to minimize any storming that may occur, create helpful norms and processes, and take action to produce important results for students. There are several tools that can be used to strengthen the quality of an ATP's plans and actions.

How Often Should an Action Team for Partnerships Meet?

An ATP should conduct just the right number of meetings—not too many and not too few—on a realistic schedule. There will be full-team meetings, committee meetings, and periodic reports to the School Council or School Improvement Team and other school groups. An ATP should consider the following recommendations about team meetings and reports.

- The full ATP should meet on a regular schedule, at least monthly for one or two hours. The full ATP meetings are used to plan and schedule activities, coordinate actions, evaluate results, identify and solve problems, and celebrate progress. The meetings should be organized with agendas that reinforce teamwork and team spirit and that keep the activities in the One-Year Action Plan moving forward.

- Whole team meetings may be used to orient new team members to the One-Year Action Plan, build team identity and spirit, review and revise the One-Year Action Plan for the year, monitor the progress of committees from month to month, plan publicity and other communication strategies, evaluate activities that were implemented, conduct end-of-year reviews and evaluations, celebrate progress, plan and write a new One-Year Action Plan, and conduct other ATP responsibilities.

- ATP committees focused on the six types of involvement or on selected school improvement goals should meet as often as needed to plan and implement the activities in the One-Year Action Plan for which they are responsible. Committee meetings may be used to check responsibilities and needs for implementing upcoming activities (e.g., facilities, materials, publicity, or outreach or assistance from the full ATP, School Improvement Team, or others), evaluate completed activities, celebrate successes, plan improvements, design the committee's activities for the full ATP's next One-Year Action Plan, and conduct other committee responsibilities.

- The chair or, optimally, co-chairs of the full ATP and the ATP committees will prepare the agendas for the meetings, secure a room, remind members of the meeting, invite special guests, conduct the meeting, and take other leadership roles. (See ABCs of Action Team Leadership, pp. 112-118 in this *Handbook*.)

- The chair, co-chairs, or designated members of the ATP should report regularly (at least twice a year) to the School Council or School Improvement Team, the full faculty, the PTA or PTO, and to other groups so that all teachers, parents, students, and members of the community know about the school's plans, activities, and progress on partnerships. These also are occasions to gather information and ideas for needed changes and improvements and to recruit leaders and participants for various activities.

The chair, co-chairs, or designated members of the ATP should publicize the plans, activities, and progress on partnerships to all families, students, and the community in school or community newsletters, on websites, with banners or posters, in other media, and in various forums to increase understanding, participation, and support for partnerships. (See How to Organize Your Action Team for Partnerships, pp. 215-216 in this *Handbook*.)

What Tools Help
an Action Team for Partnerships
Conduct Its Activities?

To fulfill its responsibilities and to develop and strengthen its program of partnerships from year to year, an Action Team for Partnerships (ATP) should address the questions in the first column. Planning and evaluation tools in this *Handbook* described in the second column may be used to answer the questions.

QUESTIONS TO ANSWER

1. This school's ATP is already conducting some family involvement activities. How can we take stock of the activities that teachers are doing individually, at particular grade levels, and that are being conducted by various groups schoolwide?

2. This school has a School Improvement Plan that identifies key goals. How can our ATP link family and community involvement to our school's long-term goals for improvement?

3. There are so many parent and community involvement activities to choose from. How can our ATP organize a good and realistic plan for this school year?

4. This school is implementing its One-Year Action Plan. How will our ATP know if we are making progress?

TOOLS TO USE

1. *Starting Points*. Conduct an inventory of present practices for the six types of involvement (see pp. 208-211).

2. *Three-Year Outline.* Create a long-term vision of how school-family-community partnerships will be implemented over time to contribute to student success (see pp. 336-342).

3. *One-Year Action Plan*. Write an annual plan with a detailed schedule of activities and specific responsibilities for members of the Action Team for Partnerships. See pages 343-352 for the alternative forms for the One-Year Action Plan.

4. *End-of-Year Evaluation*. Reflect on progress and new challenges at the end of the school year (see pp. 353-364).

Use *A Measure of School, Family, and Community Partnerships* to learn how well activities are implemented (see pp. 330-335).

Write the next One-Year Action Plan.

Many other tools to help ATPs organize their work are in this chapter. Pages 106-118 include guidelines for organizing committees, conducting team meetings, setting communication ground rules, evaluating team processes, and improving team leadership. Also see other information for district and state leaders to assist ATPs in Chapter 7.

What Will the Action Team for Partnerships Be Named?

A school may simply call its team the Action Team for Partnerships (ATP) or select an alternative name. Some team names are the School, Family, and Community Partnership Team or the Home, School, Community Partnership Team. Or a school may choose a unique name for the ATP such as Parent-Educator Network (PEN), Teachers Getting Involved With Families (TGIF), Partners in Education (PIE), Partners for Student Success (PASS), Partners for Progress (PFP), Teachers and Parents for Students (TAPS), or other names that refer to partnerships.

Some names should *not* be chosen. Titles should be avoided that refer only to parents or that suggest that the ATP is conducting only a "parent program." Names such as The Parent Team or Bringing Parents to School would *not* be good team names. An ATP needs a name that conveys the fact that educators, families, and the community will work together because of their shared interests in the success of all students.

How Does an Action Team for Partnerships Differ From the School Council or School Improvement Team?

School councils, improvement teams, and other decision-making or advisory groups identify school goals and write and oversee broad plans. School councils are usually agents for change that draw the big picture of school improvement and set goals for excellence. Most School Councils do not stipulate detailed schedules, nor do they delegate responsibilities for implementing specific school, family, and community partnership activities.

The ATP accounts for and takes responsibility for planning and conducting family and community involvement activities. The ATP reports to the School Council or School Improvement Team about how family and community connections are supporting specific school improvement goals and whether and how progress on partnerships is made each year.

For example, a School Council may set a goal to improve students' math skills. This broad goal affects the actions that teachers and administrators take to improve the math curriculum and instruction. The goal to improve students' math skills also affects family and community involvement. The ATP will include in the One-Year Action Plan for partnerships some activities that involve all families and the community in helping students focus on math, enjoy learning math, complete math homework, share math progress and successes and other math-related activities.

If the school receives Title I federal funds, the ATP, the One-Year Action Plan for partnerships, and the implementation of that plan fulfill and exceed Title I's requirements for family and community involvement. The pledges in this chapter (see pp. 122-126) formalize an agreement for teachers, students, parents, and administrators to work together as partners to help all students succeed in school. By organizing and implementing a partnership program, the ATP assists the school administration and School Council or School Improvement Team to meet family and community involvement requirements for Title I funding.

Could the School Council Be the Action Team for Partnerships?

If a School Council or School Improvement Team is very large, a designated subset of teachers, parents, and an administrator may serve as the Action Team for Partnerships. In most schools, however, the School Improvement Team or School Council is limited in size and has defined responsibilities for advising the principal about school goals and for overseeing all aspects of the school's program and progress.

Most School Councils need an ATP as an action arm to plan and implement family and community involvement activities. The ATP (like any other work group or special committee) reports to the School Council on a regular schedule about its progress on family and community involvement and obtains input and ideas from the council for the annual One-Year Action Plan. One member of the School Council may also serve on the ATP as a *linking member* to ensure that the School Council is always aware of the plans and activities for partnerships and how to support those activities.

When different people serve on the School Council and the ATP, individual leaders are protected from trying to do too many things and burning out. Also, an ATP ensures that more teachers, administrators, parents, and community partners develop leadership skills over time.

How Does the Action Team for Partnerships Differ From the PTA or PTO?

A school benefits by having an Action Team for Partnerships *and* a PTA, PTO, Home-School Association, or other parent association. A PTA/PTO helps develop parent leaders and brings parents' voices to many school decisions and activities. Typically, however, a PTA/PTO does not guide or direct school administrators or teachers to organize and improve communications with all families on student learning, homework, report card grades, curriculum matters, tests and assessments, post-secondary planning, and other important school topics.

The ATP writes an annual One-Year Action Plan for family and community involvement that extends the PTA/PTO agenda to include activities that teachers, administrators, counselors, community partners, or others conduct to help all parents understand their children's work and learning opportunities each year. An officer or representative of the PTA/PTO should be a member or co-chair of the Action Team for Partnerships to make sure that the two groups are working in concert.

How May the Action Team Approach Be Used to Organize Comprehensive School Reform?

Schools with ambitious goals for whole-school change may organize a Partnership School-Comprehensive School Reform (CSR) model. In the Partnership School-CSR model, *four* or *five* action teams are organized, instead of only an Action Team for Partnerships, as shown in Figure 3.2. Each action team writes and implements annual action plans to attain a major school improvement goal. For example, a school may have an Action Team for Math (ATM), an Action Team for Reading (ATR), an Action Team for Attendance (ATA), and an Action Team for Partnerships (ATP).

On each action team, teachers, administrators, school staff, parents, and members of the community work together. Each team's action plans must include specific, scheduled activities for improving the curriculum, instructional approaches, assessments, and classroom management to attain each selected school goal. In addition, each team's action plans must include activities for the six types of family and community involvement to help the school and students reach the selected goals.

In a Partnership School-CSR model, schools may select various academic and behavioral goals for their own students, but all schools must include one goal to strengthen and sustain a positive climate of school, family, and community partnerships. The ATP plans and implements connections with families and communities for the six types of involvement that are not addressed by the action teams for the selected academic and behavior goals.

Note

1. This chapter draws some information from Epstein, J. L. (2001). Strategies for action in practice, policy, and research. In *School, family, and community partnerships: Preparing educators and improving schools*. Boulder, CO: Westview Press.

Figure 3.2

Action Team for Partnerships
Structure for Comprehensive School Reform (CSR)

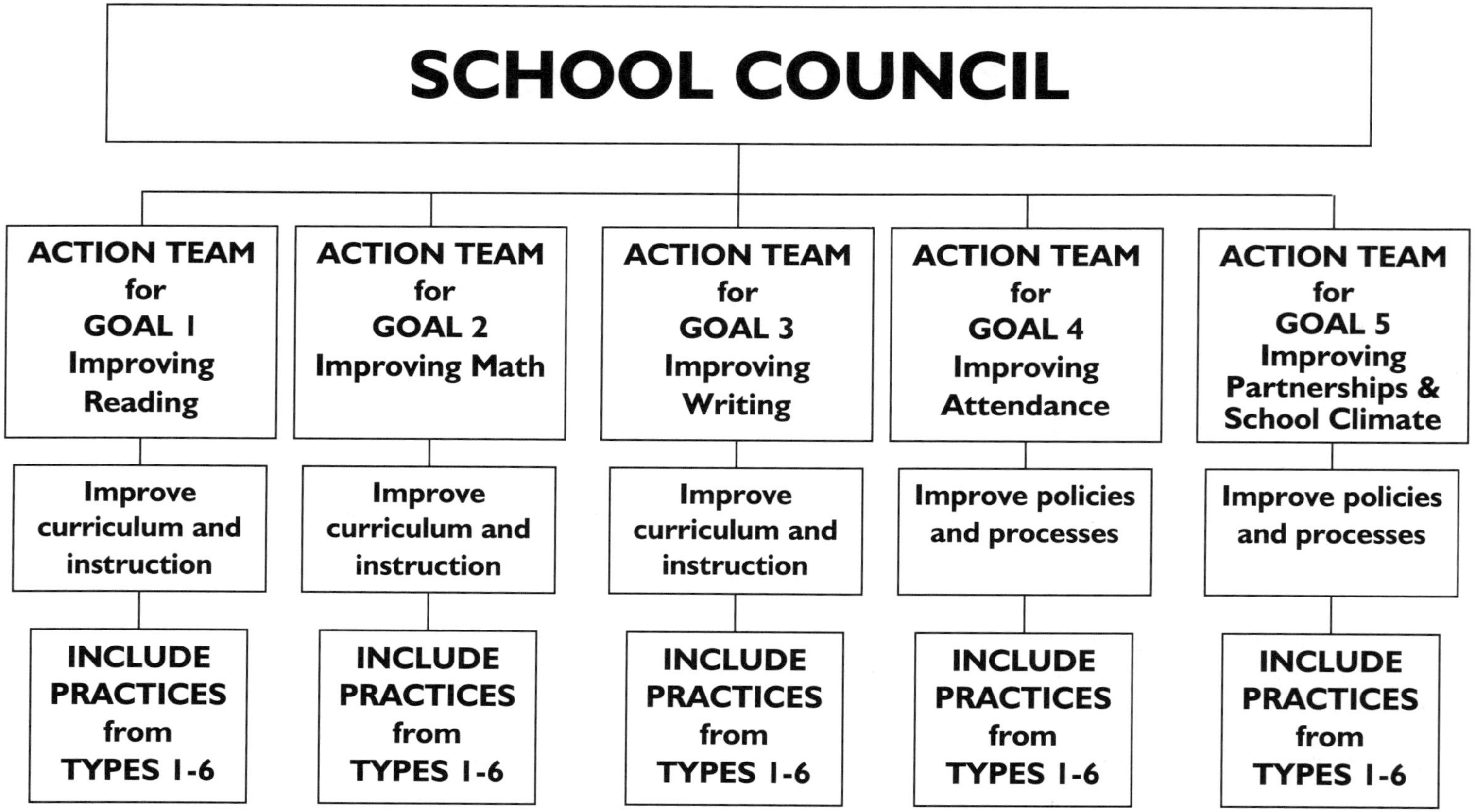

SCHOOL COUNCIL

ACTION TEAM for GOAL 1 Improving Reading
→ Improve curriculum and instruction
→ INCLUDE PRACTICES from TYPES 1-6

ACTION TEAM for GOAL 2 Improving Math
→ Improve curriculum and instruction
→ INCLUDE PRACTICES from TYPES 1-6

ACTION TEAM for GOAL 3 Improving Writing
→ Improve curriculum and instruction
→ INCLUDE PRACTICES from TYPES 1-6

ACTION TEAM for GOAL 4 Improving Attendance
→ Improve policies and processes
→ INCLUDE PRACTICES from TYPES 1-6

ACTION TEAM for GOAL 5 Improving Partnerships & School Climate
→ Improve policies and processes
→ INCLUDE PRACTICES from TYPES 1-6

References

Epstein, J. L., & Sheldon, S. B. (2002). Present and accounted for: Improving student attendance through family and community involvement. *Journal of Educational Research*.

Hirsh, S., & Valentine, J. W. (1998). *Building effective middle level teams*. Reston, VA: National Association of Secondary School Principals.

Ten Steps to Success in School, Family, and Community Partnerships

✔ **Create an Action Team for Partnerships**

✔ **Obtain funds and official support**

✔ **Provide training to all members of the Action Team for Partnerships**

✔ **Identify starting points— present strengths and weaknesses**

✔ **Develop a Three-Year Outline and vision for partnerships**

✔ **Write a One-Year Action Plan**

✔ **Enlist staff, parents, students, and the community to help conduct activities**

✔ **Evaluate implementations and results**

✔ **Conduct annual celebrations and report progress to all participants**

✔ **Continue working toward a comprehensive, ongoing, goal-oriented program of partnerships**

Checklist: Are You Ready?

GETTING STARTED WITH AN ACTION TEAM FOR PARTNERSHIPS

The chair or co-chairs of the Action Team for Partnerships (ATP) will guide these activities.

CHECK ☑ WHEN YOUR SCHOOL ATP COMPLETES THE FOLLOWING:

❏ **Select the members of the ATP** including 6 to 12 members, with teachers, parents, principal, and others selected for their interest in and commitment to positive school, family, and community connections

❏ **Identify the chair or co-chairs of the Action Team for Partnerships**

❏ **Select the ATP's committee structure to focus on each of the six types of involvement or on four school improvement goals and identify the chair or co-chairs of each committee**

❏ **Complete an inventory of present practices** for each of the six types of involvement. Discuss the inventory with teachers, parents, students, and others and obtain their ideas about partnership activities that should be maintained, improved, and added. (See *Starting Points,* pp. 208-211.)

❏ **Complete a Three-Year Outline** of broad goals for partnerships focused on the six types of involvement or specific school improvement goals to show how the school's program of partnerships will develop over time

❏ **Complete a One-Year Action Plan** specifying partnership activities for each of the six types of involvement or for four school improvement goals, who is responsible for implementing the involvement activities, when they will be conducted, and what results are expected

❏ **Establish a reasonable schedule for meetings of the full ATP** (e.g., monthly or every other month) and a reasonable schedule for meetings of the committees that will work on the six types of involvement or on partnerships for school improvement goals

Decide how often and in what ways the ATP will report to the following groups and schedule these connections:

> ❏ The school council or school improvement team
> ❏ The full faculty
> ❏ All parents
> ❏ Parent association (e.g., PTA, PTO, Home-School, or other groups)
> ❏ The community (e.g., organizations, media)
> ❏ District leaders, school board, other district offices

❏ **Design and schedule a "kickoff" activity** to effectively convey the message to all educators, families, and students that the school is a "partnership school."

Who Are the Members of the
Action Team for Partnerships?

School Year_____

What skills, talents, and experiences do members bring to the Action Team for Partnerships? For example, who has art, music, computer, financial, writing, or teaching talents? Who makes many contacts with community groups and organizations? Who is well suited to be a chair or co-chair of the ATP or of one of the ATP committees?

List the names, addresses, and positions (e.g., teacher, parent, administrator, student) of the 6 to 12 members of the Action Team for Partnerships. Discuss and note the strengths and talents each one brings to the ATP. On the next page, identify the ATP's committee structure and leadership positions.

Name: _____ Position: _____ Telephone: _____
Address: _____ Best Time to Call: _____
Strengths/Talents: _____ E-mail _____
_____

Name: _____ Position: _____ Telephone: _____
Address: _____ Best Time to Call: _____
Strengths/Talents: _____ E-mail: _____
_____

Name: _____ Position: _____ Telephone: _____
Address: _____ Best Time to Call: _____
Strengths/Talents: _____ E-mail: _____
_____

Name: _____ Position: _____ Telephone: _____
Address: _____ Best Time to Call: _____
Strengths/Talents: _____ E-mail: _____
_____

Name: _____ Position: _____ Telephone: _____
Address: _____ Best Time to Call: _____
Strengths/Talents: _____ E-mail: _____
_____

Name: _____ Position: _____ Telephone: _____
Address: _____ Best Time to Call: _____
Strengths/Talents: _____ E-mail: _____
_____

(If you have more than six members on the ATP, make additional copies of this form.)

ATP Committee Structure and Leaders

School Year_____

Check ☑ the committee structure that the ATP will use to organize its One-Year Action Plan and activities on school, family, and community partnerships. Then fill in the ATP and committee leaders. *Check and fill in ONLY ONE COLUMN of this form.*

❏ **This ATP will organize SIX committees for the TYPES of involvement.** See Three-Year Outline—Form T, One-Year Action Plan—Form T, and End-of-Year Evaluation—Form T

LEADERS THIS YEAR
Chair/Co-chairs of ATP

_____

_____

Chair/Co-chairs of Committees

Type 1-Parenting

_____

_____

Type 2-Communicating

_____

_____

Type 3-Volunteering

_____

_____

Type 4-Learning at Home

_____

_____

Type 5-Decision Making

_____

_____

Type 6-Collaborating With the Community

_____

_____

❏ **This ATP will organize FOUR committees for selected school improvement GOALS.** See Three-Year Outline—Form G, One-Year Action Plan—Form G, and End-of-Year Evaluation—Form G

LEADERS THIS YEAR
Chair/Co-chairs of ATP

_____

_____

Chair/Co-chairs of Committees

Goal 1 (Academic): _____

_____

_____

Goal 2 (Academic): _____

_____

_____

Goal 3 (Behavioral): _____

_____

_____

Goal 4 (Climate of Partnership):

_____

_____

Give a copy of this information to every team member and other school leaders.

First ATP Meeting of the School Year

The Action Team for Partnerships (ATP) implements school, family, and community connections to increase student success. The full ATP meets at least once a month to plan, monitor, evaluate, and improve activities. ATP committees may meet more often to prepare for specific partnership activities.

At its first meeting of the school year, the ATP must lay a strong foundation on which to build an effective partnership program. The agenda for the first meeting of the year may include the following topics, discussions, and actions.

- **Determine shared leadership responsibilities and select team leaders**
  Leaders may include
  - *Chairperson* or *cochairs* (cochairs are recommended)
  - *Recorder* of the minutes for each meeting
  - *Liaison* or link to the school council to report the plans and events of the ATP
  - *Liaison* or link to the PTA or PTO to include the activities of the parent organization in the ATP's One-Year Action Plan for partnerships
  - *Promoter* or *publicist* to let teachers, other staff, families, students, and the community know of action team plans, events, and progress
  - *Other roles* as needed or desired
  - Review or select the ATP's committee structure and *committee leaders* to organize specific activities in the ATP's One-Year Action Plan

- **Establish a communication system**
  - Create and distribute a phone and address list of ATP members to all members and other school leaders.
  - Set a regular schedule (dates, time, place) for meetings.
  - Establish or review the team's ground rules for communicating at meetings (see p. 109 in this *Handbook*).
  - Decide how team members will inform the team if they are unable to attend a meeting.
  - Decide how the team will provide minutes of each meeting to absent team members.
  - Plan how the team will keep the whole school community informed of partnership plans, activities, and progress.
  - Conduct a team-building activity to celebrate members' strengths, talents, and commitment to the work of the team.

- **Review the One-Year Action Plan for partnerships**
  - Discuss ATP committee responsibilities for the school year.
  - Revise activities as needed through the year.

- **Begin implementing the planned partnership activities**
  Help the appropriate ATP committees and leaders with upcoming activities:
  - Which activities are scheduled during the next month?
  - Who is in charge of each of these activities?
  - What needs to be done to prepare for the upcoming activities?
  - Who will help implement each activity?
  - How will the team evaluate the effectiveness of each activity?

- **Discuss the date, time, place, and agenda for the next ATP meeting**

COMMUNICATION GROUND RULES

Communication ground rules are rules of behavior and interaction that team members agree to use to conduct meetings, manage discussions, and share ideas with each other.

What ground rules should the Action Team for Partnerships (ATP) set to help team members communicate effectively?

How should we communicate at ATP meetings?

Example: Give everyone an opportunity to share his or her ideas.

1.

2.

3.

4.

5.

How should team members communicate with each other between meetings?

Example: E-mail the agenda to all members before each team meeting.

1.

2.

3.

4.

5.

Put a ★ next to the three most important rules for communicating at ATP meetings and the three most important rules for communicating between meetings.

Discuss the top choices and compile a final list of rules for communication that all team members agree are most important for the ATP to follow.

What Do Successful Action Teams for Partnerships Do?

Good Teams...

Help members communicate with each other

- Develop respect for one another's strengths and talents
- Establish ground rules for communicating with team members
- Identify clear roles and responsibilities for all team members
- Create a spirit of cooperation, encouragement, and appreciation
- Rise above school politics to communicate with all faculty, staff, and families about partnership activities

Plan goal-oriented partnerships

- Write an ambitious One-Year Action Plan with clear goals and objectives for family and community involvement
- Link partnership activities to school improvement plans and goals
- Identify and obtain needed resources for planned activities

Conduct useful meetings

- Create an appropriate meeting schedule for the full ATP and for ATP committees
- Follow a focused agenda at each meeting
- Start and end meetings on time

Make decisions collegially and share leadership

- Establish guidelines for decision making
- Agree to disagree with ideas, not people
- Discuss and solve problems; build consensus
- Share leadership to implement planned activities

Continue to improve partnerships

- Celebrate successful partnership activities and results
- Identify areas for improvement
- Write new One-Year Action Plans for partnerships every year
- Replace team members who leave
- Adjust roles and responsibilities as needed

ANNUAL REVIEW OF TEAM PROCESSES

School Year: _____

Discuss: How well is your ATP working as a team? How should teamwork improve?

TEAM PROCESS	RECOMMENDATION C = Continue N = Need to Improve	COMMENTS / SUGGESTIONS
MEMBERSHIP		
• ATP members include teachers, parents, administrators, and others		
• ATP leaders fill useful roles (e.g., chair, cochairs, recorder, committee chairs)		
• New members of the ATP are oriented to the team and to their responsibilities		
SCHEDULES		
• Full ATP meets on a regular schedule		
• Time/place for meetings worked well		
• ATP committees meet as needed		
ORGANIZATION		
• Agendas of meetings are well planned and cover important content		
• Minutes of meetings are provided to all members who could not attend		
• At ATP meetings, all members contribute their ideas		
• At ATP committee meetings, all members contribute their ideas		
• Team members work well as a team, listen to each other, and disagree respectfully		
PROGRAM IMPLEMENTATION		
• Activities in the One-Year Action Plan are implemented on schedule		
• The ATP's budget for partnerships is adequate		
• The ATP is making progress in informing and involving more families		
• All team members take responsibility for leading or assisting with family and community involvement activities		
• ATP members encourage all teachers, school staff, parents, students, and others to participate in some involvement activities		
• Activities are evaluated for quality and results		
• The ATP communicates with other groups at school to report plans and progress on partnerships (e.g., school council, faculty, parent organization, school board, local media, others)		

• **LOOKING AHEAD.** What is one way that the ATP could become even more effective next year in leading the school's program of school, family, and community partnerships?

The ABCs of Action Team Leadership

This section outlines the qualities and responsibilities of the chair or co-chairs of the Action Team for Partnerships (ATP).

Good leadership is essential for a well-functioning ATP.

Team leaders are expected to:

A—Accept leadership

B—Be ready to share leadership

C—Communicate with all partners

D—Develop good plans

E—Evaluate progress

F—Foster team spirit

A

ACCEPT LEADERSHIP

The chair or co-chairs of the Action Team for Partnerships (ATP) accept leadership of the team with enthusiasm and a sense of purpose. The leaders manage, coordinate, and facilitate the work of the ATP. Team leaders:

- Schedule meetings of the full ATP at least once a month or more often as needed to ensure progress

- Develop agendas and conduct ATP meetings

- Provide copies of the One-Year Action Plan for partnerships, minutes of all meetings, and other important documents to all team members

- Guide committee leaders in implementing activities for the six types of involvement or for selected school goals and oversee committee's progress

- Replace members who leave the ATP each year and orient new members to the team's plans, procedures, and their responsibilities

- Prepare for transitions by sharing ATP plans, materials, evaluations, and other history with the next ATP chair or co-chairs

B

BE READY TO SHARE LEADERSHIP

The chair or co-chairs of the Action Team for Partnerships (ATP) recognize that many leaders and helpers are needed for a successful program of partnerships. Team leaders

- **Decide**, with the full team, the committee structure that the ATP will use to organize its work (see pp. 87-90 in this *Handbook*)

- **Set ground rules**, with the full team, for good communications at ATP meetings (see p. 109 in this *Handbook*)

- **Identify** chairs or co-chairs and members of the selected committees

- **Delegate responsibilities** to the leaders of each committee to call upon other teachers, administrators, families, community partners, and students to conduct and participate in planned activities

- **Share responsibilities** with other members of the ATP to report progress on partnerships to the School Council and other groups at school and in the community

- **Share credit** for the team's progress and successes with all team members and with others who lead, help, and participate in partnership activities

C

COMMUNICATE WITH ALL PARTNERS

The chair or co-chairs of the Action Team for Partnerships (ATP) communicate with all partners about the work of the ATP. Team leaders

- Communicate with **all members of the ATP**

- Keep the **principal** and **school faculty** informed of progress and challenges. Help **new faculty** and **long-term substitute teachers** understand and participate in partnership activities

- Share information with the **School Council** or **School Improvement Team** about the ATP's plans and progress for family and community involvement linked to school improvement goals

- Include **PTA/PTO representatives** as ATP members, committee chairs, and active participants, and PTA/PTO activities in the One-Year Action Plan for partnerships

- Use newsletters and other vehicles to inform **all families** about the annual plans for school, family, and community partnerships and how all are welcome to assist and participate

- Communicate with the media to **inform the public** of the school's work on partnerships

- Talk with a **district facilitator** for partnerships about the school's program, progress, challenges, and help needed

D

DEVELOP GOOD PLANS

The chair or co-chairs of the Action Team for Partnerships (ATP) guide team members to create excellent plans for school, family, and community partnerships. Team leaders and the ATP

- **Write annual plans** for family and community involvement linked to school improvement goals

- Select activities for family and community involvement that **meet the needs of the students and families served by the school**

- Include family and community involvement activities that **create a welcoming climate of partnership** at the school

Tools to develop good plans include

- **Starting Points—at the start of the partnership program** and as needed to inventory the school's partnership practices (see pp. 208-211 in this *Handbook*)

- **Three-Year Outline—every year or as needed** to identify long-term goals for the school's partnership program (see pp. 336-342 in this *Handbook*)

- **One-Year Action Plan—every year** to continue, add, and improve partnership activities for all six types of involvement that are linked to the school improvement plan and to specific school improvement goals (see pp. 343-352 in this *Handbook*)

E

EVALUATE PROGRESS

The chair or co-chairs of the Action Team for Partnerships (ATP) guide the full team and assist committees to evaluate the quality of the partnership program and practices. Team leaders

- **Implement** planned activities on schedule

- **Assist** committee members to overcome or remove obstacles to progress

- Periodically **revisit** the One-Year Action Plan to update plans and committee responsibilities

- **Reach out** to a district facilitator for partnerships when assistance is needed

- Select useful ways to **evaluate** the **quality** of team processes, outreach to families and the community, and results of involvement activities

Tools to evaluate progress include

- **Measure of School, Family, and Community Partnerships** to assess the quality of family and community involvement practices (see pp. 330-335 of this *Handbook*)

- **End-of-Year Evaluation—every spring** to assess the strengths and weaknesses of the school's partnership program and to help develop the next One-Year Action Plan (see pp. 353-364 in this *Handbook*)

- **Annual Review of Team Processes** to assess how well the ATP organizes its work and how ATP members work together (see p. 111 in this *Handbook*)

F

FOSTER TEAM SPIRIT

The chair or co-chairs of the Action Team for Partnerships (ATP) encourage collaboration and cooperation among team members and other partners. Team leaders

- **Respect** the ideas of all team members

- **Inspire** team members to work well together

- **Help** team members develop leadership skills

- **Encourage** team members to set high expectations to involve all families in productive ways

- **Lead by example** with enthusiasm, fairness, humor, and common sense and with good organizational, communication, and problem-solving skills

- **Assist** others at the school to see the "big picture" of school, family, and community partnerships

- **Celebrate** successes with all team members and other partners

Action Team Discussion on Meeting Key Challenges to Excellent Partnerships

This activity helps an Action Team for Partnerships (ATP) discuss how to involve diverse groups of families and the community in children's education by meeting key challenges for the six types of involvement.

The chair or cochairs of an ATP or a district facilitator for partnerships should guide this discussion with the whole ATP, small groups, or ATP committees. A recorder in each group should take notes on important ideas. Small groups may address different challenges and then reconvene as a whole group to combine ideas.

Make sure that all members of the ATP have opportunities to share examples and ideas. (NOTE: This activity may be completed at one meeting or over the course of several ATP meetings.)

1. Involving Hard-to-Reach Families

All families are hard to reach some of the time, but some families pose particular challenges that must be solved to involve them in their children's education and to create a climate of partnership at the school.

- Which groups of families in this school are the hardest to reach?

- What are the main reasons for the low involvement of these families?

- What strategies and activities might improve this school's outreach and the families' involvement?

Hard-to-Reach Families	Main Reasons	How Might We Involve These Families?
_____	_____	_____
	_____	_____
	_____	_____
_____	_____	_____
	_____	_____
	_____	_____
_____	_____	_____
	_____	_____
	_____	_____
_____	_____	_____
	_____	_____
	_____	_____
_____	_____	_____
	_____	_____

School, Family, and Community Partnerships by J. L. Epstein et al., © 2002 Corwin Press, Inc.
Photocopying permissible for local school use only.

2. Improving Practices of Partnership by Meeting Key Challenges

Explore the following challenges for each type of involvement. Discuss the following:

- Which activities might help your school meet each challenge?
- How might all families be involved?
- Who might take leadership for these activities? (NOTE: Leaders may be members of the ATP or other teachers, administrators, parents or other family members, community members, or support staff who will work with the ATP or one of its committees.)
- Note: If the challenge has been resolved, consider improvements or discuss a new challenge at the school.

Type 1-Parenting

Challenge: Help families understand each stage of their children's development.

Activity: _____

Ways to reach all families: _____

Possible leaders: _____

Challenge: Provide information from workshops to all families who cannot attend.

Activity: _____

Ways to reach all families: _____

Possible leaders: _____

Type 2-Communicating

Challenge: Help families understand their children's report cards.

Activity: _____

Ways to reach all families: _____

Possible leaders: _____

Challenge: Set conference schedules so that all families can attend.

Activity: _____

Ways to reach all families: _____

Possible leaders: _____

Type 3-Volunteering

Challenge: Recruit, organize, and train volunteers to help students and the school.

Activity: _____

Ways to reach all families: _____

Possible leaders: _____

Challenge: Schedule events at various times so all parents can attend.

Activity: _____

Ways to reach all families: _____

Possible leaders: _____

Type 4-Learning at Home

Challenge: Provide families information on the skills required for students to pass each class, grade, or course.

Activity: _____

Ways to reach all families: _____

Possible leaders: _____

Challenge: Design and use interactive homework for students to share their work and ideas with family partners.

Activity: _____

Ways to reach all families: _____

Possible leaders: _____

Type 5-Decision Making

Challenge: Create an active, representative parent association (e.g., PTA or PTO).

Activity: _____

Ways to reach all families: _____

Possible leaders: _____

Challenge: Enable parents and teachers to work together on committees, including the Action Team for Partnerships.

Activity: _____

Ways to reach all families: _____

Possible leaders: _____

Type 6-Collaborating With the Community

Challenge: Identify community resources to assist families, students, and the school.

Activity: _____

Ways to reach all families: _____

Possible leaders: _____

Challenge: Help students, educators, and families contribute to the community.

Activity: _____

Ways to reach all families: _____

Possible leaders: _____

Sample Pledges, Compacts, or Contracts

Pledges, compacts, or contracts are symbolic agreements that formally recognize that students, families, teachers, and administrators must work together to help students succeed each year in school. The form, content, and wording of pledges must be appropriate for the preschool, elementary, middle, and high school levels. The items should reflect the developmental stages of the students, the organizational characteristics of the schools, and the situations of families.

Pledges, compacts, or contracts should include parallel forms for parents, students, teachers, and administrators. By signing parallel pledges, everyone becomes aware of their common goals, shared responsibilities, and personal commitments.

It helps to do the following:

- Use the term "pledge" instead of "compact" or "contract" to recognize the voluntary, good-faith nature of these commitments.

- Keep the list of commitments short and clear, including 5 to 10 items.

- Include a short cover letter signed by the principal that explains to students, families, and teachers that pledges are *part of* a comprehensive program of school, family, and community partnerships.

- Provide each partner with signed copies of all pledges.

- Implement school practices that enable parents, students, teachers and administrators to fulfill the commitments in the pledges. For example, if parents are asked to communicate with the school, then the school must provide parents with clear information and easy avenues for contacting teachers, counselors, or administrators. If parents are asked to volunteer, then the school must establish an effective program to recruit, welcome, and train volunteers.

- Include an "open" item that students and families can insert to tailor the pledge to their own situations, interests, and needs. For example, add one more "pledge" for partnerships that tells something you will do this year.

- Discuss the content of pledges annually with students, families, teachers, and others; obtain input; and revise as needed.

- Develop a full program of partnerships including the six types of involvement. Pledges are one of many Type 2-Communicating activities that strengthen school, family, and community connections.

The sample pledges in this section may be tailored to match your school's policies and goals for students and for partnerships. Topics for parallel pledges include student effort, behavior, attendance, communications from school to home and home-to-school, parent-teacher conferences, volunteers, homework, study habits, appropriate dress, and specific school improvement goals.

SCHOOL-FAMILY-COMMUNITY PARTNERSHIPS

PARENT PLEDGE

✓ I will help my child to do well in school. I will encourage my child to work hard and cooperate with teachers and other students.

✓ I will send my child to school on time each day with a positive attitude about school and about being a student. If my child is absent due to illness, I will see that the missed work is made up.

✓ I will read notices from the school and communicate with teachers or others about questions that I have about school programs or my child's progress. I will participate in parent-teacher-student conferences and other school events.

✓ I will check to see that my child completes the homework that is assigned. I will encourage my child to discuss homework, classwork, report card grades, and academic goals with me.

✓ I will volunteer to work at school *or* at home to conduct activities to assist my child and the teacher, class, and community. I will encourage my child to contribute talents and time to home, school, and community.

SIGNATURE_____ DATE_____
                        Parent/Guardian

SCHOOL-FAMILY-COMMUNITY PARTNERSHIPS

STUDENT PLEDGE

✓ I will do my best in school. I will work hard and cooperate with my teachers and other students.

✓ I will come to school on time each day with a positive attitude about school and about being a student. If I am absent due to illness, I will make up classwork or homework that I missed.

✓ I will take notices home from school promptly and deliver notices to my teacher from home. I will participate in parent-teacher-student conferences and inform my family about school activities and events.

✓ I will complete my homework assignments. I will discuss homework with my family to share what I am learning in class. I will discuss my report card grades and academic goals with my family.

✓ I will welcome volunteers to my school and work with parents or others who assist me, my classmates, my teacher, or my school. I will contribute my talents and time to my family, school, and community.

SIGNATURE_____ DATE_____
             Student

SCHOOL-FAMILY-COMMUNITY PARTNERSHIPS

TEACHER PLEDGE

✓ I will help all of my students do their best in school. I will encourage each student to work hard, develop his or her talents, meet high expectations, and cooperate with teachers and students.

✓ I will come to school each day with a positive attitude about my students and their families and with well-prepared classroom lessons to assist students' learning. I will help students and families understand and fulfill the school's attendance policies.

✓ I will communicate clearly and frequently so that all families understand school programs and their children's progress. I will enable families to contact me with questions about their children. I will conduct at least one parent-teacher-student conference with each family.

✓ I will use interactive homework that enables students to discuss and demonstrate skills at home that we are learning in class. I will guide families to monitor their children's homework and to discuss report card grades and academic goals with their children.

✓ I will arrange ways for parents and other volunteers to use their time and talents to assist my students at school, in my class, or at home. I will vary schedules to encourage families to attend events, assemblies, and celebrations at school.

SIGNATURE_____ DATE_____
           Teacher

School, Family, and Community Partnerships by J. L. Epstein et al., © 2002 Corwin Press, Inc.
Photocopying permissible for local school use only.

SCHOOL-FAMILY-COMMUNITY PARTNERSHIPS

ADMINISTRATOR PLEDGE

✓ I will encourage all students to do their best in school. I will encourage each student to work hard, develop his or her talents, meet high expectations, and cooperate with teachers, the school staff, and other students.

✓ I will come to school each day with a positive attitude about my faculty, the students, and their families and communities. I also will help my faculty, families, and students understand, contribute to, and fulfill the school's attendance and other policies.

✓ I will communicate clearly and frequently so that all families understand the school's programs and their children's progress. I will encourage families to contact teachers and administrators with questions and ideas about their children and about school programs. I also will support and assist teachers to conduct at least one parent-teacher-student conference with each family each year.

✓ I will assist teachers, families, and students to understand and discuss homework policies, report card grades, and academic goals and support other activities that encourage family involvement in student learning.

✓ I will arrange ways for parents or other volunteers to use their time and talents to assist students and the school. I also will encourage families to attend events, assemblies, and celebrations at school.

✓ I will help develop a comprehensive program of school, family, and community partnerships at this school.

SIGNATURE_____ DATE_____
    Administrator

School, Family, and Community Partnerships by J. L. Epstein et al., © 2002 Corwin Press, Inc.
Photocopying permissible for local school use only.

4

Conducting Workshops

This chapter provides an outline and agenda for two workshops: Team-Training Workshops and End-of-Year Celebration Workshops. The workshops may be conducted by state coordinators, district facilitators, staff development organizations, or school leaders. Both workshops are designed for Action Teams for Partnerships (ATPs) or other audiences interested in developing programs of partnership. The workshops provide attendees with a common vocabulary, a common background, and processes that enable educators, parents, and others to talk and work together to build their programs of partnership.

Team-Training Workshops are conducted to provide members of new ATPs with the background they need to understand the six types of involvement, meet challenges to excellence, and link partnership activities to results. This information will help ATPs get started in planning and implementing their partnership programs. With a strong background in school, family, and community partnerships, ATPs will be prepared to take leadership at their schools to work with parents, family members, and others in the community to help students succeed at higher levels.

Facilitators and team leaders also may offer workshops to other administrators, teachers, parents, and community members who want or need to know more about the importance of school, family, and community partnerships; how to work more effectively with all families; and how to assist and support schools' Action Teams for Partnerships.

This chapter includes the agenda for a one-day workshop on school, family, and community partnerships. Notes are provided for facilitators on how to present key topics, and pages are indicated to use as overheads, handouts, and activities. The morning of the one-day workshop begins with a warm-up activity, followed by information and activities on (a) the six types of involvement, (b) challenges that must be resolved to reach all families, (c) expected results from excellent partnerships, and (d) structures for Action Teams for Partnerships. The afternoon of the one-day workshop enables each Action Team for Partnerships to apply the information learned in the morning by writing a draft One-Year Action Plan for partnerships for their own school. The draft plan is considered an "exit ticket" for attendees to leave the workshop. Facilitators should keep copies of their schools' draft plans in order to assist the ATPs in completing their final One-Year Action Plans with input from others at their schools.

The one-day workshop may be shortened to a few hours to present an overview of the types of involvement, challenges, and results of partnerships. Or, the workshop may be extended to two days to give participants more time and opportunities to share ideas and information, to take stock of their present practices and needs, and to write their One-Year Action Plans.

End-of-Year Celebration Workshops are conducted to recognize and share progress in improving school, family, and community partnerships. These workshops may include presentations on best practices, panel discussions on problems and solutions, school exhibits, and time to develop plans for the next school year. An agenda for a one-day celebration and planning workshop is outlined, along with ideas for sessions and panels to help schools' ATPs share ideas, report progress, and plan ahead. End-of-Year Celebration Workshops may be shortened to a half-day, part-day, or evening activity, depending on the time available and the number of schools involved.

End-of-Year Celebration Workshops should promote exchanges of ideas that help ATPs continue their work on partnerships and improve their next One-Year Action Plans for the new school year. Time may be provided at these workshops for ATPs to update their schools' Three-Year Outlines or long-term visions for partnerships and to begin to draft their next One-Year Action Plans. These workshops should help district facilitators recognize and reinforce the hard work that is done by schools' ATPs and encourage new and better work every year.

Team-Training Workshop

Sample Agenda

A one-day workshop for school Action Teams for Partnerships (ATPs) provides background information and activities on school, family, and community partnerships in the morning and guides teams of teachers, parents, and administrators from each school to write draft One-Year Action Plans for partnerships in the afternoon.

In the workshop, presentations on key topics are followed by group activities for participants to show how they can apply each topic to their own schools. The information and exercises develop the participants' understanding of school, family, and community partnerships. The topics increase in complexity from the six types of involvement to challenges to excellence, results of partnerships, and the organization of a well-functioning team. These four topics prepare participants to produce a workshop product—a draft One-Year Action Plan for partnerships.

The draft One-Year Action Plan is the exit ticket for attendees to leave the workshop. The teams will take the draft plans back to their schools for input from others (e.g., School Improvement Team, faculty, parent association). Then, they will complete a final version of the One-Year Action Plan. District facilitators should keep copies of all draft plans to help the schools' teams to review their ideas, gather input from others, and complete a final One-Year Action Plan.

Following is a sample one-day training workshop agenda. The agenda is followed by "Notes for Facilitators" with key points to present on the framework of six types of involvement, meeting the challenges, reaching results, action team structures, and writing action plans. Depending on the amount of time for training, the agenda may be shortened or extended.

Pages in the *Handbook* to use for each segment of the workshop are noted in parentheses. These pages may be copied for transparencies, handouts, and activities for participants.

The workshop topics give ATPs the basics to plan and implement their schools' partnership programs. Facilitators may add examples of practices to meet the special needs of the participants. For example, if elementary, middle, *and* high school ATPs attend, facilitators should include ideas for different grade levels in the presentations on the six types of involvement, meeting challenges, and results of partnerships, including attention to the importance of family and community involvement to ease students' transitions from one school level to the next. If schools have School Councils or School Improvement Teams, facilitators should make clear that the ATPs link directly with the decision-making body. The ATP serves as the School Council's action arm or work group to implement activities for family and community involvement that will promote the attainment of the goals specified in the school improvement plan. Facilitators may add other topics to the workshop agenda to address specific needs or interests of the participants.

TEAM-TRAINING WORKSHOP

Sample Agenda

SCHOOL, FAMILY, AND COMMUNITY CONNECTIONS:
STRENGTHENING YOUR PROGRAM OF PARTNERSHIPS

Date
Location

8:00-8:30   Registration and Refreshments

8:30-8:45   Greetings and Introductions

8:45-9:00   Warm-Up Activity (p. 206)

9:00-9:45   Facilitator Presentation: Framework of Six Types of Involvement
(pp. 165-171)
Group Activity: Starting Points Inventory (pp. 208-211)

9:45-10:30   Facilitator Presentation: Meeting the Challenges (pp. 178-183)
Group Activity: Jumping Hurdles (p. 212)

10:30-10:45 Break

10:45-11:30 Facilitator Presentation: Linking Practices to Results (pp. 184-193)
Group Activity: School Goals and Results of Partnerships (p. 213)

11:30-12:00 Facilitator Presentation: Action Team Structures and Team Members
(pp. 200-202)
Group Activity: How to Organize Your Action Team for Partnerships
(p. 215)

12:00-12:45 Lunch (provided or on own)

12:45-1:00   Facilitator Presentation: Guidelines for Writing One-Year Action Plans
(See pp. 142-144 for Facilitators only.)

1:00-3:00   Team Activity and Work Period: Writing Your School's Draft One-Year Action
Plan for the Next School Year (pp. 343-348 or 349-352)

3:00-3:30   Questions, Answers, and Next Steps:
Information on the National Network of Partnership Schools (See Chapter 10)
Workshop Evaluation (pp. 155-156)

NOTE FOR FACILITATORS:
Handbook pages for transparencies, handouts, and group activities are shown in
parentheses. Remove these notations when you prepare the agenda for your workshop.

TEAM-TRAINING WORKSHOP

SCHOOL, FAMILY, AND COMMUNITY CONNECTIONS: STRENGTHENING YOUR PROGRAM OF PARTNERSHIPS

Preplanning: Facilitators should review this *Handbook*, paying particular attention to the guidelines in this chapter and the workshop materials for presentations, discussions, and activities in Chapter 5.

Time: A one-day Team-Training Workshop requires six to eight hours, including time for registration, breaks, and lunch.

At least three hours (morning sessions) are required to present the background information that Action Teams for Partnerships (ATP) need to proceed in writing One-Year Action Plans for partnerships and in implementing a successful partnership program.

Two or three hours (afternoon sessions) are needed for ATPs (including teachers, parents, and administrators) to draft a One-Year Action Plan for partnerships for the next school year.

If attendees must obtain lunch on their own, facilitators should adjust the time of the afternoon sessions on the agenda to give adequate time for lunch and add more time at the end of the day.

Materials: Overhead projector, screen, microphone(s), chart paper for recording responses, tables, chairs, name tags

Meal(s) or snacks

Optional: Projector for PowerPoint presentation(s), VCR and TV for video(s)

Handouts: An agenda
Paper copies of the transparencies that are used
Other useful information, materials (e.g., notepaper, pens)
A workshop evaluation
(See workshop agenda, p. 130, for specific handouts.)

ATPs attending the workshop should bring their schools' goals or improvement plans.

After the workshop, the ATP will collect reactions to the draft plans from other teachers, parents, and administrators about desired partnership activities and consider suggestions for the final version of the One-Year Action Plan.

Other Services: Door prizes or table centerpieces may be awarded at the end of the day. Stipends to schools, planning grants, continuing education credits, and other incentives or recognitions may be awarded.

Transportation and child care services may be needed by the parents on the ATP.

Overview: Facilitators should balance the presentation of new information with opportunities for attendees to think and talk about the information and apply the new ideas and concepts to their own schools. In the following sections of this chapter, guidelines are given for presentations by facilitators followed by activities by the workshop participants. The goal of the workshop is to help attendees

- Understand the framework of the six types of involvement

- Recognize the starting points of present practices at their schools

- Understand that they must meet specific challenges to conduct a high-quality program of productive partnerships with all families

- Know that different practices of partnership lead to specific school goals and results

- Understand the structure and members of an Action Team for Partnerships

- Develop a One-Year Action Plan for family and community involvement for the next school year

In a one-day workshop, information is presented, several applications and discussions are conducted, and a draft One-Year Action Plan is written for later discussion at their schools. If the workshop is shortened (e.g., a three-hour workshop), basic information is shared and some applications are conducted. If the workshop is extended to two days or if a series of training activities are conducted, additional guidance and other in-depth discussions and planning activities from the *Handbook* may be included.

Ultimately, all Action Teams for Partnerships must write a One-Year Action Plan for partnerships. Work that is not completed at a workshop must be finished at another workshop or at the school site.

Facilitators should obtain copies of each school's final One-Year Action Plan to help the Action Team for Partnerships develop its program of school, family, and community partnerships.

COMPONENTS OF A TEAM-TRAINING WORKSHOP
NOTES FOR FACILITATORS

I. WARM-UP ACTIVITY (10-15 minutes)

GOAL: Begin the day with a short activity that focuses attendees on the benefits of working in partnership (or use the alternative activity that focuses attendees on successful partnerships they know). The following describes how to conduct a warm-up activity, with some suggested words for facilitators in **bold**.

1. Distribute copies of warm-up activity. One example of a warm-up activity is "Are Two Heads Better Than One?" (see pp. 206-207). Ask participants to work *alone* on this puzzle for two minutes. Call "Time." Then ask the participants to work with one or more partners at their tables for two minutes to complete the activity. Call "Time" again. Ask participants to call out their answers for items 1, 2, and so on to 20.

2. Ask: **How did working together compare with working alone on this activity?** List or listen to the responses. Possible replies: "Working with partners made the task easier." "We used each other's ideas, skills, and talents." "I didn't feel totally responsible for completing the task." "It was more fun." Many other responses are possible.

3. Explain: **The same results occur when teachers, parents, students, and others work together to develop a comprehensive program of school, family, and community partnerships for their school. Today's workshop will help you see how to create and conduct an ongoing, positive program of partnerships. You will be offered ways to organize your work as an Action Team for Partnerships (ATP) in order to implement activities, monitor progress, and improve school, family, and community connections over time. By working together, your team will benefit from everyone's ideas and efforts, and your school will have a program of partnerships that keeps improving year after year.**

ALTERNATIVE WARM-UP ACTIVITY (10-15 minutes)

1. Ask attendees to pick a partner nearby. Assign: **Think of *one* successful activity that you have used or heard about to involve families at school or at home. You have three minutes each to share one example.** Time this. After three minutes, ask the other partner to share an example.

2. Call "Time." Ask: **Raise your hands if you heard a good idea that might be conducted at school to increase partnerships. At home? In the community? With large groups of parents? Small groups? Individually with one parent or family at a time? In the early grades? Older elementary? Middle grades? High school? All grades?** Attendees will raise their hands to indicate the many different ways that family involvement can occur.

3. Explain: **The workshop today will help all of us understand the many different types of involvement that are needed in a comprehensive program of partnerships. We will better understand the practices that you are already conducting in your school, and we will consider which practices you might want to add to your programs to help meet your school's specific goals for student success. You will learn how to organize your work as an Action Team for Partnerships in order to implement**

activities, monitor progress, and improve school, family, and community connections over time. By working together, your team will benefit from everyone's ideas and efforts, and your school will have a program of partnerships that keeps improving year after year.

II. FRAMEWORK OF SIX TYPES OF INVOLVEMENT

GOAL: Present an overview of Epstein's framework of six types of involvement to help all Action Teams for Partnerships or other audiences share a common perspective and vocabulary about school, family, and community partnerships.

HANDBOOK: Refer to the following pages in the *Handbook* to prepare your presentation:

- Review Chapters 1 and 2.
- Review pages 134-136 in this chapter.
- Make transparencies from the materials in Chapter 5, pages 165-171.

GROUP ACTIVITY HANDOUT: *Starting Points.* Make copies of pages 208-211 for all attendees.

INFORMATION TO PRESENT (25 minutes):

What Research Says

Some facilitators start a workshop with a quick review of results from research conducted in many nations, including the United States. See pages 161-162 in Chapter 5. Present page quickly. Ask participants to think of whether these findings pertain to their school(s) and their experiences. Point out that these results of research on program development are important for this workshop. Facilitators may add comments or examples, as time permits.

If the workshop time is short, facilitators should skip the overheads on research results and proceed directly to the Keys to Successful Partnerships. Facilitators may incorporate the research findings in their introductory comments with a concise summary: Research shows that educators, parents, and students want family and community involvement. Programs of partnership must be developed to reach all families; activities must be linked to school goals for student success; all teachers must inform and involve their students' families in children's education; programs of partnership must be customized to meet the goals and needs of each school; and programs must improve over time.

Overlapping Spheres of Influence

Present the theoretical model of overlapping spheres of influence to show that children learn and grow at home, at school, and in the community. The external structure of the model shows three spheres of influence that support children's learning and development. The three contexts may be pushed apart or pulled together by the philosophies and activities of schools, families, and communities. See page 163.

If you wish to go deeper into the model, you can show the internal connections and communications of educators, families, and students that may occur. See page 164.

134

If workshop time is restricted, skip this overhead and summarize the theory of overlapping spheres of influence, which states that students learn and grow at home, at school, and in the community. Proceed directly to the Keys to Successful Partnerships.

Keys to Successful Partnerships

Explain that research shows that six major types of involvement are important to help educators, parents, other family members, and the community work as partners in children's education. The six types of involvement or "keys" create a comprehensive program of school, family, and community partnerships. (See p. 165.) Activities for the six types of involvement— *parenting, communicating, volunteering, learning at home, decision making,* and *collaborating with the community*—occur in the overlapping areas of the spheres of influence and demonstrate that home, school, and community share responsibilities for student success.

Types 1, 2, 3, 4, 5, and 6

Present each type of involvement in turn to introduce the major ways that schools connect with families and communities to help students succeed. (See pp. 166-171.) Include examples of activities for each type of involvement. Tailor the examples of partnership practices to meet the special needs and interests of those attending your workshops. For example, if elementary, middle, and high school ATPs attend, include examples of activities and challenges that arise at different grade levels. Ask the audience to be thinking of the activities that are presently conducted for each type of involvement in their own schools or in the schools they supervise. (More examples of activities for each type are found on pp. 14, 172-177.)

GROUP ACTIVITY (20 minutes):

Give a copy of *Starting Points: An Inventory of Present Practices* (pp. 208-211) to all attendees. Tell the participants that you know they are already conducting some activities to involve families and community groups in school programs. This is their "starting point," as of today.

Explain that it helps to account for present practices in order to plan for the future. Ask them to look at the inventory called *Starting Points* and think about their own school's partnership programs. Ask each table or small group of participants to begin with a different type of involvement so that all six types are covered throughout the room. Ask each group to check the activities in their assigned sections of *Starting Points* that their schools *presently* conduct. Explain that the inventory is not a test. No school is expected to conduct all the activities listed for each type of involvement. The participants may add other activities for each type of involvement on the blank lines provided.

Explain that only one person from each school team needs to do the writing, but everyone should have a copy of *Starting Points*. Groups that finish checking activities for the type of involvement they were assigned may continue with other sections of *Starting Points* that interest them, as time permits.

After about 15 minutes (or available time), ask two or three participants to report to the full group the reflections or thoughts that came to mind as they completed the checklist for the assigned type of involvement. Ask them to give their names and their affiliations. Possible reflections include: "We conduct some activities in some grades but not others." "We include some families but don't reach everyone." "Some of our activities are done well; others are weak." "We need to work on Type 4 activities that involve parents with children at home."

Many other thoughts and reactions are possible. The action teams may complete the rest of *Starting Points* at their schools.

NOTE: Action Teams for Partnerships may be sent *Starting Points* <u>before</u> the workshop and asked to bring the completed inventories with them. If this is done, the group activity at the workshop is for participants at each table to share and discuss their reflections and ideas about the six types of involvement that are presently conducted at their schools. Then, one person at each table is asked to discuss with the whole group one reflection about their schools' current partnership practices for one type of involvement.

Summary: Ask for questions about the framework of the six types of involvement. Summarize some of the main conclusions that were discussed in the reflections on *Starting Points:*

- Some partnership practices are useful at all grade levels; other activities will change as students move from grade to grade.
- Students must be part of the partnership.
- Progress is incremental. Improvements and additions are based on each school's starting point.

Reinforce: To close this section of the workshop, reinforce the fact that the attendees have shown they are familiar with all six types of involvement and that many of their schools are already conducting some family and community involvement activities. The framework of the six types of involvement helps organize ideas about present practices and about needed improvements.

Note: If the attendees talked with and listened to one another about *Starting Points*, let them know that they have done a good job in beginning to think about school, family, and community partnerships. The next section of the workshop will focus on meeting key challenges for excellent practices of the six types of involvement.

III. MEETING THE CHALLENGES

GOAL: Present an overview of the important challenges that *must be met* for each type of involvement in order to have an excellent program of partnerships. By meeting the key challenges, schools will be able to involve more families in their children's education, not just the families who are easiest to reach or who become involved on their own.

HANDBOOK: Refer to the following pages in the *Handbook* to prepare your presentation:

- Review Chapter 1, page 15.
- Review this chapter, pages 136-137.
- Make transparencies from the materials in Chapter 5, pages 178-183.

GROUP ACTIVITY HANDOUTS: *Jumping Hurdles.* Make copies of page 212 for all attendees.

INFORMATION TO PRESENT (25 minutes):

Challenges to Types 1, 2, 3, 4, 5, and 6

Explain that many schools presently conduct some activities for the six types of involvement but that most schools do not reach all families, at all grade levels, in ways that are family-friendly and that produce important results. Discuss one or two key challenges for each type of involvement to illustrate the kinds of actions and activities that must be taken to involve all families at school and at home in their children's education.

The challenges to the six types of involvement include some important redefinitions that are needed to understand school, family, and community partnerships in the 21st century. The redefinitions help educators and parents look at some common involvement activities in new ways.

NOTE: In a short workshop or basic presentation, information on the challenges can be incorporated in the overview of the six types of involvement.

GROUP ACTIVITY (20 minutes):

Give a copy of *Jumping Hurdles* (p. 212) to all attendees. Ask partners or groups to identify *one* very successful family or community involvement activity at their school (or at a school they supervise), a challenge that was faced, how the challenge was solved, and how they would improve the activity even more if it were conducted again. One person should record ideas. After 10 to 12 minutes of discussion, ask for two or three volunteers to share their reports with the full group.

Summary: Ask for questions about meeting the challenges to excellent partnerships.
Summarize the main challenges that are very important in developing programs of partnership, particularly getting information to families who cannot come to meetings at the school building, reaching families in their own languages and at appropriate reading levels, designing more opportunities for volunteers at the school and in other locations, increasing parent-child interactions on homework, increasing representatives from all neighborhoods on school committees, and identifying many useful resources and connections in the community.

Reinforce: The challenges to reach all families must be met to have a successful program.

Note: The six types of involvement and challenges to excellence must be understood, but it is important to move the discussion to the next question: Why should schools conduct and improve programs of family and community involvement? The answer: To help promote important RESULTS for students, families, and schools.

Let workshop participants know that they have worked hard and earned a break.

BREAK (15 minutes):

Give workshop participants information on restrooms in the facility and announce clearly *when* they should return for the next session. Be sure to start the next session on time.

IV. REACHING RESULTS

GOAL: Present information on how school, family, and community partnerships help produce desired results and contribute to the attainment of school improvement goals.

HANDBOOK: Refer to the following pages in this *Handbook* to prepare your presentation:

- Review Chapter 1, page 16.
- Review this chapter, pages 138-140.
- Make transparencies from the materials in Chapter 5. See pages 184-193.

GROUP ACTIVITY HANDOUTS: *School Goals and Results of Partnerships.* Make copies of page 213 for all attendees. (Or use the alternative activity, **Get Ready for Action**, p. 214).

INFORMATION TO PRESENT (20 minutes):

Partnership Practices Produce Different Results

Each of the six types of involvement leads to some DIFFERENT RESULTS. Explain that each type of involvement leads to some different results for students, parents, and teachers. Pages 184-189 summarize results for students, parents, and teachers from research and fieldwork. Point out that not every activity or every type of involvement affects student achievement. Some activities do not directly affect student learning, but may produce other desired results. To develop an excellent program of partnerships, it is necessary to know *which* results may be expected from specific activities for the six types of involvement.

Quickly point out one or two results from each overhead that may be of most interest to the workshop participants. For example, note that Type 1-Parenting activities can be selected to increase parents' understanding of school policies about attendance and on-time arrival, and what to do if students are ill and absent. Studies show that targeted activities for parents can, if well-implemented, help improve student attendance. Continue to quickly highlight one or two important results for each type of involvement.

Partnership Practices Contribute to Specific Results

All six types of involvement may be targeted to reach SPECIFIC RESULTS. Explain that although each type of involvement leads to some different results, it also is possible to design activities for all six types of involvement to focus on specific, desired results. Pages 190-193 summarize how activities for the six types of family and community involvement may be selected to promote specific goals of improving reading, math, attendance, and the school climate of partnerships. For example, if an elementary school set a goal to help students improve reading, a One-Year Action Plan for partnerships may include activities for all six types of involvement that focus directly on improving reading. Similarly, plans may be written using all or some types of family and community involvement to help students improve skills in math or other subjects, attendance, behavior, or other school goals.

Reaching Results in Middle and High Schools.

If the workshop includes teams from middle or high schools, include some examples of how the six types of involvement can help reach school improvement goals in middle or high schools (pp. 252-257 in Chapter 6). For example, if a middle or high school set a goal to improve the success of students' transitions to their new school, activities for all six types of involvement can be targeted to help incoming students adjust to their new school. Highlight other middle and high school goals and sample practices to reach those goals.

GROUP ACTIVITY (25 minutes):

Give a copy of *School Goals and Results of Partnerships* (p. 213) to all attendees. Ask partners or groups to identify *one* important academic or behavior goal *for students* at their school(s). This should be a goal that is in the school improvement plan or that is recognized as important for students at the school. Discuss and record how the school will measure progress toward the selected goal and what indicator will show that students reached the selected goal. It may be that specific statistics (e.g., test scores, report card grades, attendance rates, disciplinary referrals) are collected at the school and that a target can be set to show improvement from one year to the next. Discuss and record which family and community partnership activities for some or all six types of involvement could be implemented to help students reach the selected goal. One person should record ideas.

An alternative group activity for this time period is *Get Ready for Action* (p. 214). Ask partners or groups to list four goals that are important in their own schools: two academic goals for students, one nonacademic goal for students (such as improving attendance, discipline, safety, etc.), and, as required and already listed on the activity, the goal of maintaining a welcoming climate of partnerships. For this activity, the attendees should select *ONE of the academic or nonacademic goals for student success* and write it in the "Goal" box. One person should record ideas. Participants should list some of the family and community involvement activities for each type of involvement presently implemented at their schools that may contribute to reaching the selected goal. Then, they should brainstorm ideas on new family and community activities that might be implemented to increase attention to the selected goal.

For either activity, tell the workshop participants that their work on the activity will give them a head start on the afternoon activity of writing a One-Year Action Plan for partnerships. After about 15 to 18 minutes of discussion, ask two or three participants to share their reports with the full group. Attendees should listen to determine if the practices of partnership would directly affect the stated goal.

Summary: Ask for questions on how different types of involvement may help reach various school improvement goals or how all types can be targeted to produce results on the same goal. Check that the participants understand that (a) not every involvement activity will lead to the same results (e.g., not every activity will increase student achievement test scores), but (b) if carefully selected and well-implemented, activities for all six types of involvement may be targeted to produce results to reach specific school improvement goals.

Reinforce: Family and community involvement activities must be tightly linked to the desired goals—for example, involvement activities about *attendance* to increase *attendance*, involvement activities about *writing* to improve *writing*, and so on.

Note: Let the Action Teams for Partnerships know that they need to help others at their schools understand the importance of developing a goal-oriented program of school, family, and community partnerships. Then, family and community involvement will be seen as contributing to school improvement goals, *not* as a separate plan or program. The One-Year Action Plans that participants will write in the afternoon will link family and community involvement to goals for student success in their own schools.

V. ACTION TEAM STRUCTURE

GOAL: Present information on how an Action Team for Partnerships is linked to the School Council or School Improvement Team and how the team can organize its work in committees to conduct its work on school, family, and community partnerships.

HANDBOOK: Refer to the following pages in this *Handbook* to prepare your presentation:
- Review Chapter 1, pages 18-19.
- Review this chapter, pages 140-142.
- Make transparencies from pages 200-202 in Chapter 5.

GROUP ACTIVITY HANDOUTS: How to Organize Your Action Team for Partnerships. Make copies of pages 215-216 for all attendees.

INFORMATION TO PRESENT (15 minutes):

Two Ways to Organize a School's Program of Partnerships
Explain that there are two major ways to organize leadership on school, family, and community partnerships. The attendees will choose (or the facilitator may already have chosen) one of these approaches for organizing the Action Team for Partnerships. The decision about how the team will be organized is linked to the tools the team will use to write its One-Year Action Plan for partnerships and to evaluate progress.
Show the two diagrams of team structures. Point out the different designs for team and committee structures.
NOTE: If, based on school or district requirements, the facilitator already has selected one of the structures for the Action Team for Partnerships, then show and describe *only* the diagram for the selected structure described below. If the participants are going to choose the team structure that will work best for their school(s), then show and describe the two diagrams for Action Team for Partnerships, Structures T (Types) and G (Goals), described below.

Structures of the Action Team for Partnerships
Show that the top box of the chart recognizes that the School Council or School Improvement Team is the main advisory or decision-making group for the school. The next box shows that the ATP is the "action arm" of the School Council. The ATP plans and implements family and community involvement activities that support school improvement plans and goals. One member of the ATP may also be a member of the School Council. The ATP makes scheduled reports to the School Council about plans and progress on partnerships. (See Chapter 3 for detailed information on the composition and responsibilities of the Action Team for Partnerships.)

Two organizational charts illustrate how the Action Team for Partnerships may organize its committees in order to conduct the family and community involvement activities that are planned each year.

Action Team for Partnerships: Structure T (Types)

- Serves as the "action arm" of the School Council (or School Improvement Team)
- Committees are based on the six types of involvement
- Activities for each type of involvement lead to important results
- Each committee will have a chair or cochairs from the ATP and will engage other teachers, parents, administrators, community partners, and students in various planned activities for each of the six types of involvement

Action Team for Partnerships: Structure G (Goals)

- Serves as the "action arm" of the School Council (or School Improvement Team)
- Committees are based on four improvement goals:
  Two academic or curricular goals
  One nonacademic goal (attendance, behavior, safety, etc.)
  One goal for creating a welcoming climate for partnerships
- Activities to achieve each goal cover some or all the six types of involvement
- Each committee will have a chair or cochairs from the ATP and will engage other teachers, parents, administrators, community partners, and students in various planned activities for family and community involvement for each goal

Notes To Facilitators

1. If there is no official planning or advising council at a school, the ATP takes the lead role in deciding which goals are important and how school, family, and community partnership activities will be organized to help reach these goals. (If there is no School Council or similar body, workshop presenters may remove the top box from these charts.)

2. A third team structure may be used in schools that are organizing comprehensive school reform (CSR) or whole school change. This requires four or five Action Teams instead of only the Action Team for Partnerships. For more information on the Partnership Schools-CSR model and team structure, see Chapter 3, pages 101-102.

Members of the Action Team for Partnerships

Explain the essential members and positions of an Action Team for Partnerships, including educators and parents, and options for other team members. Quickly describe options for the terms of office and leadership roles.

Explain that other teachers, administrators, parents, students, and members of the community work with the ATP's committees on various activities.

GROUP ACTIVITY (15 minutes):

Give a copy of *How to Organize Your Action Team for Partnerships* (pp. 215-216) to all attendees. One person should record ideas.

IF a district facilitator has decided that all schools will use the same structure for their Action Teams for Partnerships, have workshop attendees mark the correct box (A or B) in Section 1 and proceed as directed. Otherwise, ask each team to discuss which team structure it will use. Check box A if the school will use Team Structure T (Types), with committees for the six types of involvement. OR, check box B if the school will use Team Structure G (Goals), with committees for four improvement goals. Those who check box B also will list the four school improvement goals that will be addressed in the One-Year Action Plan for Partnerships.

Ask each team to discuss and answer questions 2, 3, 4, and 5 to plan how its school's ATP will be organized and how it will operate effectively with leaders, meetings, committees, and connections with others at the school.

Groups may continue their discussions of team structures, leaders, meetings, committees, or other workshop topics during lunch.

Final decisions about the structure of the Action Team for Partnerships, its members, meetings, leaders, committees, and communications should be made with input from others at the school.

Summary: Ask for questions about how to organize an Action Team for Partnerships and about members of the team. Let all teams know that the structure they select for the Action Team for Partnerships and its committees is linked to the way the team will write its One-Year Action Plan for partnerships and the way it will conduct and evaluate its work.

- Action Team for Partnerships Structure T (Types) is linked to the One-Year Action Plan-Form T (Types) and the End-of-Year Evaluation-Form T (Types).

- Action Team for Partnerships Structure G (Goals) is linked to the One-Year Action Plan-Form G (Goals) and the End-of-Year Evaluation-Form G (Goals).

Reinforce: It is important for all teams to complete the activity, *How to Organize Your Action Team for Partnerships*, so that team meetings and reports proceed smoothly.

Note: Having completed the basic topics (types, challenges, results, and team structure), the workshop attendees are ready to write a draft One-Year Action Plan for partnerships.

LUNCH

Provide information about lunch and *when* attendees must return to the workshop for the start of the afternoon session. Be sure to start the afternoon session on time.

VI. WRITING ONE-YEAR ACTION PLANS FOR PARTNERSHIPS

GOAL: The afternoon of a Team-Training Workshop is devoted to helping schools' Action Teams for Partnerships write their draft One-Year Action Plans for partnerships for the next full school year. The ATPs will take the draft plans back to their schools for input from others and complete the final version of their One-Year Action Plans for partnerships.

HANDBOOK: Refer to the following pages in this *Handbook* to guide school action teams to write their One-Year Action Plans:

- Review this chapter, pages 142-144.
- Make transparencies of the One-Year Action Plan form(s) that will be used at the workshop from pages 343-348 or 349-352 in Chapter 9.

GROUP ACTIVITY HANDOUTS: One-Year Action Plans: Workshop leaders may preselect one of the One-Year Action Plan forms to use with their school teams or provide both forms.

- One-Year Action Plan-Form T (Types), pages 343-348, is used with Action Team for Partnerships Structure T (Types). This tool organizes family and community involvement activities by the six types of involvement.
- One-Year Action Plan-Form G (Goals), pages 349-352, is used with Action Team for Partnerships Structure G (Goals). This tool organizes family and community involvement activities for four school improvement goals: two academic goals, one nonacademic goal, and one goal of creating a welcoming climate of partnerships.

INFORMATION TO PRESENT (15 minutes):

Guidelines for Writing One-Year Action Plans

Show and discuss the One-Year Action Plan (Form T *or* Form G). Both forms ask for details about which family and community involvement activities will be conducted, when each activity is scheduled, what preparation is needed, which types of involvement are tapped, what results are expected, and who is responsible for or will help conduct the planned activities.

Make sure that attendees understand that they will write a draft One-Year Action Plan for the next school year.

IF FORM T is selected: Teams will complete the six pages of Form T—one for each type of involvement. Teams may refer to the *Starting Points* inventory from the morning activity and to the other workshop handouts to identify (a) family and community involvement activities that the school presently conducts and wants to continue, and (b) new family and community activities for the six types of involvement to engage more families and reach important results.

IF FORM G is selected: Teams will complete the four pages of Form G—one for each improvement goal (two academic goals, one nonacademic goal, and one goal for creating a welcoming climate of partnerships). Teams should use their School Improvement Plans or knowledge about needed improvement to select the academic and nonacademic goals. All Action Teams for Partnerships address the fourth goal of creating a welcoming climate of partnerships. Teams may refer to their ideas on *School Goals and Results of Partnerships* from the morning session. Teams also may refer to *Starting Points* and other handouts to identify present and new family and community involvement activities that directly address each goal.

Ask for examples of the four goals that the various teams will address in their One-Year Action Plans to see if all teams understand that they may choose the academic and nonacademic goals to meet needs at their schools, improving reading, math, writing, science, or other subjects, improving discipline, reducing suspensions, or increasing safety. See that they understand that every team will have one page of the One-Year Action Plan that shows how they will improve and maintain a welcoming climate of partnerships.

Remind the teams that across the four pages of Form G, activities for all six types of involvement should be represented, although not every goal will include activities for all types.

GROUP ACTIVITY (At least two hours):

Each Action Team for Partnerships will complete a draft One-Year Action Plan (Form T *or* Form G) for its own school. Workshop leader(s) may consult with each team to answer any questions. If district leaders (or state leaders) attend the workshop, they may draft a One-Year Leadership Plan during this period that outlines their goals and activities including how they will assist schools with their partnership programs. (See pp. 280-286.)

Summary: Ask for questions about the sections of the One-Year Action Plan. Check all draft plans as they are completed and before teams leave the workshop. If possible, make copies of the draft plans at the workshop so that the team and the facilitator have copies.

Reinforce: Each team will take the draft plan back to the school to discuss with the School Council or School Improvement Team, the faculty, the parent organization, or other interested partners. Input and ideas can be considered for the final version of the One-Year Action Plan, which should be appended to the School Improvement Plan (as appropriate). If help is needed, the district facilitator may visit the school and assist the Action Team for Partnerships to complete the final version of the One-Year Action Plan.

Note: All members of the Action Team for Partnerships and other school leaders should have copies of the final version of the One-Year Action Plan for partnerships for easy reference. District facilitators for school, family, and community partnerships also should have copies of each school's final One-Year Action Plan for partnerships to assist schools with their plans throughout the year. Some district superintendents and other leaders (e.g., Title I leaders) also want copies of the plans to understand how schools are progressing with their partnership programs.

VII. QUESTIONS, ANSWERS, AND NEXT STEPS (30 MINUTES)

GOAL: Help the workshop attendees see how much they accomplished in one day to increase their knowledge, skills, and plans for school, family, and community partnerships.

Summary: Review the day's activities and the topics that were discussed including the theoretical model of overlapping spheres of influence, the framework of the six types of involvement, challenges to meet to reach all families, ways to link school, family, and community partnerships to important results, how to organize the Action Team for Partnerships, and how to a draft a One-Year Action Plan so that family and community involvement help reach important school goals.

- Ask for questions concerning any of the topics of the day.
- Ask participants to share some ideas about the next steps they will take when they return to their schools.

- Facilitators should outline the steps they will take to follow up the workshop to help schools' Action Teams for Partnerships with their work. Facilitators may announce a deadline for completing the final version of the One-Year Action Plans. Also, facilitators should provide clear information on how workshop attendees can contact them for additional information or assistance.

- Facilitators also can provide information on how schools that have not yet joined the National Network of Partnership Schools at Johns Hopkins University may do so (see Chapter 10, pp. 365-369). This may include information on the benefits and requirements of the Network and how to obtain a membership form. Facilitators may provide the website address of the National Network for workshop attendees to obtain more information and online resources on school, family, and community partnerships (www.partnershipschools.org).

End-of-Year Celebration Workshop

Sample Agenda

An End-of-Year Celebration Workshop is a good way to recognize the progress that Action Teams for Partnerships (ATPs) make each year and to help ATPs plan ahead to improve their partnership programs in the next school year.

The following pages present a sample agenda for a one-day End-of-Year Celebration Workshop, where participants share their schools' best practices, discuss problems and solutions, and begin to prepare their schools' next One-Year Action Plans. Also provided are notes and guidelines to help facilitators plan and conduct successful End-of-Year Celebration Workshops.

At an End-of-Year Celebration Workshop, each school is invited to display information on practices that were implemented to promote school, family, and community partnerships. Exhibits may be set up on tables and include posters, charts, photographs, slides, video- or audiotapes, handouts, or other communications. ATPs are asked to label their activities according to the six types of involvement so that those who visit the displays will see how they might use or adapt an activity to strengthen particular aspects of their own schools' partnership programs. Attendees are given time to hear presentations, visit exhibits, and talk with each other about their activities.

Facilitators may adapt the sample agenda from a full day to a few hours, depending on the time available and the number of schools that are involved. The agenda may be shortened or lengthened depending on the work that has been accomplished, the number of problem-solving panels, the time needed for small group discussions about future One-Year Action Plans, and other factors.

Decisions vary about how to organize End-of-Year Celebrations. Some school districts with over 20 schools' Action Teams for Partnerships have organized full-day, half-day, luncheon, or dinner End-of-Year Celebrations. Some state departments of education conduct annual conferences on partnerships, where experienced schools and districts display and discuss their best practices to assist new Action Teams for Partnerships with their initial plans. Some districts conduct celebration and planning workshops at other times during the school year to precede the writing of School Improvement Plans.

Facilitators should note that tables and chairs for participants, microphones for presenters, tables and other audiovisual equipment for exhibits, name tags, and folders for information and notes are needed at End-of-Year Celebration Workshops.

At End-of-Year Celebration Workshops, facilitators may give directions and announce deadlines for schools' Action Teams for Partnerships to complete End-of-Year Evaluations of their partnership programs and to write new One-Year Action Plans for the next school year. Other details and options are included in the notes and guidelines on the following pages.

ONE-DAY END-OF-YEAR CELEBRATION WORKSHOP

Sample Agenda

SCHOOL, FAMILY, AND COMMUNITY PARTNERSHIPS: CELEBRATING PROGRESS AND PLANNING AHEAD

Date
Location

8:30-9:00	Registration and Refreshments
9:00-9:30	Greetings and Introductions
9:30-10:30	Action Teams for Partnerships (ATPs): Presentations of Best Practices (by individual schools or by groups of schools from geographic areas)
10:30-10:45	Break
10:45-11:15	Continuation—ATPs' Presentations of Best Practices
11:15-12:00	Gathering Ideas—Visits to School Exhibits
12:00-1:00	Lunch (provided or on own)
1:00-2:00	Meeting the Challenges—Panel Presentations
2:00-3:00	Continuation Plans—Preparing for the Next School Year: Writing New One-Year Action Plans
3:00-3:30	Wrap Up/Report Out/Final Announcements Workshop Evaluation

ONE-DAY END-OF-YEAR CELEBRATION WORKSHOP

Sample Agenda

NOTES FOR FACILITATORS

8:30-9:00   Registration and Refreshments

9:00-9:30   Greetings and Introductions
Overview and goals for the day

9:30-11:15   Action Teams for Partnerships (ATPs): Presentations of Best Practices (by individual schools or groups of schools from geographic areas)
See guidelines on ADVANCED PLANNING for this time segment (pp. 152-153)

    9:30-10:00   Schools Selected to Present Best Practices on Type 1-Parenting and Type 2-Communicating

May include presentations on a particularly effective parenting program that gets information to those who cannot come to events at school, an effective newsletter that includes two-way communications from home to school and school to home, an innovative parent-teacher-student conference schedule in high school, or other successful Type 1 and Type 2 activities that meet important challenges such as including all families and helping the school understand students' families.

    10:00-10:30   Schools Selected to Present Best Practices on Type 3-Volunteering and Type 4-Learning at Home

May include presentations on a particularly successful way to engage volunteers at school and at home; a way for students to share their homework and ideas in math, science, English, or other subjects with their families; or other successful Type 3 and Type 4 activities that meet important challenges such as linking volunteers and activities at home to specific goals for student learning.

    10:30-10:45   Break

    10:45-11:15   Schools Selected to Present Best Practices on Type 5-Decision Making and Type 6—Collaborating With the Community

May include presentations on particularly effective practices that parent leaders use to gather and give information to the families they represent, unusual community partnerships that reach families and students, or other successful Type 5 and Type 6 activities that meet important challenges such as increasing representation of leaders from all neighborhoods and identifying resources in all segments of the community that increase the quality of school programs or services to students and families.

11:15-12:00   Gathering Ideas—Visits to School Exhibits

Facilitators may meet with ATPs before the End-of-Year Celebration to discuss the most effective practices and modes of presentation for the school displays. ATPs may prepare short and clear summaries as handouts that would help other schools adopt or adapt the practices. Summaries should include names and phone numbers to call with any questions. These may be collated in an annual collection of "Bright Ideas" or "Promising Practices" and distributed throughout the school district.

12:00-1:00   Lunch (provided or on own)

1:00-2:00   Meeting the Challenges—Panel Presentations
(See guidelines on ADVANCED PLANNING for this time segment, pp. 153-154.)

2:00-3:00   Continuation Plans—Preparing for the Next School Year
Writing New One-Year Action Plans

Each school's ATP meets to consider the various issues discussed in the morning, at the exhibits, and by the panels. The teams may bring to the workshop their Three-Year Outlines or long-term goals for partnerships, current One-Year Action Plans, and School Improvement Plans. ATPs may discuss how to update the three-year vision for partnerships or what should be included in the new One-Year Action Plan for partnerships for the next school year. These discussions, decisions, and plans may begin at the workshop and continue at the school sites so that the ATPs complete their next One-Year Action Plans before the end of the present school year. This will ensure that the ATPs will be ready to carry on their program of school, family, and community partnerships when the new school year begins.

Each ATP should select a reporter to share ideas in the wrap-up.

3:00-3:30   Wrap-Up

Action Team Updates: The reporters from each ATP will present one or two ideas from the discussion period to indicate the new directions and next steps that the ATP will take in the next school year.

Final Announcements: Facilitators must plan their final announcements.

- Awards, appreciations, and door prizes may be distributed.
- Deadlines for End-of-Year Evaluations and new One-Year Action Plans may be announced.
- Schools should be reminded how to contact the facilitator for assistance.
- Other announcements may include information on how to obtain professional credit for attending the workshop (if appropriate) or where to place the workshop evaluations (p.155), or other issues that the facilitator wants to discuss.

Advanced Planning for an End-of-Year Celebration Workshop

Guidelines for Facilitators

Facilitators must do some *advanced planning* with the Action Teams for Partnerships that will participate in two segments of the End-of-Year Celebration Workshop: (a) presentations of best practices and (b) presentations by panelists on meeting the challenges for successful programs of partnership.

ADVANCED PLANNING for

9:30-11:15   Action Teams for Partnerships (ATPs):
              Presentations of Best Practices
              (by individual schools or groups of schools)

Before the End-of-Year Celebration Workshop, facilitators should identify especially promising practices at various schools and grade levels. Presenters for the End-of-Year Celebration Workshop should be selected to represent different schools and different grade levels to share outstanding activities for the six types of involvement.

Presenters should be notified ahead of time, informed of strict time limits for their presentations in each segment, and guided in good presentation skills. ATP chairpersons, other effective speakers, or groups of speakers may represent the schools in these presentations. They may use visual displays such as overheads, slides, charts, banners, or handouts. The print or pictures must be large enough for all to see. Some presentations have included choral speakers, poems, songs, dances, and skits to demonstrate particular family and community involvement activities.

Some facilitators select themes for the workshop each year and guide participants to present information on outstanding partnership activities that relate to the theme (e.g., partnerships for helping produce results for improving students' reading or math or partnerships that engage families with diverse cultural and linguistic backgrounds). Facilitators should clarify at the workshop that a few activities were selected for presentation, but that many other good practices are featured in the exhibits for every school.

The time from 9:30 to 11:15 a.m. can be planned in 15-minute segments for presentations on best practices for each of the six types of involvement, with a 15-minute break in the middle. For example, if two presenters were asked to share the time from 9:30 to 10:00 to describe their schools' outstanding activities for Type 1 and Type 2, each would have 10 minutes to speak, with five minutes for questions from the audience for each speaker. If four presenters were asked to share the same time period (e.g., two presenters for Type 1 and two presenters for Type 2), each would have five minutes to describe their schools' activities, with five minutes of questions from the audience for each pair. Facilitators must decide how to use the time (a total of one and a half hours for all presentations) and guide presenters accordingly.

Some facilitators ask clusters of schools (e.g., five clusters of four schools in a district of 20 schools) that have met about their programs of partnership throughout the school year to make presentations for each other on their outstanding family and community involvement activities. Under this plan, the 9:30 to 11:15 a.m. time period at the End-of-Year Celebration Workshop can be divided to give each cluster of schools equal time for presentations on selected best practices. Facilitators should meet with each cluster of ATP chairpersons to decide which practice(s) they will present at the workshop in the allotted time. Across clusters, all six types of involvement should be represented.

It is the facilitator's responsibility at the workshop to keep presenters *on time.* This can best be accomplished by planning the presentations *prior to the workshop.* A successful workshop meets its agenda; an unsuccessful workshop lets presenters to go on and on, beyond the allotted time. It sometimes is necessary to signal presenters when they have one minute left to conclude their presentations.

ADVANCED PLANNING for
1:00-2:00 Meeting the Challenges—Panel Presentations

Facilitators should identify especially important topics that have posed challenges to the Action Teams for Partnerships (ATPs) throughout the year. Usually, schools struggle with similar or related problems, and some schools solve them sooner than others and in varied ways. It should be made clear that the topics selected for the workshop are not the only important issues or problems, but that they highlight a few challenges that may be particularly helpful to discuss. Topics may address

- How to solve challenges linked to each type of involvement

- How to organize the leadership and work of the ATP

- How to report on partnerships to the School Improvement Team

- How to link partnerships to school improvement goals

- How principals can support the work of ATPs (a panel of principals)

- How to evaluate the results of specific partnership practices

- How parents view and contribute to the partnership program (a panel of parents)

Panel participants should be selected to represent various views and different solutions. Panels may include teachers, parents, students, principals, district leaders, community partners, or others. Panel members should be selected for particular topics from varied grade or school levels prior to the workshop, informed of the time allotted, and guided in effective presentation skills.

Three to five panels may be scheduled in one hour, with three to five participants on each panel sharing their experiences and observations. Time should be included for questions from the audience. For example, speakers would have about five minutes for their summaries if there were three panels each with three people from different schools. About 15 minutes would remain for questions from the audience. A smaller number of topics or fewer participants would give more time for presentations and for questions. Facilitators must decide how to use the time (one hour) and select panels accordingly.

At one workshop, for example, two panels were scheduled to share this time period. One panel consisted of eight people (four speakers from each of two schools) who discussed how they organized the work and meetings of their Action Teams for Partnerships. They addressed four questions to help other schools that were still struggling to create an effective team structure: Who is on your Action Team for Partnerships, when do you find time to meet, how do you keep in touch with your School Improvement Team, faculty, and families, and what budget or fund-raising is needed to support the work of your action team? In the one-half hour for this panel's presentation, two people (one from each school) addressed each of the four questions. They each spoke for about three minutes. This left about six minutes for questions from the audience. The second panel consisted of four people (two from each of two different schools). They discussed how they measure results of particular practices of partnership that they implement at their schools. Thus, in one hour, two panels addressed topics that were of interest to just about all schools attending the workshop.

Other Topics to Consider for Panel Presentations. In addition to the topics described above, the following may be addressed by panels of educators, parents, students, or other partners:

- How the six types of involvement continue or change at different grade levels

- How students view school, family, and community partnerships and the help they need to succeed in school (a panel of students)

- How to identify and connect with hard-to-reach families (invited panel of family members and educators)

- How to identify and obtain funds for programs of school, family, and community partnership activities

- How a School Council or School Improvement Team works effectively

- What topics should be covered in the cluster meetings of schools during the next school year

- Other important issues

SAMPLE A

A General Evaluation of Team-Training Workshops or End-of-Year Celebration Workshops

Evaluation

WORKSHOP ON SCHOOL, FAMILY, AND COMMUNITY PARTNERSHIPS

Date_____

Location_____

Please circle how much you agree or disagree with each statement.

	Strongly Disagree	Disagree	Agree	Strongly Agree
Structure				
The goals of this workshop were clear.	SD	D	A	SA
The goals of this workshop were met.	SD	D	A	SA
Time was used well.	SD	D	A	SA
Content				
I gained many ideas that will help improve school, family, and community partnerships at my school.	SD	D	A	SA
There were opportunities to share ideas with others.	SD	D	A	SA
Overall, this workshop was worthwhile.	SD	D	A	SA
Facilities				
The room was suitable.	SD	D	A	SA
Refreshments were satisfactory.	SD	D	A	SA

Which part of this workshop was most useful to you?

_____

_____

_____

What assistance or follow-up would you like?

_____

_____

_____

Thank you for your reactions!

SAMPLE B

Reactions to Specific Topics in Team-Training Workshops

Evaluation

WORKSHOP ON SCHOOL, FAMILY, AND COMMUNITY PARTNERSHIPS

Date_____

Location_____

How helpful were these workshop topics?	Very Helpful	Helpful	Not Helpful
Background			
1. Understanding the six types of involvement and examples of practices	_____	_____	_____
2. Understanding the challenges that must be met for excellent partnerships	_____	_____	_____
3. Linking the six types of involvement to school goals and results	_____	_____	_____
4. Organizing an Action Team for Partnerships	_____	_____	_____
Team Discussions			
1. Taking stock of your present partnership practices	_____	_____	_____
2. Gathering ideas for your school's One-Year Action Plan for partnerships	_____	_____	_____

Other comments or ideas on the workshop:

_____

_____

_____

What assistance or follow-up would you like?

_____

_____

_____

Thank you for your reactions!

156

5

Selecting Materials for Presentations and Workshops

This chapter is divided into two sections: Transparencies and Handouts and Small Group Activities for Workshops.

The first section provides charts, diagrams, and summaries that may be used as transparencies on overhead projectors or as printed handouts in presentations and discussions with teachers, parents, and others. For the technologically inclined, these pages can be scanned for a computer file, made into color transparencies, or activated for PowerPoint presentations. If necessary, wording may be revised to match vocabulary used in specific schools, districts, or states. Background information for many of the charts is in Chapter 1 of this *Handbook.*

The second section provides the small group activities to use in one-day workshops to ensure that attendees understand the presentations on each topic and can apply the information to their own school(s).

The materials in this chapter should be used with the directions for workshop presentations in Chapter 4.

Transparencies and Handouts

Short Summary of Research on Partnerships

The first page summarizes a few important, common results of basic research on school, family, and community partnerships from studies conducted in 20 nations, including the United States. The second page summarizes what research says about developing strong programs of school, family, and community partnerships.

Theoretical Model of Overlapping Spheres of Influence

External Structure. This shows the three contexts that influence children's learning and development. The areas of overlap indicate that the family, school, and community share responsibility for children. Various practices, philosophies, histories, and other forces create more or less overlap—more or fewer connections of individuals in the three contexts. The practices and extent of overlap change over time.

Internal Structure. This shows the interactions that may occur when people in schools, families, and communities communicate and work together. The child is the central focus of and actor in these interactions. The connections of home, school, and community may be at an institutional level—involving all families, children, educators, and the community—or at the individual level—involving one teacher, parent, child, community partner, or a small group.

Keys to Successful Partnerships

This is a one-page summary of the six types of involvement.

Summaries of the Six Types of Involvement, Challenges, and Results

The Six Types of Involvement. Six pages outline a few topics that define each type of involvement.

Sample Practices for Each Type. Six pages provide examples of common activities for each type of involvement that have been effectively implemented in many elementary, middle, and high schools.

Sample Challenges and Redefinitions for Each Type. Six pages show a few examples of program-design features that schools must address in order to have a truly successful program of partnerships. The redefinitions summarize new ways to think about involvement activities.

Sample Results From Each Type for Students, Parents, and Teachers. Six pages offer a few examples of benefits that have been measured or observed for each type of involvement. The lists alert participants to the fact that different results are linked to each type of involvement.

Four more pages provide examples of how the six types of involvement may guide the selection of activities for families and communities to help reach specific school improvement goals. The examples show how to use the six types of involvement to help students improve reading skills, math skills, and behavior in school and to help schools create a welcoming climate of partnerships. (Examples of goal-oriented activities for the six types of involvement for middle and high schools are included in Chapter 6.)

Summary Charts of Types, Challenges, and Results. The charts on the six types of involvement, challenges, and results are useful for making transparencies for use in presentations and workshops. Some leaders prefer to use a shorter set of pages on the types, challenges, and results for printed handouts. Six pages summarize sample activities, challenges, redefinitions, and expected results for each type of involvement. These pages with small print *should not* be made into transparencies for presentations because they are hard to read from a distance.

The charts on the six types, challenges, and results are drawn from the tables in Chapter 1 of this *Handbook.* Workshop leaders should encourage participants to raise questions and think of other examples of practices, challenges, needed redefinitions, and results that they have observed or measured. The charts should help Action Teams for Partnerships understand and select practices for their partnership programs that will maximize the chances of reaching goals that have been set in their own schools. See Chapter 4 for detailed instructions on how and when to use the charts in workshop presentations.

Action Team Structures

These pages illustrate two ways to organize the work of an Action Team for Partnerships. The charts assume that there is a School Council or School Improvement Team to which the Action Team for Partnerships reports. If there is no such decision-making or advisory body that sets goals and priorities for the school, remove the top box from these charts.

Members of the Action Team for Partnerships

This chart shows who should serve on an Action Team for Partnerships, including parents, teachers, administrators, support staff, community partners, students (at the high school level), and others. The number of team members, leadership roles, and terms of office is flexible, depending on conditions and constraints in each school.

Levels of Commitment to Partnerships

Two pages list and explain the levels of commitment to partnerships. All six types of involvement are important as "types," not "levels." They lead to different, important results for students, families, and schools. There are, however, levels of commitment that increase from caring to civility, clarity, cooperation, and collaboration. A comprehensive program of partnerships will include all six types of involvement and work toward the highest level of commitment—collaboration.

WHAT DO WE KNOW
from U.S. and international studies of school, family, and community partnerships?

- **Parents vary in how much they presently are involved.**

- **Parents are most concerned about their children's success in school.**

- **Students need multiple sources of support to succeed in school and in their communities.**

- **Teachers and administrators are initially resistant to increasing family involvement.**

- **Teachers and administrators need inservice, preservice, and advanced education.**

- **Schools must reach out in order to involve all families.**

What does research say about the DEVELOPMENT OF PROGRAMS of school, family, and community partnerships?

- **Programs and practices of partnership make a difference in whether, how, and which families are involved in their children's education.**

- **Subject-specific practices involve families in ways that directly assist students' learning and success.**

- **Teachers who use practices of partnership are more likely to report that all parents can help their children. These teachers are less likely to stereotype single parents, poor parents, or those with less formal education as unable to help.**

- **Programs will be most useful to schools and to families if they are customized, comprehensive, and continually improved to help meet important goals for students.**

Theoretical Model
OVERLAPPING SPHERES OF INFLUENCE OF
FAMILY, SCHOOL, AND COMMUNITY ON CHILDREN'S LEARNING
External Structure

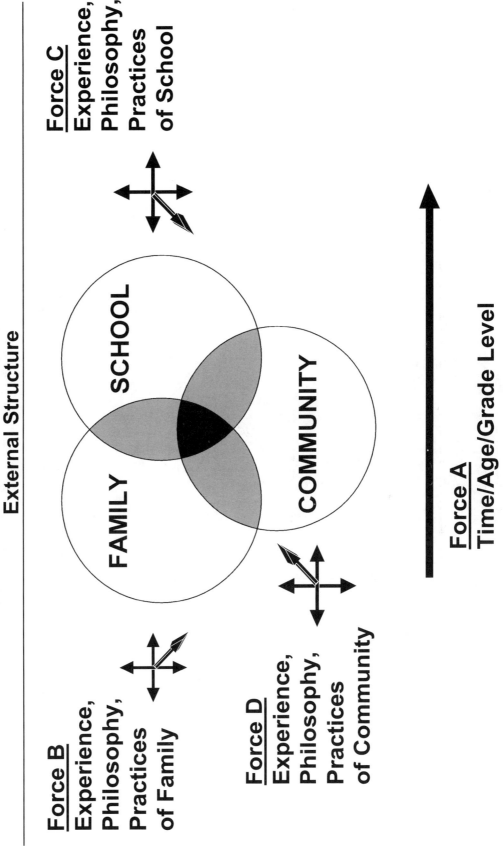

Force A
Time/Age/Grade Level

Force B
Experience,
Philosophy,
Practices
of Family

Force C
Experience,
Philosophy,
Practices
of School

Force D
Experience,
Philosophy,
Practices
of Community

SCHOOL

FAMILY

COMMUNITY

Theoretical Model
OVERLAPPING SPHERES OF INFLUENCE*
Internal Structure

FAMILY   SCHOOL

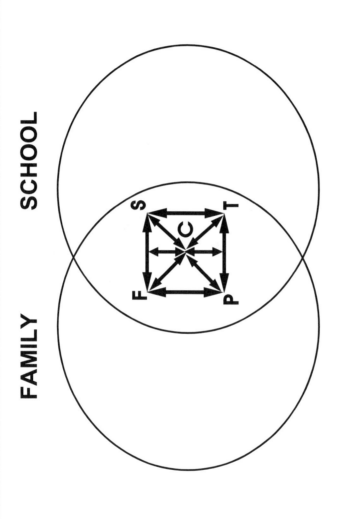

KEY: *Inter*-institutional interactions (in overlapping area)

F = Family   C = Child   S = School   P = Parent   T = Teacher

Interactions include those at the institutional level (e.g., all families, children, educators, and entire community) and at the individual level (e.g., one parent, child, teacher, community partner).

*Note: In the full model, the internal structure is extended to include the community (Co) and individual business and community agents (A), and interactions in the non-overlapping areas.

THE KEYS TO SUCCESSFUL
SCHOOL, FAMILY, AND COMMUNITY PARTNERSHIPS
EPSTEIN'S SIX TYPES OF INVOLVEMENT

PARENTING: Assist families with parenting and child-rearing skills, understanding child and adolescent development, and setting home conditions that support children as students at each age and grade level. Assist schools in understanding families.

COMMUNICATING: Communicate with families about school programs and student progress through effective school-to-home and home-to-school communications.

VOLUNTEERING: Improve recruitment, training, work, and schedules to involve families as volunteers and audiences at the school or in other locations to support students and school programs.

LEARNING AT HOME: Involve families with their children in learning activities at home, including homework and other curriculum-related activities and decisions.

DECISION MAKING: Include families as participants in school decisions, governance, and advocacy through PTA/PTO, school councils, committees, action teams, and other parent organizations.

COLLABORATING WITH THE COMMUNITY: Coordinate community resources and services for students, families, and the school with businesses, agencies, and other groups, and provide services to the community.

School, Family, and Community Partnerships by J. L. Epstein et al., © 2002 Corwin Press, Inc.   165
Photocopying permissible for local school use only.

Type 1
PARENTING

Basic Responsibilities of Families

✔ **Housing, health, nutrition, clothing, safety**

✔ **Parenting skills for all age levels**

✔ **Home conditions that support children as students at all grade levels**

✔ **Information and activities to help schools understand children and families**

Type 2

COMMUNICATING

Basic Responsibilities of Schools

SCHOOL-TO-HOME

✔ **Memos, notices, report cards, conferences, newsletters, phone calls, computerized messages, e-mail, websites**

✔ **Information to help families**
- **Understand school programs and children's progress**
- **Understand student tests and assessments**
- **Choose or change schools**
- **Choose or change courses, placements, programs, and activities**

HOME-TO-SCHOOL

✔ **Two-way channels of communication for questions and interactions**

Type 3

VOLUNTEERING

Involvement at and for the School

VOLUNTEERS

In School or Classroom

✔ **Assist administrators, teachers, students, or parents as mentors, coaches, boosters, monitors, lecturers, chaperones, tutors, leaders, or demonstrators, and in other ways**

For School or Classroom

✔ **Assist school programs and children's progress from any location at any time**

AUDIENCES

✔ **Attend assemblies, performances, sports events, recognition and award ceremonies, celebrations, and other events**

Type 4

LEARNING AT HOME

Involvement in Academic Activities

Information for Families on

✔ **How to help at home with homework**

✔ **Required skills to pass each subject**

✔ **Curriculum-related decisions**

✔ **Other skills and talents**

Type 5
DECISION MAKING
Participation and Leadership

✔ **Advisory groups**
- **School Council**
- **School Improvement Team**
- **Title I Advisory Council**
- **School-Site Management Team**

✔ **Action Team for Partnerships**

✔ **PTA/PTO**
- **Membership, participation, leadership, representation**

✔ **Other school or district committees**

✔ **Independent school advisory groups**

Type 6

COLLABORATING
WITH THE COMMUNITY

✔ **Connections to enable the community to contribute to schools, students, and families**

  - **Business partners**
  - **Cultural and recreational groups**
  - **Health services**
  - **Service or volunteer groups**
  - **Senior citizen associations**
  - **Faith-based organizations**
  - **Government and military agencies**
  - **Other groups and programs**

✔ **Connections to enable schools, students, and families to contribute to the community**

Sample Practices—Type 1

PARENTING

Assist Families With Parenting Skills and Setting Home Conditions to Support Children as Students, and Assist Schools to Understand Families

✔ Workshops, videotapes, computerized phone messages, website pages, and other strategies to provide information on parenting and child development at each age and grade level

✔ Parent education and other courses or training for parents (e.g., GED, family literacy, college, or training programs)

✔ Family support programs to assist families with health, nutrition, and parenting, including clothing swap shops, food co-ops, parent-to-parent groups

✔ Family room or family resource center for parent meetings, volunteer activities, videos, publications, and other information for parents

✔ Home visiting programs or neighborhood meetings to help families understand schools and to help schools understand families

✔ Annual survey for families to share information and concerns with schools about their children's goals, strengths, and special talents

Sample Practices—Type 2

COMMUNICATING

Conduct Effective Communications From School to Home and From Home to School About School Programs and Children's Progress

✔ Conferences with every parent at least once a year with follow-ups as needed

✔ Language translators to assist families as needed

✔ Folders of student work sent home weekly or monthly for parent review and comments

✔ Parent and student pickup of report cards

✔ Regular schedule of useful notices, memos, phone calls, and other communications

✔ Effective newsletters including information about school events, student activities, and parents' questions, reactions, and suggestions

✔ Clear information on all school policies, programs, reforms, assessments, and transitions

✔ Clear information about choosing schools, and selecting courses, programs, and activities within schools

✔ Annual survey of families' reactions to school programs and students' needs

Sample Practices—Type 3

VOLUNTEERING

Organize Volunteers and Audiences to Support the School and Students

✔ Annual survey to identify interests, talents, and availability of volunteers

✔ Parent room or family center for volunteer work, meetings, and resources for families

✔ Class parents, telephone tree, or other structures to provide all families with needed information

✔ Parent or grandparent patrols to increase school safety

✔ Annual review of schedules for students' performances, sports events, and assemblies for daytime and evening audiences

Sample Practices—Type 4

LEARNING AT HOME

Involve Families With Their Children in Homework and Other Curriculum-Related Activities and Decisions

✔ Information for families on required skills in all subjects at each grade

✔ Information on homework policies and how to monitor and discuss schoolwork at home

✔ Information on how to assist students with skills that they need to improve

✔ Regular schedule of interactive homework that requires students to demonstrate and discuss what they are learning in class

✔ Calendars with daily or weekly activities for parents and students to do at home or in the community

✔ Summer learning packets or activities

✔ Family participation in helping students set academic goals each year and plan for college or work

Sample Practices—Type 5

DECISION MAKING

Include Families as Participants in School Decisions, and Develop Parent Leaders and Representatives

✔ Active PTA/PTO or other parent organizations, advisory councils, or committees (e.g., curriculum, safety, personnel) for parent leadership and participation

✔ Action Team for Partnerships to oversee the development of the school's program of the six types of family and community involvement

✔ Networks to link all families with parent representatives

✔ Quick surveys or phone calls to obtain parents' input and reactions to school policies

✔ District-level advisory councils and committees

✔ Information on school or local elections for school representatives

✔ Independent advocacy groups to lobby for school reform and improvements

School, Family, and Community Partnerships by J. L. Epstein et al., © 2002 Corwin Press, Inc.
Photocopying permissible for local school use only.

Sample Practices—Type 6

COLLABORATING WITH THE COMMUNITY

Coordinate Resources and Services From the Community for Families, Students, and the School, and Provide Services to the Community

✔ **Information for students and families on community health, cultural, recreational, social support, and other programs or services**

✔ **Information on community activities that link to learning skills and talents, including summer programs for students**

✔ **School-business partnerships to attain school improvement goals**

✔ **Participation of alumni in school programs for students**

✔ **"One-stop" shopping for family services through partnerships of school, counseling, health, recreation, job training, and other agencies**

✔ **Service to the community by students, families, and schools (e.g., art, music, drama, and other activities for senior citizens; recycling projects; or tutoring or coaching programs)**

School, Family, and Community Partnerships by J. L. Epstein et al., © 2002 Corwin Press, Inc.
Photocopying permissible for local school use only.

Challenges—Type 1

PARENTING

✔ **Provide information to *all* families who want it or who need it, not just to the few who attend workshops or meetings at the school building**

✔ **Enable families to share information with schools about their background, culture, children's talents, goals, and needs**

✔ **Make all information about parenting age-appropriate, usable, and linked to children's success**

Redefinitions

"Workshop" is not only a *meeting* on a topic held at the school building at a particular time, but also the *content* of a topic to be viewed, heard, or read at convenient times and varied locations.

Challenges—Type 2

COMMUNICATING

✔ **Make all memos, notices, and other print and nonprint communications clear and understandable for all families**

✔ **Consider parents who do not speak English well, do not read well, or need large type**

✔ **Obtain ideas from families to improve the design and content of major communications such as newsletters, report cards, and conference schedules**

✔ **Establish an easy-to-use two-way channel for communications from school to home and from home to school**

Redefinitions

"Communications about school programs and student progress" are not only from school to home but also include two-way, three-way, and many-way channels of communication that connect schools, families, students, and the community.

Challenges—Type 3

VOLUNTEERING

✔ **Recruit widely for volunteers so that *all* families know that their time and talents are welcome**

✔ **Make flexible schedules for volunteers, assemblies, and events to enable working parents to participate**

✔ **Provide training for volunteers and match time and talent with school needs**

✔ **Recognize parent and other volunteers for their assistance at school and in other locations**

Redefinitions

"Volunteer" not only means someone who comes to school during the day, but also anyone who supports school goals and children's learning in any way, at any place, and at any time.

Challenges—Type 4

LEARNING AT HOME

✔ Design and implement a regular schedule of interactive homework (e.g., weekly or twice a month) for which students take responsibility to discuss important things they are learning with their families

✔ Coordinate family-linked interactive homework assignments if students have several teachers

✔ Involve families and their children in all important curriculum-related decisions

Redefinitions

"Homework" not only means work that students do alone, but also interactive activities that students share with others at home or in the community, linking schoolwork to real life.

"Help" at home means how families encourage, listen, react, praise, guide, monitor, and discuss schoolwork with their children, not how they "teach" children school subjects.

Challenges—Type 5

DECISION MAKING

✔ **Include parent leaders from all racial, ethnic, socioeconomic, and other groups in the school**

✔ **Offer training to enable parent leaders to develop skills to serve as representatives of other families**

✔ **Include student representatives along with parents on decision-making committees**

Redefinitions

"Decision making" means a process of partnership—sharing views, solving problems, and taking action toward shared goals, not just a power struggle between conflicting ideas.

Parent "leader" means a representative who shares information with and obtains ideas from other families and community members, not just a parent who attends school meetings.

Challenges—Type 6

COLLABORATING WITH THE COMMUNITY

✔ **Match business and community volunteers and resources with school goals**

✔ **Solve turf problems of roles, responsibilities, funds, and places for collaborative activities**

✔ **Inform all families and students about community programs and services**

✔ **Ensure equal opportunities for students and families to obtain services and participate in community programs**

Redefinitions

"Community" is rated not only by low or high social or economic qualities, but also by strengths and talents of people and organizations available to support students, families, and schools.

"Community" includes not only families with children in the schools, but also all who are interested in and affected by the quality of education.

"Community" means not only the neighborhoods where students' homes and schools are located, but also other neighborhoods or locations that influence their learning and development.

Results—Type 1
PARENTING*

RESULTS FOR STUDENTS

- Awareness of family supervision
- Respect for parents
- Positive personal qualities, habits, beliefs, and values taught by family
- Balance between time spent on chores, other activities, and homework
- Regular attendance
- Awareness of importance of school

RESULTS FOR PARENTS

- Self-confidence about parenting
- Knowledge of child and adolescent development
- Adjustments in home environment as children proceed through school
- Awareness of own and others' challenges in parenting
- Feeling of support from school and other parents

RESULTS FOR TEACHERS

- Understanding of families' backgrounds, cultures, concerns, goals, needs, and views of their children
- Respect for families' strengths and efforts
- Understanding of student diversity
- Awareness of own skills to share information on child development

*This chart refers to results of well-designed and well-implemented Type 1 practices.

School, Family, and Community Partnerships by J. L. Epstein et al., © 2002 Corwin Press, Inc.

Results—Type 2

COMMUNICATING*

RESULTS FOR STUDENTS

- Awareness of own progress in subjects and skills
- Knowledge of actions needed to maintain or improve grades
- Understanding of school programs and policies
- Informed decisions about courses and programs
- Awareness of own role as courier and communicator in school-family partnerships

RESULTS FOR PARENTS

- Understanding of school programs and policies
- Monitoring and awareness of child's progress in subjects and skills
- Responses to student problems
- Ease of interactions and communications with school and teachers
- High rating of school quality

RESULTS FOR TEACHERS

- Diversity of communications with families
- Ability to communicate clearly
- Use of network of parents to communicate with all families
- Ability to understand family views and elicit help with children's progress

*This chart refers to results of well-designed and well-implemented Type 2 practices.

Results—Type 3
VOLUNTEERING*

RESULTS FOR STUDENTS

- Skills in communicating with adults
- Skills that are tutored or taught by volunteers
- Awareness of many skills, talents, occupations, and contributions of parents and other volunteers

RESULTS FOR PARENTS

- Understanding of the teacher's job
- Self-confidence about ability to work in school and with children
- Awareness that families are welcome and valued at school
- Specific skills of volunteer work
- Use of school activities at home
- Enrollment in programs to improve own education

RESULTS FOR TEACHERS

- Organization, training, and use of volunteers
- Readiness to involve families in new ways, including those who do not volunteer at school
- Awareness of parents' talents and interests in school and children
- Individual attention to students because of help from volunteers

*This chart refers to results of well-designed and well-implemented Type 3 practices.

Results—Type 4

LEARNING AT HOME*

RESULTS FOR STUDENTS

- **Skills, abilities, and test scores linked to homework and classwork**
- **Homework completion**
- **Positive attitude about homework and school**
- **View of parent as more similar to teacher and of home as more similar to school**
- **Self-confidence in ability as learner**

RESULTS FOR PARENTS

- **Knowledge of how to support, encourage, and help student at home each year**
- **Discussions at home of school, classwork, homework, and future plans**
- **Understanding of instructional program and what child is learning in each subject**
- **Appreciation of teacher's skills**
- **Awareness of child as a learner**

RESULTS FOR TEACHERS

- **Varied designs of homework including interactive assignments**
- **Respect for family time**
- **Recognition of helpfulness of single-parent, dual-income, and all families in motivating and reinforcing student learning**
- **Satisfaction with family involvement and support**

*This chart refers to results of well-designed and well-implemented Type 4 practices.

Results—Type 5

DECISION MAKING*

RESULTS FOR STUDENTS

- Awareness of representation of families in school decisions
- Understanding that student rights and interests are protected
- Specific benefits linked to policies enacted by parent organizations

RESULTS FOR PARENTS

- Awareness of school, district, and state policies
- Input on policies affecting children's education
- Feeling of ownership of school
- Awareness of parents' voices in school decisions
- Shared experiences and connections with other families

RESULTS FOR TEACHERS

- Awareness of perspectives of families in policy development and school decisions
- Acceptance of equality of family representatives of school committees and in leadership roles

*This chart refers to results of well-designed and well-implemented Type 5 practices.

School, Family, and Community Partnerships by J. L. Epstein et al., © 2002 Corwin Press, Inc.

Results—Type 6

COLLABORATING WITH THE COMMUNITY*

RESULTS FOR STUDENTS

- **Skills and talents from enriched curricular and extracurricular experiences**
- **Knowledge and exploration of careers and options for future education and work**
- **Self-confidence, feeling valued by and belonging to the community**
- **Positive relationships with adults in the community**

RESULTS FOR PARENTS

- **Knowledge and use of local resources to increase skills and talents or to obtain needed services**
- **Interactions with other families in community activities**
- **Awareness of community's contributions to school**
- **Participation in activities to strengthen the community**

RESULTS FOR TEACHERS

- **Knowledge and use of community resources to enrich curriculum and instruction**
- **Skill in working with mentors, business partners, community volunteers, and others to assist students and teaching practice**
- **Knowledge of referral processes for families and children with needs for specific services**

*This chart refers to results of well-designed and well-implemented Type 6 practices.

ELEMENTARY SCHOOL EXAMPLES

for a One-Year Action Plan
to **IMPROVE READING**

TYPE 1 Workshops for parents on various ways to read aloud with young children

TYPE 2 Parent-teacher-student conferences on reading goals at the start of the school year and on reading progress midyear

TYPE 3 Reading-partner volunteers, guest readers of favorite stories, and other organized, ongoing read-with-me activities

TYPE 4 Weekly interactive reading homework activities for all students to read aloud for a family partner, show links of reading and writing, go over vocabulary and spelling words, and other reading activities

TYPE 5 PTA/PTO support for a family room or parent center to provide information on children's reading, and to conduct book swaps, make book bags for read-at-home programs, create family books, and sponsor other reading activities

TYPE 6 Donations from business partners of books for classrooms, for the school library, or for children to take home

... AND MANY OTHER IDEAS FOR EACH TYPE OF INVOLVEMENT

ELEMENTARY SCHOOL EXAMPLES
for a One-Year Action Plan
to **IMPROVE MATH SKILLS**

TYPE 1 Workshops for parents to explain new math standards and tests and to demonstrate and discuss how math skills are taught to students

TYPE 2 Articles for parents in school or class newsletters by students and math teachers on interesting math topics and skills

TYPE 3 Volunteer math tutors to assist students who need one-on-one tutoring and extra help with specific math skills

TYPE 4 Weekly interactive homework assignments for students to demonstrate mastery of a math skill for family partners and to discuss how each skill is used in everyday situations

TYPE 5 PTA/PTO-sponsored Family Math Night for fun and learning

TYPE 6 After-school programs funded by business and community partners to provide students with extra help and enrichment activities in math

. . . AND MANY OTHER IDEAS FOR EACH TYPE OF INVOLVEMENT

ELEMENTARY SCHOOL EXAMPLES
for a One-Year Action Plan
to **IMPROVE STUDENT BEHAVIOR**

TYPE 1   Parent-to-parent group meetings on student behavior, age-appropriate discipline, and related topics

TYPE 2   Student-of-the-month assembly, bulletin board, and luncheon with family partners to recognize students for good or improved behavior, character, and citizenship

TYPE 3   Volunteers for school patrols in hallways, in the cafeteria, on the playground, or in other locations to increase or maintain students' good behavior

TYPE 4   Monthly interactive homework assignments for students to talk with parents or other family partners about selected character traits, values, and behaviors

TYPE 5   PTA/PTO-sponsored speaker series for parents on student development, with mental health, medical, and other specialists

TYPE 6   Community connections with students on problem-solving and conflict resolution skills to reduce bullying and other problem behaviors

. . . AND MANY OTHER IDEAS FOR EACH TYPE OF INVOLVEMENT

ELEMENTARY SCHOOL EXAMPLES

for a One-Year Action Plan
to **CREATE A CLIMATE OF PARTNERSHIPS**

TYPE 1 Low-cost immunization shots and health examinations for students to assist parents with these school requirements

TYPE 2 Student-led parent-teacher conferences to communicate with all parents about student progress

TYPE 3 Resource directory to identify the available time and talents of parents and other volunteers to assist teachers and school staff throughout the year

TYPE 4 Information for and exchanges with parents on homework policies, how to help at home, and whom to call with questions

TYPE 5 PTA/PTO potluck dinners combined with School Improvement Team meetings to encourage more parents to participate in decision making

TYPE 6 "Salute the Arts" fair for students and families where community artists demonstrate drawing and painting, music, dance, and crafts and offer information on community-based art programs and museums

. . . AND MANY OTHER IDEAS FOR EACH TYPE OF INVOLVEMENT

TYPE 1—PARENTING
BASIC RESPONSIBILITIES OF FAMILIES

- Housing, health, nutrition, clothing, safety

- Parenting skills for all age levels

- Home conditions that support children as students at all grade levels

- Information and activities to help schools understand children and families

CHALLENGES

Provide information to all families who want it or who need it, not only to the few who attend workshops or meetings at the school building

Enable families to share information with schools about background, culture, talents, goals, and needs

REDEFINITIONS

"Workshop" is not only a meeting on a topic held at the school building, but also the content of that meeting to be viewed, heard, or read at convenient times and varied locations.

RESULTS FOR STUDENTS

- Balance time spent on chores, homework, and other activities
- Regular attendance
- Awareness of importance of school

RESULTS FOR PARENTS

- Self-confidence about parenting as children proceed through school
- Knowledge of child and adolescent development

RESULTS FOR TEACHERS and SCHOOLS

- Understanding of families' goals and concerns for children
- Respect for families' strengths and efforts

SUMMARY

TYPE 2—COMMUNICATING
BASIC RESPONSIBILITIES OF SCHOOLS

SCHOOL-TO-HOME COMMUNICATIONS

- Memos, notices, report cards, conferences, newsletters, phone calls, computerized messages

- Information on school programs, tests, and children's progress

- Information to choose or change schools, courses, programs, or activities

HOME-TO-SCHOOL COMMUNICATIONS

- Two-way channels of communication for questions and interactions

CHALLENGES

Make all memos, notices, and other print and nonprint communications clear and understandable for ALL families

Obtain ideas from families to improve the design and content of communications such as newsletters, report cards, and conference schedules

REDEFINITIONS

"Communications about school programs and student progress" are not only from school to home, but also from home to school and with the community.

RESULTS FOR STUDENTS

- Awareness of own progress in subjects and skills
- Knowledge of actions needed to maintain or improve grades
- Awareness of own role as courier and communicator in partnerships

RESULTS FOR PARENTS

- High rating of quality of the school
- Support for child's progress and responses to correct problems
- Ease of interactions and communications with school and teachers

RESULTS FOR TEACHERS and SCHOOLS

- Ability to communicate clearly
- Use of network of parents to communicate with all families

TYPE 3—VOLUNTEERING
INVOLVEMENT AT AND FOR THE SCHOOL

- **In schools or classrooms: Assist administrators, teachers, students, or parents as aides, tutors, coaches, lecturers, chaperones, and other leaders**

- **For schools or classrooms: Assist school programs and children's progress from any location at any time**

- **As audiences: Attend assemblies, performances, sports events, recognition and award ceremonies, celebrations, and other events**

CHALLENGES

Recruit widely, provide training, and create flexible schedules for volunteers so that all families know that their time and talents are welcomed and valued

REDEFINITIONS

"Volunteer" not only means those who come during the school day, but also those who support school goals and children's learning any way, any time.

RESULTS FOR STUDENTS

- **Skills that are tutored or taught by volunteers**
- **Skills in communicating with adults**

RESULTS FOR PARENTS

- **Understanding of the teacher's job**
- **Self-confidence about ability to work in school and with children**
- **Enrollment in programs to improve own education**

RESULTS FOR TEACHERS and SCHOOLS

- **Readiness to involve all families in new ways, not only as volunteers**
- **More individual attention to students because of help from volunteers**

TYPE 4—LEARNING AT HOME
INVOLVEMENT IN ACADEMIC ACTIVITIES

INFORMATION FOR FAMILIES ON

- How to help at home with homework

- Required skills to pass each subject

- Curriculum-related decisions

- Other skills and talents

CHALLENGES

Design and implement interactive homework for which students take responsibility to discuss important classwork and ideas with their families

REDEFINITIONS

"Homework" not only means work that students do alone, but also interactive activities that students share and discuss with others at home.

"Help" at home means how families encourage and guide children, not how they "teach" school subjects.

RESULTS FOR STUDENTS

- Skills, abilities, and test scores linked to classwork; homework completion
- View of parent as more similar to teacher, and home in sync with school
- Self-confidence in ability as learner and positive attitude about school

RESULTS FOR PARENTS

- Discussions with child about school, classwork, homework, and future plans
- Understanding curriculum, what child is learning, and how to help each year

RESULTS FOR TEACHERS and SCHOOLS

- Respect of family time and satisfaction with family involvement and support
- Recognition that single-parent, dual-income, and low-income families can encourage and assist student learning

SUMMARY

TYPE 5—DECISION MAKING PARTICIPATION AND LEADERSHIP

- PTA/PTO membership, participation, leadership, representation

- Advisory councils, school improvement teams

- Title I councils, school-site management teams, other committees

- Independent school advisory groups

CHALLENGES

Include parent leaders from all racial, ethnic, socioeconomic, and other groups in the school

Offer training for parent leaders to develop leadership skills

Include student representatives along with parents in decision making

REDEFINITIONS

"Decision making" means a process of partnership to share views and take action toward shared goals for school improvement and student success, not a power struggle.

RESULTS FOR STUDENTS

- Awareness that families' views are represented in school decisions
- Specific benefits linked to policies enacted by parent organizations

RESULTS FOR PARENTS

- Awareness of and input to policies that affect children's education
- Shared experiences and connections with other families

RESULTS FOR TEACHERS and SCHOOLS

- Awareness of families' perspectives in policies and school decisions
- Acceptance of equality of family representatives on school committees

TYPE 6—COLLABORATING WITH THE COMMUNITY

- **COMMUNITY CONTRIBUTES TO SCHOOLS, STUDENTS, AND FAMILIES**
  Business partners, agencies, cultural groups, health services, recreation, and other groups and programs

- **SCHOOLS, STUDENTS, AND FAMILIES CONTRIBUTE TO COMMUNITY**
  Service learning, special projects to share talents and solve local problems

CHALLENGES

Solve problems of turf, responsibilities, funds, and goals

Inform all families and students about community programs and services, and ensure equal opportunities for services and participation

REDEFINITIONS

"Community" includes not only families with children in the schools, but also all who are interested in and affected by the quality of education.

Communities are rated not only on economic qualities, but also on the strengths and talents available to support students, families, and schools.

RESULTS FOR STUDENTS

- Knowledge, skills, and talents from enriched curricular and extracurricular experiences and explorations of careers

- Self-confidence and feeling valued by and belonging to the community

RESULTS FOR PARENTS

- Knowledge and use of local resources to increase skills and talents or to obtain needed services for family

- Interactions with other families, and contributions to community

RESULTS FOR TEACHERS and SCHOOLS

- Knowledge and use of community resources for improving curriculum and instruction

- Strategies to enable students to learn about and contribute to the community

Action Team for Partnerships
Structure T (Focus on Types)

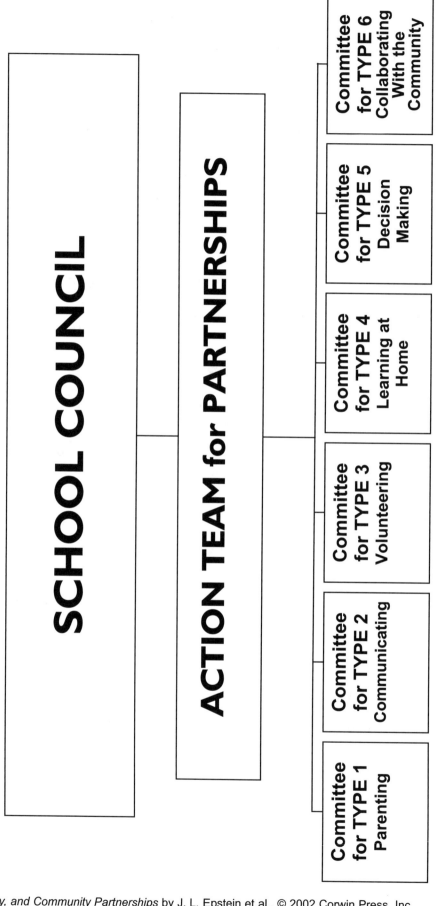

SCHOOL COUNCIL

ACTION TEAM for PARTNERSHIPS

Committee for TYPE 1 Parenting

Committee for TYPE 2 Communicating

Committee for TYPE 3 Volunteering

Committee for TYPE 4 Learning at Home

Committee for TYPE 5 Decision Making

Committee for TYPE 6 Collaborating With the Community

Action Team for Partnerships
Structure G (Focus on Goals)

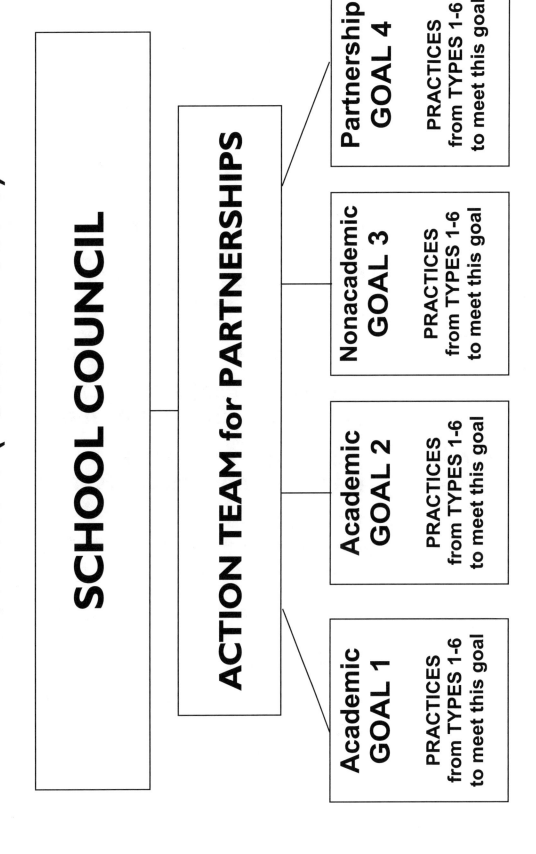

SCHOOL COUNCIL

ACTION TEAM for PARTNERSHIPS

Academic **GOAL 1**

PRACTICES from TYPES 1-6 to meet this goal

Academic **GOAL 2**

PRACTICES from TYPES 1-6 to meet this goal

Nonacademic **GOAL 3**

PRACTICES from TYPES 1-6 to meet this goal

Partnership **GOAL 4**

PRACTICES from TYPES 1-6 to meet this goal

Members of the Action Team for Partnerships

How Many?	6-12 members
Who?	2-3 teachers or more
	2-3 parents/family members or more
	Representatives may include parent liaison, PTA/PTO officer, parents with children in different grades, families from various neighborhoods
	Principal
	1-2 students (in high school)
	1-2 other members (e.g., nurse, counselor, community members)
Terms?	2-3 years (renewable) Replacements made as needed
	At least one member also serves on the school improvement team or school council
Leaders?	Chair or co-chairs are team members who communicate well with educators *and* families
	Other members serve as chairs or co-chairs of committees for each type of involvement or for specific school goals

All features are flexible to fit school conditions and needs.

Levels of Commitment
to School, Family, and Community
Partnerships

CAN YOU "C" THE CONNECTIONS?

1. Care

2. Civility / Courtesy

3. Clarity

4. Cooperation

5. Collaboration

Understanding Levels of Commitment to

SCHOOL, FAMILY, and COMMUNITY PARTNERSHIPS

1. *CARE.* We care about the children and each other at this school. Families feel welcome at the school. Educators feel welcome in the community.

2. *CIVILITY / COURTESY.* We respect each other at this school and recognize our shared responsibilities for children. Teachers and families talk with and listen to each other.

3. *CLARITY.* We conduct clear and useful two-way communications about school programs, children's progress, families' talents and needs, community activities, and other topics important to families, students, the school, and the community. Our communications can be understood by all families, and all families are able to communicate easily with teachers and administrators.

4. *COOPERATION.* We assist each other and the students. Families, educators, and community members are comfortable working with each other. We work together to improve the school, strengthen families, and ensure student success. We try to solve problems, and we are open to new ideas.

5. *COLLABORATION.* We maintain a comprehensive program of school, family, and community partnerships. We use an action team approach that enables educators, parents, students, and community members to work together over time to design, implement, and improve activities for the six types of involvement. We work as partners to help students at all grade levels reach important goals. We encourage discussion and debate on important issues. We celebrate progress and continually plan improvements in activities to involve all families.

 School, Family, and Community Partnerships by J. L. Epstein et al., © 2002 Corwin Press, Inc.

Small Group Activities for Workshops

This chapter includes the following small group activities to use after each topic in a workshop on school, family, and community partnerships. The activities can be completed by schools' Action Teams for Partnerships sitting together at workshop tables. The activities show the workshop leader that the participants understood each presentation and that they can think about how each topic (i.e., types of involvement, challenges, results, team structure) applies to their own schools.

The activities should be reproduced and provided to every participant. See Chapter 4 for detailed directions on how to introduce and use these activities.

Workshop Warm-Up

This word puzzle is a quick activity to help participants see the results of working together with teachers, parents, administrators, and other partners compared with working alone.

Starting Points

This inventory is used as a small group activity following a presentation on the six types of involvement.

Jumping Hurdles

This small group activity is used following a presentation on how to meet key challenges to excellent partnerships.

School Goals and Results of Partnerships

This small group activity is used following a presentation on the expected results of the six types of involvement.

Get Ready for Action

This alternative small group activity may be used following a presentation on expected results of the six types of involvement.

How to Organize Your Action Team for Partnerships

This small group activity is used following a presentation on how Action Teams for Partnerships may be structured to help participants think about how they will work as a team at their schools.

NOTE: See Chapter 9 to select the One-Year Action Plan (Form T-Types or Form G-Goals) for Action Teams for Partnerships to use at the Team-Training Workshop. Also see pages 140-144 in Chapter 4 for information on how to select the One-Year Action Plan for the schools at a workshop.

Workshop Warm-Up

ARE TWO HEADS BETTER THAN ONE?

1.	wire
	just
		11.	often
			      not
			often
			      not
			often

2.	ANKLE	12.	MIGR**A**INE
3.	night fly	13.	you just me
4.	WAY ——— PASS	14.	once upon a time N | E ... S
5.	END N D	15.	GOLDEN GATE H_2O
6.	SS SS SS SS SS NE1?	16.	RASINGINGIN
7.	VAD ERS	17.	<u>1 3 5 7 9</u> WHELMING
8.	esroh riding	18.	**ALL** world
9.	DO 12" OR	19.	a chance n
10.	GIVE GET GIVE GET GIVE GET GIVE GET	20.	USE APPLAUS (in a circle)

An Inventory of Present Practices of School, Family, and Community Partnerships

Karen Clark Salinas, Joyce L. Epstein, and Mavis G. Sanders
National Network of Partnership Schools, Johns Hopkins University

This inventory will help you identify your school's present practices for each of the six types of involvement that create a comprehensive program of school, family, and community partnerships. At this time, your school may conduct all, some, or none of the activities listed. Not every activity is appropriate for every school or grade level. You may write in other activities that you conduct for each type of involvement.

The Action Team for Partnerships (ATP) should complete this inventory, with input from the teachers, parents, School Improvement Team, and others, as appropriate. These groups have different knowledge about all of the present practices of partnership in your school.

After you complete the inventory, you will be ready to write a Three-Year Outline and One-Year Action Plan of how your school will work to increase, improve, or maintain activities for each of the six types of involvement.

Directions: Check the activities that your school conducts and circle all of the grade levels presently involved. Write in other activities for each type of involvement that your school conducts.

To assess how well each activity is implemented, add these symbols next to the check-box: * (for very well implemented with all families), + (a good start with many families), - (needs improvement).

TYPE 1 – PARENTING: BASIC RESPONSIBILITIES OF FAMILIES   **At Which Grades?**
Assist families with parenting skills and setting home conditions to support children as students, and assist schools to understand families

❑ We sponsor parent education workshops and other courses or training for parents.   K 1 2 3 4 5 6 7 8 9 10 11 12

❑ We provide families with information on child or adolescent development.   K 1 2 3 4 5 6 7 8 9 10 11 12

❑ We conduct family support programs with parent-to-parent discussion groups.   K 1 2 3 4 5 6 7 8 9 10 11 12

❑ We provide families with information on developing home conditions that support learning.   K 1 2 3 4 5 6 7 8 9 10 11 12

❑ We lend families books or tapes on parenting or videotapes of parent workshops.   K 1 2 3 4 5 6 7 8 9 10 11 12

❑ We ask families about children's goals, strengths, and talents.   K 1 2 3 4 5 6 7 8 9 10 11 12

❑ We sponsor home visiting programs or neighborhood meetings to help families understand schools and to help schools understand families.   K 1 2 3 4 5 6 7 8 9 10 11 12

❑ _____   K 1 2 3 4 5 6 7 8 9 10 11 12

❑ _____   K 1 2 3 4 5 6 7 8 9 10 11 12

❑ _____   K 1 2 3 4 5 6 7 8 9 10 11 12

❑ _____   K 1 2 3 4 5 6 7 8 9 10 11 12

School, Family, and Community Partnerships by J. L. Epstein et al., © 2002 Corwin Press, Inc.
Photocopying permissible for local school use only.

TYPE 2 – COMMUNICATING: BASIC RESPONSIBILITIES OF SCHOOLS **At Which Grades?**

Conduct effective communications from school to home and from home to school about school programs and children's progress

❑ We have formal conferences with every parent at least once a year.   K 1 2 3 4 5 6 7 8 9 10 11 12

❑ We provide language translators to assist families as needed.   K 1 2 3 4 5 6 7 8 9 10 11 12

❑ We provide clear information about report cards and how grades are earned.   K 1 2 3 4 5 6 7 8 9 10 11 12

❑ Parents pick up report cards.   K 1 2 3 4 5 6 7 8 9 10 11 12

❑ Our school newsletter includes:

     ❑ A calendar of school events   K 1 2 3 4 5 6 7 8 9 10 11 12

     ❑ Student activity information   K 1 2 3 4 5 6 7 8 9 10 11 12

     ❑ Curriculum and program information   K 1 2 3 4 5 6 7 8 9 10 11 12

     ❑ School volunteer information   K 1 2 3 4 5 6 7 8 9 10 11 12

     ❑ School policy information   K 1 2 3 4 5 6 7 8 9 10 11 12

     ❑ Samples of student writing and artwork   K 1 2 3 4 5 6 7 8 9 10 11 12

     ❑ A column to address parents' questions   K 1 2 3 4 5 6 7 8 9 10 11 12

     ❑ Recognition of students, families, and community members   K 1 2 3 4 5 6 7 8 9 10 11 12

     ❑ Other _____   K 1 2 3 4 5 6 7 8 9 10 11 12

❑ We provide clear information about selecting courses, programs, and/or activities in this school.   K 1 2 3 4 5 6 7 8 9 10 11 12

❑ We send home folders of student work weekly or monthly for parent review and comments.   K 1 2 3 4 5 6 7 8 9 10 11 12

❑ Staff members send home positive messages about students on a regular basis.   K 1 2 3 4 5 6 7 8 9 10 11 12

❑ We notify families about student awards and recognition.   K 1 2 3 4 5 6 7 8 9 10 11 12

❑ We contact the families of students having academic or behavior problems.   K 1 2 3 4 5 6 7 8 9 10 11 12

❑ Teachers have easy access to telephones to communicate with parents during or after school.   K 1 2 3 4 5 6 7 8 9 10 11 12

❑ Teachers and administrators have e-mail and/or a school website to communicate with parents.   K 1 2 3 4 5 6 7 8 9 10 11 12

❑ Parents have the telephone numbers and/or e-mail addresses of the school, principal, teachers, and counselors.   K 1 2 3 4 5 6 7 8 9 10 11 12

❑ We have a homework hotline for students and families to hear daily assignments and messages.   K 1 2 3 4 5 6 7 8 9 10 11 12

❑ We conduct an annual survey for families to provide reactions to school programs and share information and concerns about students.   K 1 2 3 4 5 6 7 8 9 10 11 12

❑ _____   K 1 2 3 4 5 6 7 8 9 10 11 12

❑ _____   K 1 2 3 4 5 6 7 8 9 10 11 12

❑ _____   K 1 2 3 4 5 6 7 8 9 10 11 12

❑ _____   K 1 2 3 4 5 6 7 8 9 10 11 12

TYPE 3 – VOLUNTEERING: INVOLVEMENT AT AND FOR THE SCHOOL
Organize volunteers and audiences to support the school and students

At Which Grades?

❑ We conduct an annual survey to identify interests, talents, and availability of volunteers.
K 1 2 3 4 5 6 7 8 9 10 11 12

❑ We have a parent room or family center for volunteer work, meetings, and resources for families.
K 1 2 3 4 5 6 7 8 9 10 11 12

❑ We encourage families and the community to be involved at school by:

  ❑ Assisting in the classroom (tutoring, grading papers, etc.)
  K 1 2 3 4 5 6 7 8 9 10 11 12

  ❑ Helping on trips or at parties
  K 1 2 3 4 5 6 7 8 9 10 11 12

  ❑ Giving talks (careers, hobbies, etc.)
  K 1 2 3 4 5 6 7 8 9 10 11 12

  ❑ Checking attendance
  K 1 2 3 4 5 6 7 8 9 10 11 12

  ❑ Monitoring halls, or working in the library, cafeteria, or other areas
  K 1 2 3 4 5 6 7 8 9 10 11 12

  ❑ Leading clubs or activities
  K 1 2 3 4 5 6 7 8 9 10 11 12

  ❑ Other _____
  K 1 2 3 4 5 6 7 8 9 10 11 12

❑ We provide ways for families to be involved at home or in the community if they cannot volunteer at school.
K 1 2 3 4 5 6 7 8 9 10 11 12

❑ We have a program to recognize our volunteers.
K 1 2 3 4 5 6 7 8 9 10 11 12

❑ We organize class parents or neighborhood volunteers to link with all parents.
K 1 2 3 4 5 6 7 8 9 10 11 12

❑ We schedule plays, concerts, games, and other events at different times of the day or evening so that all parents can attend some activities.
K 1 2 3 4 5 6 7 8 9 10 11 12

❑ _____
K 1 2 3 4 5 6 7 8 9 10 11 12

❑ _____
K 1 2 3 4 5 6 7 8 9 10 11 12

❑ _____
K 1 2 3 4 5 6 7 8 9 10 11 12

TYPE 4 – LEARNING AT HOME: INVOLVEMENT IN ACADEMIC ACTIVITIES
Involve families with their children in homework and other curriculum-related activities and decisions

At Which Grades?

❑ We provide information to families on required skills in all subjects.
K 1 2 3 4 5 6 7 8 9 10 11 12

❑ We provide information to families on how to monitor and discuss schoolwork at home.
K 1 2 3 4 5 6 7 8 9 10 11 12

❑ We provide information on how to assist students with skills that they need to improve.
K 1 2 3 4 5 6 7 8 9 10 11 12

❑ We have a regular schedule of interactive homework that requires students to demonstrate and discuss what they are learning with a family member.
K 1 2 3 4 5 6 7 8 9 10 11 12

❑ We ask parents to listen to their child read or to read aloud with their child.
K 1 2 3 4 5 6 7 8 9 10 11 12

❑ We provide calendars with daily or weekly activities for families to do at home and in the community.
K 1 2 3 4 5 6 7 8 9 10 11 12

❑ We help families help students set academic goals, select courses and programs, and plan for college or work.
K 1 2 3 4 5 6 7 8 9 10 11 12

❑ _____
K 1 2 3 4 5 6 7 8 9 10 11 12

❑ _____
K 1 2 3 4 5 6 7 8 9 10 11 12

❑ _____
K 1 2 3 4 5 6 7 8 9 10 11 12

TYPE 5 – DECISION MAKING: PARTICIPATION AND LEADERSHIP
Include families as participants in school decisions, and develop parent leaders and representatives

At Which Grades?

❑ We have an active PTA, PTO, or other parent organization.

K 1 2 3 4 5 6 7 8 9 10 11 12

❑ Parent representatives are on the school's advisory council, improvement team, or other committees.

K 1 2 3 4 5 6 7 8 9 10 11 12

❑ We have an Action Team for Partnerships to develop a goal-oriented program with practices for all six types of involvement.

K 1 2 3 4 5 6 7 8 9 10 11 12

❑ Parent representatives are on district-level advisory councils or committees.

K 1 2 3 4 5 6 7 8 9 10 11 12

❑ We develop formal networks to link all families with their parent representatives for decision making.

K 1 2 3 4 5 6 7 8 9 10 11 12

❑ We involve all parents to get input and ideas on school policies.

K 1 2 3 4 5 6 7 8 9 10 11 12

❑ We provide information on school or local elections for school representatives.

K 1 2 3 4 5 6 7 8 9 10 11 12

❑ We involve parents in selecting school staff.

K 1 2 3 4 5 6 7 8 9 10 11 12

❑ We involve parents in revising school and/or district curricula.

K 1 2 3 4 5 6 7 8 9 10 11 12

❑ _____

K 1 2 3 4 5 6 7 8 9 10 11 12

❑ _____

K 1 2 3 4 5 6 7 8 9 10 11 12

❑ _____

K 1 2 3 4 5 6 7 8 9 10 11 12

TYPE 6 – COLLABORATING WITH THE COMMUNITY
Coordinate resources and services *from* the community for families, students, and the school, and provide services *to* the community

At Which Grades?

❑ We provide a resource directory for parents and students with information on community agencies, programs, and services.

K 1 2 3 4 5 6 7 8 9 10 11 12

❑ We provide information on community activities that link to learning skills and talents, including summer programs for students.

K 1 2 3 4 5 6 7 8 9 10 11 12

❑ We work with local businesses, industries, and community organizations on programs to enhance student skills.

K 1 2 3 4 5 6 7 8 9 10 11 12

❑ We offer after-school programs for students, with support from community businesses, agencies, or volunteers.

K 1 2 3 4 5 6 7 8 9 10 11 12

❑ We sponsor intergenerational programs with local senior citizen groups.

K 1 2 3 4 5 6 7 8 9 10 11 12

❑ We provide "one-stop" shopping for family services through partnerships of school, counseling, health, recreation, job training, and other agencies.

K 1 2 3 4 5 6 7 8 9 10 11 12

❑ We organize service *to* the community by students, families, and schools.

K 1 2 3 4 5 6 7 8 9 10 11 12

❑ We include alumni in school programs for students.

K 1 2 3 4 5 6 7 8 9 10 11 12

❑ Our school building is open for use by the community after school hours.

K 1 2 3 4 5 6 7 8 9 10 11 12

❑ _____

K 1 2 3 4 5 6 7 8 9 10 11 12

❑ _____

K 1 2 3 4 5 6 7 8 9 10 11 12

❑ _____

K 1 2 3 4 5 6 7 8 9 10 11 12

❑ _____

K 1 2 3 4 5 6 7 8 9 10 11 12

JUMPING HURDLES

All Action Teams for Partnerships face challenges in developing programs of school, family, and community partnerships. Can you think of a successful family or community involvement activity that your school presently conducts and a challenge that was met in order to implement this activity?

- List ONE SUCCESSFUL ACTIVITY that your school conducts to involve families or the community in students' education at home, at school, or in the community.

- Identify ONE CHALLENGE or obstacle that your school faced in implementing this activity.

- Briefly describe how your school SOLVED that challenge.

- Note one NEXT STEP that your school could take to make the activity even more successful.

ONE SUCCESSFUL FAMILY or COMMUNITY INVOLVEMENT ACTIVITY

_____

_____

_____

_____

CHALLENGE?

_____

_____

_____

SOLUTION?

_____

_____

_____

_____

NEXT STEPS?

_____

_____

_____

School Goals and Results of Partnerships

HOW MIGHT THE SIX TYPES OF INVOLVEMENT
HELP YOUR SCHOOL REACH ITS GOALS?

ONE ☆ MAJOR ☆ GOAL THAT OUR SCHOOL HAS SET IS:_____

_____

_____

_____

MEASURABLE RESULTS: How will you know if your school reaches THIS goal? What measures (e.g., tests, surveys, portfolios, interviews, attendance lists) will your school use to evaluate and document progress? _____

_____

_____

_____

PARTNERSHIP PRACTICES: Identify specific partnership activities that directly link to the goal. Some goals will be helped by practices from all *six* types of involvement; others may be helped by practices from just three or four types. Fill in family and community involvement activities only if they will help reach THIS goal.

Activities to help reach THIS goal

Type 1—Parenting _____

_____

Type 2—Communicating _____

_____

Type 3—Volunteering _____

_____

Type 4—Learning at Home _____

_____

Type 5—Decision Making _____

_____

Type 6—Collaborating With the Community _____

_____

Get Ready for Action

Use this activity to begin to think about your school's program of school, family, and community partnerships.

- Identify *four* goals from your school improvement plan that will be the focus of the school's family and community involvement program.

    Academic goal #1: _____

    Academic goal #2: _____

    Nonacademic goal for students: _____

    Partnership goal (required): _____Develop a welcoming climate of partnerships_____

- With a partner, select *one* of the four goals above and write it in the "Goal" box. Together, list family and community involvement activities that your school *presently* implements to reach the selected goal.

- Then, brainstorm *new* family and community involvement activities that your school could implement this year to help reach the selected goal.

- Remember: Include examples for as many of the six types of involvement as possible.

Goal:	
	Current family and community involvement activities that help reach THIS goal:	*New* family and community involvement activities that may help reach THIS goal:
Type 1		
Type 2		
Type 3		
Type 4		
Type 5		
Type 6		

- Next, use these ideas to begin to write your school's One-Year Action Plan for partnerships.

HOW TO ORGANIZE YOUR
ACTION TEAM FOR PARTNERSHIPS

Complete this activity with your team. Review and update periodically.

1. How will your school's Action Team for Partnerships (ATP) organize its work? (check **A** or **B**)

☐ **A.** We will organize our ATP's One-Year Action Plan and committees based on the *six types of involvement.* Our ATP will have six committees, one for each type of involvement.

☐ **B.** We will organize our ATP's One-Year Action Plan and committees based on *school improvement goals.* Our ATP will have *four* committees to develop family and community involvement for two academic goals, one behavior goal, and for the goal of creating a positive climate for partnerships.

B1. *Which four goals* will your ATP committees address to involve students' families and community in important ways?

Goal 1 (Academic) _____

Goal 2 (Academic) _____

Goal 3 (Nonacademic) _____

Goal 4 (*Required*) Develop a welcoming climate of partnerships

2. Who will be the members and leaders of the Action Team for Partnerships (ATP)?
(There should be 6-12 members of the ATP. See pp. 85-86 of this *Handbook.*)

Required:

Administrator(s) _____

Teachers (at least 2) _____

Parents/family (at least 2) _____

Student(s) (at the high school level) _____

Optional:

Other school staff _____

Community partners _____

Who will be ATP chair or co-chairs? _____
_____

3. When will the *whole* Action Team for Partnerships (ATP) meet?
(The ATP should meet at least monthly. See pp. 96-97 of this *Handbook.*)

How often? _____ Day _____ Time _____ Place _____

How will information from the ATP meetings be shared with absent members?
_____

4. Who will be the leaders and helpers of ATP committees, and when will ATP committees meet?

(ATP committees should meet as often as needed to successfully implement the activities in the One-Year Action Plan for which they are responsible. See pp. 87-90 of this *Handbook*.)

ATP Committees (List the 6 types or the 4 goals)	ATP Committee Chairs or Co-chairs	Others on ATP Committees (Helpers need not be on the full ATP)	Meeting Day, Time, Place

5. How will reports about the ATP's plans and progress be presented to other groups?

Check ☑ the groups that will receive reports on the Action Team for Partnerships' plans and progress. How often will the reports be presented? In what form (e.g., oral report, computerized phone message, written summary, detailed written report, newsletter article, press release, website entry, or some other form)? Who will make the presentations?

Which Groups Will Receive Reports on ATP Plans and Progress on Partnerships?	How Often?	In What Form?	Who Will Present?
❑ School Improvement Team or council			
❑ PTA/PTO or parent organization			
❑ All parents in the school			
❑ The full faculty			
❑ Students			
❑ Community members			
❑ Local media			
❑ Others			

6

Strengthening Partnership Programs in Middle and High Schools

Middle and high schools face unique challenges in developing and maintaining comprehensive programs of school, family, and community partnerships. Typically, middle and high school teachers have more students than do teachers in the elementary grades and, therefore, must connect with more families. Families tend to live farther away from middle and high schools and cannot easily come often to the school building. Most families are unsure of how to relate to many teachers and need more information about the middle and high school curriculum, policies, and requirements for students. Students in secondary schools are trying to balance their need for guidance with their need for greater independence. Despite these complex realities, research shows that connections of home, school, and community remain important for student success in middle and high schools.

Three short articles in this chapter explore school, family, and community partnerships in middle and high schools. The first article includes examples of activities for the six types of involvement that have been useful in secondary schools. It also discusses the challenges that must be solved and the expected results of well-implemented, age-appropriate partnerships in middle and high schools.

The second article summarizes a study of over 11,000 parents of high school students. The results show that family involvement is important for student success through the 12th grade. Moreover, high schools that conducted involvement activities had more parents who were involved in their teens' education. These data indicate that, by implementing strong programs of partnerships, high schools can help families remain influential in their teens' lives in important ways.

The third article guides secondary schools, step-by-step, to take a goal-oriented approach in planning their partnership programs. Examples from middle and high schools show that Action Teams for Partnerships can write plans for family and community involvement to help schools reach specific improvement goals.

The following tools and materials also are included in this chapter.

Reaching Middle and High School Goals Through Partnerships

Use the six types of involvement to target specific goals for students and for schools. Activities are listed that illustrate how involvement activities may help students make successful transitions to the next school level, improve attendance, increase reading achievement, improve math skills, plan for postsecondary education, and create a welcoming school environment. These pages may be turned into transparencies or handouts for workshops or presentations on results of partnerships in middle and high schools. These examples supplement results of partnerships in elementary schools on pages 190-193 in this *Handbook*.

Why Partnerships Are Important in Middle and High Schools

Review the eight research results that explain why programs of school, family, and community partnerships are important in secondary schools.

Special Considerations for Middle and High Schools

Reflect on several issues to help middle and high schools' ATPs establish and sustain successful programs and practices of partnership. This summary presents six lessons learned from middle and high schools that are developing their partnership programs.

Transitions: Involving Families When Students Move to New Schools

Plan to involve students and families in activities that will ease transitions to new schools. The One-Year Action Plan for partnerships should include strategies to welcome new students and families to the school and activities to prepare students and families to move successfully to the next school level (e.g., from elementary to middle school or from middle to high school).

Improving School, Family, and Community Partnerships in Middle and High Schools

Joyce L. Epstein[1]

The goal of positive and productive family and community involvement is on every school improvement list, but few secondary schools have implemented comprehensive programs of partnership. Research suggests that the goal is an important one to reach because families and communities contribute to children's learning, development, and school success at every grade level. Presently, however, most families need more information about adolescent development, middle and high school organization, and community programs and services for teens (Dornbusch & Ritter, 1988; Eccles & Harold, 1996; Epstein & Lee, 1995; Ho & Willms, 1996; Hollifield, 1995; Hoover-Dempsey & Sandler, 1997; Rutherford, 1995).

Just about all parents want their adolescents to succeed in school, graduate from high school, and attend college or career education (Catsambis, 1998; Epstein & Lee, 1995; Sanders, Epstein, & Connors-Tadros, 1999; see also Hoover-Dempsey et al., 2001). Most, however, need better information and guidance to support their teens' success through high school. Some parents are discouraged from remaining involved when faced by the multifaceted needs and problems of adolescents; the complexities of school curricula, assessments, and organization; and the growing constraints on family time (Simon, 2001).

Studies are accumulating that show that well-designed programs of partnership can help all families support their children's education in middle and high school (Balli, Demo, & Wedman, 1998; Catsambis, 1998; Dauber & Epstein, 1993; Ho & Willms, 1996; Lee, 1994; Sanders 1998, 1999; Sanders et al., 1999; Simon, 2001; Van Voorhis, 2001). Results indicate that when secondary schools plan and implement comprehensive programs of partnership, many more families respond, including those who would not become involved on their own.

Middle and high school teachers and administrators agree that family involvement and community connections are important, but their beliefs are not always supported by action (Connors & Epstein, 1994). Three questions need to be answered to help middle and high school educators conduct more effective programs of partnership:

1. What is a comprehensive program of school, family, and community partnerships in middle and high schools?
2. How do family and community partnerships link to other aspects of successful middle and high schools?
3. How can any middle or high school develop and sustain a productive program of partnerships?

1. What Is a Comprehensive Program of Partnerships?

A comprehensive program of school, family, and community partnerships is a planned, goal-oriented, and ongoing schedule of activities that inform and involve all families and the community in ways that promote student success. Family and community involvement activities are implemented to address specific goals, meet key challenges, and produce results for students, families, and schools.

A framework of six types of family and community involvement guides schools in establishing full and productive programs of partnership (Epstein, 1995). This section summarizes the six types of involvement and discusses a few sample practices that are being conducted in middle and high schools across the country. Also noted are some of the challenges that all schools must solve to achieve successful partnerships and examples of results that can be expected from each type of involvement for secondary school students, families, and educators. Comprehensive programs of partnership include activities for all six types of involvement. Importantly, there are many choices of activities, so middle and high schools can select different ways to involve families and the community to help reach specific school goals.

Type 1-Parenting

Type 1-Parenting activities are conducted to help families strengthen parenting skills, understand adolescent development, and set home conditions to support learning at every grade level. Type 1 activities also enable families to provide information to schools so educators understand families' backgrounds, cultures, and goals for their children.

Sample Practices. Many families have questions about how to relate to and support their children through adolescence. Middle and high schools can plan and implement activities and provide services that assist families to better understand adolescent development. Among Type 1 activities, middle and high schools may conduct workshops for parents; provide short, clear summaries of important information on parenting; and organize support groups, panels, and other opportunities for parents to exchange ideas with other parents, educators, and community experts on topics of adolescent development.

Topics of interest to parents of adolescents include health, nutrition, discipline, guidance, peer pressure, preventing drug abuse, and planning for the future. Type 1 activities also provide families with information on students' transitions to middle school and to high school and on family roles and responsibilities in student attendance, college planning, career preparation, and other topics that are important for adolescents' success in school. Secondary schools may offer parents GED programs, family support sessions, family computer classes, and other learning and social opportunities for parents and for students. To ensure that families provide valuable information to the schools, teachers may ask parents at the start of each school year or periodically to share insights about their children's strengths, talents, interests, needs, and goals.

Challenges. Even if workshops are well planned, not all interested parents are able to attend. Yet, most parents can benefit from the content of workshops. One major challenge that must be met for successful Type 1 activities is to get information from workshops to parents who cannot come to meetings and workshops at the school building. This may be done with videos, tape recordings, summaries, newsletters, cable broadcasts, phone calls, and other print and nonprint communications. Another Type 1 challenge is to design procedures that enable all families to share information easily and as needed about their teens with teachers, counselors, and others.

Results. If useful information flows to and from families about adolescent development, parents will increase their confidence about parenting, students will be more aware of and benefit from parents' continuing guidance, and teachers will better understand their students' families. For example, if practices are targeted to help families send their children to school every day and on time, then student attendance will improve and lateness will decrease. If families are part of their children's transitions from elementary to middle school and from middle to high school, then more students will adjust well to their new schools, and more parents will remain involved across the grades.

Type 2-Communicating

Type 2-Communicating activities increase school-to-home and home-to-school communications about school programs and student progress through notices, memos, conferences, report cards, newsletters, phone, e-mail and computerized messages, the Internet, open houses, and other traditional and innovative communications.

Sample Practices. Families rely on communications with teachers, administrators, and counselors to follow their children's progress and problems. Middle and high schools are using traditional communications and, increasingly, new technologies to relay information to and from families. Among many Type 2 activities, middle and high schools may provide parents with clear information on each teacher's criteria for report card grades and how to interpret interim progress reports. Type 2 activities include conferences for parents with teams of teachers or parent-student-teacher conferences to ensure that students take personal responsibility for learning. Activities may be designed to improve school and student newsletters to include student work, a feature column for parents' questions, calendars of important events, and parent response forms. Many schools are beginning to use e-mail, voice mail, and websites to encourage two-way communications between families and teachers, counselors, and administrators.

Challenges. Not all communications between middle and high school educators and families are successful. One major challenge that must be met for successful Type 2 activities is to make communications clear and understandable for all families, including parents who have less formal education or who do not read English well, so that all families can understand and respond to the information they receive. Other Type 2 challenges are to know which families are and are not receiving and understanding the communications in order to design ways to reach all families, develop effective two-way channels of communication so that families can easily contact and respond to educators, and make sure that students in middle and high schools understand the important roles they play as couriers and interpreters in facilitating school and family connections.

Results. If communications are clear and useful, and if two-way channels are easily accessed, then school-to-home and home-to-school interactions will increase; more families will understand middle and high school programs, follow their children's progress, guide students to maintain or improve their grades, and attend parent-teacher conferences. If, for example, computerized phone lines are used to communicate information about daily homework, more families will know more about their children's daily assignments. If middle and high schools' newsletters include respond-and-reply forms, more families will offer ideas, questions, and comments about school programs and activities.

Type 3-Volunteering

Type 3-Volunteering activities are designed to improve recruitment, training, and schedules to involve parents and others as volunteers and as audiences at the school or in other locations to support students and school programs.

Sample Practices. Parents of older students often wonder if they could or should continue to serve as volunteers. Middle and high schools can enrich, extend, and support their curricular and extracurricular programs by organizing volunteers in new ways. Among many Type 3 activities, middle and high schools may collect information on family members' talents, occupations, interests, and availability to serve as volunteers. Parents, family members, and other volunteers may help to enrich students' subject classes; improve career explorations; serve as language translators; monitor attendance and call parents of absent students; conduct parent patrols and be morning greeters to increase school safety;

serve as boosters or supporters of extracurricular clubs; or organize and improve activities such as clothing and uniform exchanges, school stores, fairs, and many other activities. Schools may organize volunteers to serve as homeroom parents, neighborhood representatives, or sports and club contacts and establish telephone trees to help parents communicate with each other about school programs and events. Schools may establish a corps of volunteers to offer a "welcome wagon" of information about the school to students and families who enroll during the school year. Secondary schools also may create opportunities for mentors, coaches, tutors, and leaders of after-school programs to ensure that middle and high school students have experiences that build and expand their skills and talents and that keep them safe and supervised after school. Some Type 3 activities may be conducted in a parent room or family center at the school where parents obtain information, conduct volunteer work, and meet with other parents (Johnson, 1996).

Challenges. Volunteers must be well prepared to conduct specific tasks in middle and high schools, and they must feel that their efforts are appreciated. Challenges that must be met for successful Type 3 activities are to recruit volunteers widely so that parents and other family members feel welcome, make hours flexible for parents and other volunteers who work during the school day, provide needed training, and enable volunteers to contribute productively to the school, classroom, and extracurricular or after-school programs. Volunteers will be better integrated in a middle or high school program if there is a coordinator who is responsible for matching volunteers' times and skills with the needs of teachers, administrators, and students. Another Type 3 challenge is to change the definition of "volunteer" to mean anyone who supports school goals or students' learning at any time and in any place. This includes parents and family members who voluntarily come to school as audiences for students' sports events, assemblies, musical or drama presentations, and other events that support students' work. It also includes volunteers who work for the school at home, through their businesses, or in the community. A related challenge is to help adolescents understand how volunteers help their school and to encourage students to interact with volunteers who can assist them with their work and activities.

Results. If tasks are well designed and if schedules and locations for volunteers are varied, more parents, family members, and others in the community will assist middle and high schools and support students as members of audiences. More families will feel comfortable with the school and staff, more students will talk and interact with varied adults, and more teachers will be aware of and use parents' and other community members' talents and resources to improve school programs and activities. For example, if volunteers serve effectively as attendance monitors, more families will assist teens to improve attendance. If volunteers conduct a hall patrol or are active in other locations, school safety will increase and student

Answers

Are Two Heads Better Than One?

NOTE: The answers to the puzzles are for facilitators only.
Do not duplicate as a workshop handout!

1. just under the wire

2. twisted ankle, turned ankle

3. fly by night

4. highway overpass

5. making ends meet, split ends

6. tennis, anyone?

7. space invaders

8. horseback riding

9. foot in the door

10. forgive and forget

11. more often than not

12. a splitting headache

13. just between you and me

14. *Westside Story*

15. water under the bridge

16. singing in the rain

17. the odds are overwhelming, overwhelming odds

18. it's a small world after all

19. an outside chance

20. a round of applause

behavior problems will decrease due to a better student-adult ratio. If volunteers are well trained as tutors in particular subjects, student tutees will improve their skills in those subjects, and if volunteers discuss careers, students will be more aware of their options for the future. These examples reinforce the importance of organizing volunteers to conduct activities that help the school and students reach specific goals.

Type 4-Learning at Home

Type 4-Learning at Home activities involve families with their children in academic learning activities at home that are coordinated with students' classwork and that contribute to student success in school. These include interactive homework, goal setting for academic subjects, and other curricular-linked activities and decisions about courses, academic programs, and postsecondary paths.

Sample Practices. Of all the types of involvement, most families want to know more about how to help their teens at home so that they will do better in school. Middle and high school teachers and counselors can work together to enable more families to connect with teens about schoolwork and homework. Among many Type 4 activities, middle and high schools may provide information to students and to parents about the skills needed to pass each course and about each teacher's homework policies. Schools also may implement activities that help families encourage, praise, guide, and monitor their children's work by using interactive homework strategies, student-teacher-family contracts for long-term projects, summer home-learning packets, student-led conferences with parents at home on portfolios of students' writing or work in other subjects, goal-setting activities for improving or maintaining good report card grades in all subjects, specific ways to work with students at home to help them improve grades or behavior, and other approaches that keep students and families talking about schoolwork at home. Family fun and learning nights are often used as a starting point to help parents and students focus on curricular-related topics and family interactions. A systematic approach to increasing parent-teen conversations about academic subjects is found in the Teachers Involve Parents in Schoolwork (TIPS) interactive homework for the middle grades (Epstein, Salinas, & Jackson, 1995). For information on how to use interactive homework in middle and high schools, go online to www.partnershipschools.org and visit the "TIPS" section.

Challenges. Involving parents with teens on homework is difficult and parents must not be expected to teach middle and high school subjects. Middle and high school students are key to the success of family involvement in learning activities at home. One major challenge that must be met for successful Type 4 activities is to design and implement a regular schedule of interactive homework that requires students to take responsibility for discussing important things they are learning, interviewing family members, recording reactions, and sharing their work and ideas at home. Another Type 4 challenge is to create a schedule of activities that involve families regularly and systematically with students on short-term and long-term goal-setting for attendance, achievement, behavior, talent development, and plans for college or careers.

Results. If Type 4 activities are well designed and implemented, then student homework completion, report card grades, and test scores in specific subjects should improve; more families will know what their children are learning in class and how to monitor, support, and discuss homework. More students should complete required course credits, select advanced courses, and take college entrance tests. Students and teachers will be more aware of family interest in students' work.

Type 5-Decision Making

Type 5-Decision Making activities include families in developing middle and high school mission statements and in designing, reviewing, and improving school policies that affect their children and families. Family members are active participants on School Improvement Teams, committees, PTA/PTO or other parent organizations, Title I and other councils, and advocacy groups.

Sample Practices. Parents have different perspectives from teachers about many school issues. Middle and high schools can better identify and understand issues important to students and families and make better decisions by including parent representatives on various school committees. Among Type 5 activities, middle and high schools may organize and maintain an active parent association and include family representatives on all committees for school improvement (e.g., curriculum, safety, supplies and equipment, partnerships, fundraising, and postsecondary college planning and career development committees). In particular, along with teachers, administrators, students, and others from the community, parents are members of the Action Team for Partnerships, which plans and conducts family and community involvement activities linked to school improvement goals. Schools may offer parents and teachers training in leadership, decision making, policy advocacy, and collaboration. Type 5 activities help to identify and provide information desired by families about school policies, course offerings, student placements and groups, special services, tests and assessments, annual test results for students, and evaluations of school programs.

Challenges. It is important for parents to have their voices, ideas, and interests represented on school committees. One challenge that must be met for successful Type 5 activities in middle and high schools is to ensure that leadership roles are filled by parent representatives from all the major race and ethnic groups, socioeconomic groups, and neighborhoods that are present in the school. A related challenge is to help parent leaders serve as effective representatives by obtaining information from and providing information to all parents about school issues and decisions. Another Type 5 challenge is to include middle and high school student representatives along with parents in decision-making groups and leadership positions. An ongoing challenge is to help parents, teachers, and students who serve on an Action Team for Partnerships or other committees learn to trust, respect, and listen to each other as they collaborate to reach common goals for school improvement.

Results. If Type 5 activities are well implemented in middle and high schools, more families will have input to decisions that affect the quality of their children's education; students will increase their awareness that families and students have a say in school policies; and teachers will increase their understanding of family perspectives on policies and programs for improving the school.

Type 6-Collaborating With the Community

Type 6-Collaborating With the Community activities draw upon and coordinate the work and resources of community businesses; cultural, civic, and religious organizations; senior citizen groups; colleges and universities; governmental agencies; and other associations in order to strengthen school programs, family practices, and student learning and development. Other Type 6 activities enable students, staff, and families to contribute their services to the community.

Sample Practices. Students' needs and interests become more diverse in adolescence than in earlier years, and students' activities in the community become more numerous and noticeable. Middle and high schools need to identify and activate the resources, services, and opportunities in the community to fully serve students and their families. Among many Type 6 activities, middle and high schools may create useful directories that inform students and families about the availability of community programs and resources such as after-school recreation, tutorial programs, health services, cultural events, service opportunities, and summer programs. The information includes ways that students and families may gain access to community resources and programs. For example, some middle and high schools work with local businesses to organize "gold card" discounts as incentives for students to improve attendance and report card grades.

Collaborations with community businesses, groups, and agencies also strengthen the other five types of involvement. Examples include enhancing Type 1 activities by conducting parent education workshops for families at community or business locations or by having businesses provide refreshments or incentives to increase the success of school-based workshops for parents; increasing Type 2 activities by communicating about school events on the local radio and TV stations, at churches, clinics, supermarkets, laundromats, and other neighborhood locations; soliciting volunteers from businesses and the community to strengthen Type 3 activities; enriching Type 4 by offering students learning opportunities with artists, scientists, writers, mathematicians, and others whose careers link to the school curriculum; and including community members on Type 5 decision-making councils and committees.

Challenges. It is not always easy for educators to collaborate with partners outside the school. One challenge that must be met for successful Type 6 activities is to solve problems associated with community-school collaborations such as turf problems of determining who is responsible for funding, leading, and supervising cooperative activities. The initial enthusiasm and decisions for school-community partnerships must be followed by actions that sustain productive collaborations over the long term. Another Type 6 challenge is to recognize and link students' valuable learning experiences in the community to the school curricula, including lessons that build on students' nonschool skills and talents, club and volunteer work, and part-time jobs. A major challenge is to inform and involve families about community-related activities that students conduct or to expand some community activities to involve families with students. Related challenges are to help adolescents understand how community partners help their school and to engage students themselves as volunteers and in service learning in their own schools, other schools, and the community.

Results. If Type 6 activities are well implemented, the knowledge that families, students, and schools have about the resources and programs in their community will increase to help students reach important goals. If community services are better coordinated, adolescents and their families may prevent health, social, and educational problems or solve them before they become too serious. Type 6 activities also can support and enrich school curricula and extracurricular programs. For example, activities such as tutoring and mentoring can directly affect student learning and achievement.

Summary. The six types of involvement create a comprehensive program of partnerships in middle and high schools, but the implementation challenges for each type of involvement must be met in order for programs to be effective. The expected results are directly affected by the quality of the design, implementation, and content of the involvement activities. Not every practice to involve families will result in higher student achievement test scores. Rather, practices for each type of involvement can be selected to help students, families, and teachers reach specific goals such as increasing attendance, increasing homework completion, helping plan postsecondary pathways, and achieving other results (Epstein, 1995, 2001). The examples above include only a few of hundreds of suggestions that can help middle and high schools develop strong programs of partnership. For more examples of effective activities, see the other summaries in this chapter of the *Handbook* and go online to www.partnershipschools.org to visit the "Middle and High School" section.

2. How Do School, Family, and Community Partnerships Link to Other Aspects of Successful Middle and High Schools?

Good schools have qualified and talented teachers and administrators, high expectations that all students will succeed, rigorous curricula, engaging instruction, responsive and useful tests and assessments, strong guidance for every student, *and* effective school, family, and community partnerships (Balfanz & Mac Iver, 2000; Erb, 2001; McPartland, Balfanz, Jordan, & Legters, 1998; National Association of Secondary School Principals, 1996). In good schools, these elements combine to promote students' learning and to create a school climate that is welcoming, safe, caring, stimulating, and joyful for all students, educators, and families.

All the elements of successful schools are interconnected. It is particularly important for middle and high school educators to understand that partnerships are not extra, separate, or different from the "real work" of a school, but are integral to and essential for improving the quality of a school's program and student success. As one middle school principal noted, "I think that family and community involvement and school improvement should be joint efforts . . . they support each other" (Sanders, 1999, p. 35).

The following two examples show how family involvement is linked to the success of middle and high schools' academic and guidance programs.

Family and community involvement activities contribute to the quality of academic programs and student learning. National and local surveys indicate that secondary school students and their families have very high aspirations for success in school and in life. Fully 98% of a national sample of eighth-grade students say they plan to graduate from high school, and 82% plan at least some postsecondary schooling, with over 70% aiming to complete college (Epstein & Lee, 1995). Tenth-grade students have similarly high ambitions, with about 90% saying they sometimes or often talk with a parent about college (Simon, 2001). In order to help students reach their aspirations, middle and high school educators and students' families must work together to guide students to take the courses they need to complete high school and to attend college. Schools, with families' support, also must provide some students with extra help and more time to learn in coaching classes, extra-help courses, summer school, tutoring, mentoring, and other responsive programs.

Families need good information about middle and high school curricula, teachers' instructional approaches, and assessments in order to be able to discuss important academic topics with their children at home. Families and others in the community (e.g., students' part-time employers) need to know about the courses and extra services that are offered in middle and high schools in order to guide teens' decisions about academic programs. Families also need to understand how their children are progressing in each subject, how to help students set and meet learning goals, and how to work with students to solve major problems that threaten course or grade-level failure. Some middle and high schools create individual student educational plans and conferences with all students and parents (Lloyd, 1996).

Students themselves are aware that family involvement spurs their academic efforts (Connors & Epstein, 1994). Explained one 10th-grade student in a high school working to improve its partnership program,

> Parent involvement is important because if you don't have a parent to encourage you and support you—ask you about your grades, and how you're doing—then you'd think they didn't care. Then you wouldn't have that motivation to go out there and try to get a 100% or 90% (on a test), you'll take whatever you get because no one else is interested. (Sanders, 1998, p.41)

Middle and high schools use new and varied teaching strategies that are unfamiliar to most families (Mulhall, Mertens, & Flowers, 2001). These may include group activities, problem-solving processes, prewriting techniques, student-as-historian methods, interactive homework, and other innovative approaches to promote learning. Families and others in the community also need to know about major tests, report card criteria, and other state and local standards that schools use to determine students' progress and pathways through middle and high school. Some schools' Action Teams for Partnerships design evening activities for parents to learn about and try items on new performance-based assessments.

With clear information about school academic programs, more families will be able to guide students' decisions about courses, homework completion, studying for tests, and taking steps toward college or work. Moreover, if teachers, students, and parents or other family members communicate clearly and frequently through high school about students' academic programs, progress, and needs, more students will succeed at high levels and fulfill their own and their families' high expectations.

Family and community involvement activities contribute to the quality of guidance programs and student attitudes and behavior. School guidance and support services are likely to be stronger and serve students better if educators, students, and families are well connected (Christenson & Conoley, 1992). Students need to know that their guidance counselors and teachers understand and appreciate their families' cultures, hopes, and dreams. Many adolescents are trying to balance their love for their family, need for guidance, need for peer acceptance and friendship, and need for greater independence. By their actions, middle and high school educators and parents can help students see that these seemingly contradictory pressures can coexist.

Guidance counselors, school social workers, and school psychologists should meet with students' families and may serve as key contacts for parents to call if questions arise about students' academic progress, attendance, behavior, peer relations, or interactions with teachers. In some middle and high schools, guidance counselors are members of interdisciplinary teams of teachers who meet with parents and students on a regular schedule. In other schools, guidance counselors could contact parents *before* students are at serious risk of failing courses due to absence, attitudes, behavior, classwork, or homework in order to devise collaborative approaches to help students succeed in school.

Programs of school, family, and community partnerships help this agenda. For example, Sanders reports how parent volunteers in a high school explain their contributions to improving student attendance:

> We do a lot of things as attendance monitors. We make home visits, and we call parents to find out why the child is not in school. We also call to encourage parents and to let them know that they are the first and primary educators of their children. We encourage them to come in and volunteer time, find out why the child does not want to attend school, find out what the problem is. (1998, p. 36)

Sanders (1998, p. 38) also reports parents contribute to a safe and orderly high school climate and better student behavior. A parent liaison, member of the Action Team for Partnerships, and organizer of 25 volunteers for the school's parent patrol stated:

> When I first got here, I envisioned a program where parents would come in and patrol the halls, because we had kids who would not stay in classes and would not listen to the staff. So, I felt if parents were here at the school, they would work at keeping their kids in class, plus they'd help with the other kids. . . . When the kids found out . . . there was a big turnaround. And, it wasn't just fear. Some of the students were proud that their parents were part of the school.

Families need to know about the formal and informal guidance programs at their children's schools. This includes knowing the names, phone or voice-mail numbers, and e-mail addresses of their children's teachers, counselors, advocates, and administrators in order to reach them with questions about their children's progress or problems. This is particularly important at times of transition when students move from elementary to middle school and from middle to high school. With good information, parents and other family partners can assist students to adjust successfully to their new schools.

When students, guidance counselors, teachers, and parents communicate well about students' social and emotional development and special needs through the teen years, more students are likely to succeed and stay in school.

3. How Can Any Middle or High School Develop and Sustain a Productive Program of Partnerships?

Many middle and high schools are demonstrating how to design, implement, and sustain strong programs of school, family, and community partnerships (Salinas & Jansorn, 2001). Educators and parents in these schools are using the framework of the six types of involvement to ensure that families are well informed about and engaged in their children's education at school and at home. They are connecting with their communities in many ways to support the school and assist families and students. They are drawing on the research base summarized above, and they are being supported and assisted by school principals, district administrators and key staff, state leaders, and others.

In well-designed partnership programs, each middle and high school forms an Action Team for Partnerships consisting of teachers, parents, administrators, and others. Each team writes an annual action plan for partnerships, implements and oversees activities, maintains an adequate budget, evaluates the quality of partnerships, and improves plans and activities from year to year. In excellent programs, activities to involve families and community partners are linked to school improvement goals to produce the kinds of results described above (Epstein, 2001; Sanders, 2001).

This *Handbook* provides background information and research-based tools and guidelines to help all middle and high schools develop and sustain strong and productive programs of school, family, and community partnerships. Action Teams for Partnerships can use the tools to plan and evaluate family and community involvement activities to help reach middle and high school goals. Moreover, middle and high schools, school districts, and states can join the National Network of Partnership Schools at Johns Hopkins to obtain ongoing professional development for school, family, and community partnerships (see Chapter 10 in this *Handbook* and www.partnershipschools.org).

Note

1. This article extends an earlier version in Epstein, J. L. (2001). School, family, and community partnerships. In T. Erb (Ed.), *This we believe . . . and now we must act* (pp. 42-55). Westerville, OH: National Middle School Association. Another summary that addresses the same questions for elementary, middle, and high schools appears as Epstein, J. L. (2002). Family, school, and community connections. In J. W. Guthrie (Ed.), *Encyclopedia of education* (2nd ed.). New York: Macmillan. The author thanks Beth Simon for her thoughtful edits and suggestions.

References

Balfanz, R., & Mac Iver, D. J. (2000). Transforming high-poverty urban middle schools intro strong learning institutions. *Journal of Education for Students Placed at Risk, 5*(1/2), 137-158.

Balli, S. J., Demo, D. H., & Wedman, J. F. (1998). Family involvement with children's homework: An intervention in the middle grades. *Family Relations, 47,* 149-157.

Catsambis, S. (1998). *Expanding knowledge of parental involvement in secondary education: Social determinants and effects on high school academic success* (Report 27). Baltimore: Johns Hopkins University, Center for Research on the Education of Students Placed at Risk.

Christenson, S. L., & Conoley, J. C. (Eds.). (1992). *Home-school collaboration: Enhancing children's academic and social competence.* Silver Spring, MD: National Association of School Psychologists.

Connors, L. J., & Epstein, J. L. (1994). *Taking stock: The views of teachers, parents, and students on school, family, and community partnerships in high schools* (Report 25). Baltimore: Johns Hopkins University, Center on Families, Communities, Schools and Children's Learning.

Dauber, S. L., & Epstein, J. L. (1993). Parents' attitudes and practices of involvement in inner-city elementary and middle schools. In N. Chavkin (Ed.), *Families and schools in a pluralistic society* (pp. 53-71). Albany: SUNY Press.

Dornbusch, S. M., & Ritter, P. L. (1988). Parents of high school students: A neglected resource. *Educational Horizons, 66,* 75-77.

Eccles, J. S., & Harold, R. D. (1996). Family involvement in children's and adolescents' schooling. In A. Booth and J. Dunn (Eds.), *Family-school links: How do they affect educational outcomes* (pp. 3-34). Hillside, NJ: Lawrence Erlbaum.

Epstein, J. L. (1995). School/family/community partnerships: Caring for the children we share. *Phi Delta Kappan, 76,* 701-712.

Epstein, J. L. (2001). *School, family, and community partnerships: Preparing educators and improving schools.* Boulder, CO: Westview.

Epstein, J. L., & Lee, S. (1995). National patterns of school and family connections in the middle grades. In B. Ryan, G. Adams, T. Gullotta, R. Weissberg, & R. Hampton (Eds.), *The family-school connection: Theory, research and practice* (pp. 108-154). Thousand Oaks, CA: Sage.

Epstein, J. L., Salinas, K. C., & Jackson, V. (1995). *Teachers Involve Parents in Schoolwork (TIPS) in the middle grades.* Baltimore: Johns Hopkins University, Center on School, Family, and Community Partnerships.

Erb, T. O. (2001). *This we believe . . . and now we must act.* Westerville, OH: National Middle School Association.

Ho, E. S., & Willms, D. J. (1996). Effects of parental involvement on eighth-grade achievement. *Sociology of Education, 69,* 126-141.

Hollifield, J. (1995). Making the right investments. *The High School Magazine, 2*(7), 4-9.

Hoover-Dempsey, K. V., Battiato, A. C., Walker, J. M., Reed, R. P., DeJong, J. M., & Jones, K. P. (2001). Parental involvement in homework. *Educational Psychologist, 36,* 195-210.

Hoover-Dempsey, K. V., & Sandler, H. M. (1997). Why do parents become involved in their children's education? *Review of Educational Research, 67,* 3-42.

Johnson, V. R. (1996). *Family center guidebook.* Baltimore: Johns Hopkins University, Center on Families, Communities, Schools and Children's Learning.

Lee, S. (1994). *Family-school connections and students' education: Continuity and change of family involvement from the middle grades to high school.* Unpublished doctoral dissertation, Department of Sociology, Johns Hopkins University.

Lloyd, G. M. (1996). Research and practical applications for school, family, and community partnerships. In A. Booth and J. F. Dunn (Eds.), *Family-school links: How do they affect educational outcomes?* (pp. 255-264). Mahwah, NJ: Lawrence Erlbaum.

McPartland, J., Balfanz, R., Jordan, W., & Legters, N. (1998). Improving climate and achievement in a troubled urban high school through the Talent Development model. *Journal of Education for Students Placed at Risk, 3*, 337-361.

Mulhall, P. F., Mertens, S. B., & Flowers, N. (2001). How familiar are parents with middle level practices? *Middle School Journal, 33*(2), 57-61.

National Association of Secondary School Principals. (1996). *Breaking ranks: Changing an American institution.* Reston, VA: Author.

Rutherford, B. (Ed.). (1995). *Creating family/school partnerships.* Columbus, OH: National Middle School Association.

Salinas, K. C., & Jansorn, N. R. (2001). *Promising partnership practices—2001.* Baltimore: Johns Hopkins University, Center on School, Family, and Community Partnerships.

Sanders, M. G. (1998). School-family-community partnerships: An action team approach. *High School Magazine, 5*(3), 38-49.

Sanders, M. G. (1999). Improving school, family and community partnerships in urban middle schools. *Middle School Journal, 31*(2), 35-41.

Sanders, M. G. (2001). Schools, families, and communities partnering for middle level students' success. *NASSP Bulletin, 85*(627), 53-61.

Sanders, M. G., Epstein, J. L., & Connors-Tadros, L. C. (1999). *Family partnership with high schools: The parents' perspective* (Report 32). Baltimore: Johns Hopkins University, Center for Research on the Education of Students Placed at Risk.

Simon, B. S. (2001). Family involvement in high school: Predictors and effects. *NASSP Bulletin, 85*(627), 8-19.

Van Voorhis, F. L. (2001). Interactive science homework: An experiment in home and school connections. *NASSP Bulletin, 85*(627), 20-32.

Predictors and Effects of Family Involvement in High School

Beth S. Simon[1]

Reports from more than 11,000 parents of high school seniors and 1,000 high school principals were analyzed to learn about high school, family, and community partnerships. Analyses revealed that regardless of students' background and prior achievement, various parenting, volunteering, and learning at home activities positively influenced student grades, course credits completed, attendance, behavior, and school preparedness. When educators guided parents and solicited their participation, parents responded with increased involvement to support student success.

A substantial body of research examines the role of family involvement in the elementary and middle grades (Desimone, 1999; Epstein & Dauber, 1991; Ho & Willms, 1996; Schneider & Coleman, 1993; Singh, Bickley, Trivette, Keith, & Keith, 1995; Van Voorhis, 2000). Fewer studies have focused on school–family connections in high schools. Studies on partnerships at the high school level reveal that family involvement tends to decrease as children get older (Clark, 1983; Dornbusch & Ritter, 1988; George, 1995; Lee, 1994; Stevenson & Baker, 1987). Research suggests, however, that partnerships between families and schools are still important for high school students' success (Catsambis, 1998; Connors & Epstein, 1994; Dornbusch & Ritter, 1988; Lee, 1994).

Method

Important questions remain about the nature and intensity of high school, family, and community partnerships; the influence of partnerships on student success; and predictors of family and community involvement. To fill gaps in research and support educators' work in strengthening partnerships in high school, this study addressed three main questions:

1. What do school, family, and community partnerships look like in high school?

2. How do school–family connections influence student success?

3. When high schools reach out to families, do families respond with increased involvement?

Analyses were based on reports from the parents of over 11,000 high school students and from more than 1,000 high school principals in the

National Education Longitudinal Study of 1988 (NELS:88). NELS:88 followed a cohort of students as they moved from the middle grades to high school and into postsecondary schooling or careers (Ingels, Thalji, Pulliam, Bartot, & Frankel, 1994). In 1988, a nationally representative sample of 24,599 eighth-grade students from 1,052 schools was surveyed. These students were followed over time and surveyed again in their sophomore and senior years of high school. School principals and students' parents were also surveyed over time, and information was gathered on a range of topics, including characteristics and practices of school, family, and community connections. Following are summaries of key research findings on the nature of high school, family, and community partnerships, the effects of partnerships on student success, and the relationship between school outreach and family involvement.[2]

Results

What Do High School, Family, and Community Partnerships Look Like?

There are often reports that family involvement drops off by the time teenagers are in high school. Compared to partnerships in the earlier grades, high school, family, and community connections appear weak (Clark, 1983; Dornbusch & Ritter, 1988; George, 1995; Stevenson & Baker, 1987). This conclusion, though, is based on research that takes a narrow view of involvement and does not consider the wide range of partnership activities that are conducted at home, at school, and in the community.

The present study conceptualized partnerships broadly using Epstein's (1995) framework of six types of family and community involvement, which recognizes a wide range of partnership activities. Reports from parents of high school seniors and from high school principals were analyzed to learn about involvement in various types of activities, including parenting, communicating, volunteering, learning at home, decision making, and collaborating with the community. Following are selected findings that illustrate how schools, families, and communities connect during the high school years.

Type 1-Parenting. Workshops are a popular parenting activity in many high schools. More than half of the high school principals reported that their school offered workshops to parents on drug and alcohol abuse prevention, an important issue for many teens and their parents. Approximately one third of parents reported that they attended a college-planning workshop to learn about postsecondary educational opportunities and financial planning.

Type 2-Communicating. Overall, activities involving school-to-home and home-to-school communication were intermittent or infrequent. Parents and high school staff members rarely communicated about teenagers' academic performance (except for report cards), attendance, and behavior. For example, approximately two out of three parents were never contacted by the school about their child's attendance and about three out of four parents never contacted the school about their child's attendance. Parent–teacher conferences are a popular communicating activity in the elementary and middle grades. One third of high school principals, however, reported that they did not use parent–teacher conferences as a way for parents and teachers to communicate about students' progress, challenges, concerns, and future plans.

Type 3-Volunteering. Most parents volunteered their time by attending school activities with their teenagers. About two thirds of parents attended as audience members at least one school activity, and one third of those parents attended more than a few times. Fewer parents participated in the more traditional sense of volunteering (i.e., as teachers' aides, cafeteria monitors, and field trip chaperones). Parents may question how helpful they can be in the classroom; teachers may not want to be monitored by parents in the classroom; and students may not want their parents at the school, keeping tabs on them during the school day. These and other reasons may explain why, even though one third of high schools reportedly had a formal program to recruit and train volunteers, only about one in eight parents volunteered.

Type 4-Learning at Home. Parents may find it daunting to help high school students study for a trigonometry or chemistry test or review their essays on classic literature. However, approximately three out of four parents indicated that school staff never contacted them about how to help teenagers with homework. Still, two thirds of parents reported that they tried to help teenagers with homework or school projects sometimes or frequently. Many parents could benefit from guidance from teachers on how to work with their children on homework or school projects. According to principals, few parents solicited information from teachers about helping teenagers with homework or specific skills. In most high schools, fewer than one fourth of all parents asked for information to help teenagers with homework. Although some parents may feel unprepared to help their children with homework, most talked with their teenagers about school and almost all were aware of teenagers' academic progress.

Type 5-Decision Making. Many schools use a PTA or PTO as a forum for parents to give input to the high schools their teenagers attend. Nevertheless, about one third of high school principals reported that their school did not have such an organization. The absence of a PTA or PTO may restrict parents' influence on school policy decisions and contribute to the growing distance parents may feel from schools as their children move across the grades.

Type 6-Collaborating With the Community. Principals reported that community partners supported high schools in various collaborative activities.

For example, most principals reported that employers asked the school to post job listings and to recommend students for jobs. Half of the principals reported that a local business organization was involved in efforts to promote a safe and drug-free environment at the school. In terms of giving back to the community, fewer than half of the principals reported having a community-service program at their high school. Most of these principals reported that students spent two hours a week—or fewer—volunteering at a community site.

As they develop from childhood through adolescence, youth move from a family-centered world to a wider world that includes peers and other adults in the community. Adolescents increasingly rely on social networks beyond their families, yet the data revealed that many families supported teenagers' development through the last years of high school in several ways. Parents continued to monitor teenagers' potentially risky behavior, parents and teenagers spent some free time together, parents and teenagers discussed postsecondary educational plans and current school activities, and parents were aware of teenagers' progress in school. Most parents attended some school activities and many attended postsecondary planning workshops if they were offered by the high school.

In addition to the school, family, and community partnership indicators measured with the NELS:88 data, families and communities may be involved in many other activities that support adolescent learning and development. Still, the range of indicators available in the NELS:88 data revealed that families participated in various partnership activities that, as the next set of analyses shows, positively influenced a range of student outcomes, including report card grades, course credits completed, attendance, behavior, and school preparedness.

How Does Family Involvement Influence High School Success?

Families, schools, and communities all may benefit from carefully planned, well-implemented partnership activities, but the bottom line in education reform is student achievement. Educators want to know: How do partnerships affect student success? Will students earn better grades? Will they attend school more regularly and come to class more prepared to learn? Understanding how partnerships influence student success is an important step in refining partnership-program planning and research. By clarifying links between school, family, and community connections and student success, partnership-program planners can make the most effective and efficient use of resources within the home, the school, and the community, and researchers can strengthen studies with more theoretically sound measures of partnerships and results.

Studies have begun to address the influence of partnerships on student success, but many studies are weakened by limited partnership indicators (Astone & McLanahan, 1991; Lee, 1993; Steinberg, 1998; Stevenson & Baker, 1987), a limited range of student outcome measures (Ho & Willms, 1996;

Pong, 1998; Singh et al., 1995), and analyses of partnership activities and student outcomes that are tenuously linked (Ho & Willms, 1996; Pong, 1998; Singh et al., 1995). In contrast to prior research that considered only a few partnership indicators, the present study analyzed how 17 partnership practices—including various parenting, communicating, volunteering, learning at home, and decision-making activities—influenced student success. Building on research that evaluated the effects of partnerships on only a few indicators of student success, this study tested how particular partnership activities influenced the following student outcomes: English and math grades, standardized test scores, course credits completed in English and math, attendance, behavior, and school preparedness (e.g., students completed homework and brought books and a pen or pencil to class).

The results indicate that, after controlling for race and ethnicity, family structure, gender, and the powerful influence of students' prior achievement and socioeconomic status, when parents were involved in various ways, teenagers earned higher grades in English and math, completed more course credits in English and math, had better attendance and behavior, and came to class more prepared to learn. This article highlights patterns of relationships between family involvement and substantively linked student outcomes, although analyses also revealed some significant relationships between family involvement and less well-connected measures of student success.

Grades and Course Credits Completed. Regardless of teenagers' earlier grades in English and math or their family background, when parents attended college-planning workshops and when parents and teenagers talked about college planning, teenagers earned better grades in English and math and completed more course credits in English and math. Parental attendance at college-planning workshops and discussions with teenagers about college planning may have positively influenced students' grades and the number of course credits they completed for various reasons. First, teenagers may have gotten the message that their parents valued their college plans and supported their efforts to get good grades and take classes required for college admission. Second, when parents attended college-planning workshops, they may have learned the importance of grade point averages and course credits for college admission and, subsequently, encouraged or monitored their children's efforts to improve grades and take necessary courses to get into college.

Standardized Test Scores. How well students perform on standardized tests in earlier years strongly predicts how well they will perform in future years. Given how strongly prior test scores predict future test scores, there is little room for additional factors to boost or lower student test scores. The results of this study found that, even after accounting for the powerful influence of prior achievement, parents and teenagers talking about college and parents attending college-planning workshops had a small, positive influence on test scores.

Attendance. Beyond the influence of teenagers' prior attendance or background, when parents participated in various school activities with teenagers, teenagers attended school more regularly. In general, when parents attend school functions, they have the opportunity to meet other teenagers' parents and develop a parent network. As in close-knit neighborhoods where teenagers are held accountable to the community's adults—not just their own parents—parent networks may prevent teenagers from skipping school because they know that other parents may be keeping tabs on them. In addition, parents may have the opportunity to chat with teachers or high school administrators who are also attending school events. These informal conversations reinforce the link between home and school and may remind students that what they do at school may be reported to their parents.

Behavior and School Preparedness. Various involvement activities positively influenced students' good behavior and school preparedness. For example, when students reported talking with their parents about school and college planning, they also reported better behavior and were more likely to come to class prepared.[3] When parents talk with their children, they may communicate the importance that they place on education and may motivate their child's school performance. Similarly, the more time that parents and teenagers spent together, the better behaved students were and the more prepared they arrived to class. Parents may reinforce norms and rules for students' behavior through leisure activities. Teenagers may also feel motivated because what they do and how they spend their time matters to their parents.

Negative Relationships Between Family Involvement and Student Success. Some communication practices—parents contacting the school about teenagers' attendance and behavior—were negatively associated with student success. In other words, the more often parents reported contacting the schools about teenagers' attendance and behavior, the less likely it was that students were successful in school. These findings, however, do not indicate that home-to-school contacts caused teenagers to do poorly. Instead, analysis showed that parents contacted the school because teenagers were struggling. Compared with parents of teenagers who were doing well in school in Grade 10, parents of teenagers who had poor attendance, lower math and English grades, and lower standardized test scores in Grade 10 were more likely to contact the school about teenagers' behavior and attendance in Grade 12. The longitudinal data revealed that parents' contacts with the school occurred in the context of teenagers' continued school struggles.

In summary, analysis revealed positive relationships between parenting, volunteering, and learning at home activities and various measures of Grade 12 student success, including teenagers' report card grades; the number of course credits students completed; and teenagers' attendance, behavior, and school preparedness. The NELS:88 data, however, did not permit thorough analysis of the effects on student success of other aspects of partnerships, such as family involvement in school decision making and collaborations with the community. As with the parenting, volunteering, and learning at home activities tested, it is expected that family involvement in school decision making and collaborations with the community, when well planned and linked to specific outcome measures, may also improve specific indicators of student success.

By their senior year of high school, teenagers have some entrenched study habits, attitudes, and behavior patterns related to school. Nevertheless, this study shows that even through the last year of high school, and regardless of teenagers' background or achievement, families' involvement in education influences teenagers' school success. When parents support teenagers as learners in various ways, teenagers are more likely to succeed in school.

How Do High Schools Influence Family Involvement?

School and family partnerships tend to decline over the school years for many reasons. For example, the complex organization of high schools, their complicated curriculum, and the tensions of adolescence might discourage family involvement. In this study, we considered the factors that might counter this trend and increase school and family connections over the years.

To understand variation in levels of family involvement in high school, researchers have investigated the effects of students' background—including race and ethnicity, family structure, and socioeconomic status—on family involvement (Astone & McLanahan, 1991; Catsambis, 1998; Catsambis & Garland, 1997; Clark, 1983; Desimone, 1999; Goyette & Xie, 1999; Lee, 1994; Phelan, Davidson, & Yu, 1998; Pong, 1998; Singh et al., 1995). These studies reveal that students' background explains some of the variation in family involvement at the high school level. Although socioeconomic status tends to be consistently, positively related to some family involvement practices (Singh et al., 1995), it is also insignificantly related to other partnership activities (Epstein, 2001; Simon, 2000). Other background indicators, including students' race and ethnicity, family structure, gender, and prior achievement, do not always predict how families support teenagers' learning.

Although frequently analyzed, student background is not the only possible predictor of family involvement. Instead, a range of conditions may influence whether and how teenagers' families are involved in their education. By examining high school outreach activities as predictors of family involvement in teenagers' learning and development, this study builds on previous research that accounted only for students' background.

This study examined how 14 different high school outreach activities predicted family involvement. Some analysis focused on whether relationships between high school practices and family involvement activities were substantively linked (e.g., school contacts parents about helping teenagers with homework and parents working with teenagers on homework). The results show that when high schools conducted specific activities, families were more likely to be involved in particular ways. Regardless of teenagers' achievement, socioeconomic status, family structure, gender, and race and ethnicity, high school outreach activities positively predicted family involvement. In fact, in several cases, high school practices influenced family involvement more strongly than teenagers' background or achievement.

Following are a few examples of how high school programs and practices to involve families positively related to family support of teenagers as learners. These analyses focused on whether there were connections of specific school practices and parents' responses. Parents of high school students reported the following:

- When high school staff members contacted parents about teenagers' postsecondary plans, parents were more likely to attend postsecondary planning workshops and talked more frequently with teenagers about college and employment.

- When high school staff members contacted parents about volunteering, parents were more likely to volunteer as audience members at school activities.

- When high school staff members informed parents about how to help teenagers study, parents worked more often with their teenagers on homework.

- When high school staff members contacted parents about a range of school-related issues, including their teen's academic program, course selection, and plans after high school, parents talked with teenagers more often about school.

Principals' reports confirm the results from parents. High school programs and practices influenced family involvement, above and beyond the influence of school sector (public vs. private), location (urban, suburban, rural), or the percentage of teenagers receiving free or reduced-price lunch or living in single-parent homes. Specifically, high school principals reported that when high schools had a formal program to recruit and train parents as volunteers, more parents were likely to volunteer for the school. They also reported that when high schools encouraged parent–school associations, more parents joined the PTA/PTO and attended PTA/PTO meetings.

Summary

All parents want their children to succeed in school; however, not all parents know how best to support their children as learners. This study shows that high schools can reach out and increase family involvement in partnership activities. Families' involvement habits are not fixed by teenagers' senior year of high school. Instead, high school outreach practices—among other potential influences—can shift family involvement levels. Following is a summary of key findings in this research:

- Schools, families, and communities continue to partner in a range of ways through teenagers' last year of high school.

- Regardless of teenagers' achievement or background, high school and family partnerships positively influence teenagers' grades, course credits completed, attendance, behavior, and school preparedness.

- Regardless of family background or school context, when high schools reach out to involve families, families respond with increased involvement (see Table 6.1).

Table 6.1   The Influence of High School Outreach on Family Involvement

When high schools...	*Parents were more likely to...*
Contacted parents about teens' plans after high school	Attend college and career-planning workshops and talk with teens about college and careers
Contacted parents about volunteering	Volunteer as an audience member at school activities
Gave parents information about how to help teens study	Work with their teens on homework
Contacted parents about school-related issues	Talk with teens about school-related issues
Formally recruited and trained parent volunteers	Volunteer for the school
Encouraged parent-school associations	Join the PTA/PTO and attend PTA/PTO meetings

Families participate in various ways to support student learning through teens' last year of high school. High schools not only have a particular responsibility to organize partnership programs that reach out to involve all families at all grade levels but they also have the *capacity* to change the way that families support teenagers' school success.

Notes

1. An earlier version of this article was published as Simon, B. S. (2001). Family involvement in high school: Predictors and effects. *NASSP Bulletin, 85*(627), 8-19. The author thanks Joyce Epstein and Karl Alexander for their invaluable editorial comments on the larger project from which this emerged.

2. This article summarizes findings from a larger study on high school, family, and community partnerships. For the detailed report, see Simon (2000).

3. The full report also includes results from analyses of student-reported indicators of family involvement practices.

References

Astone, N. M., & McLanahan, S. S. (1991). Family structure, parental practices and high school completion. *American Sociological Review, 56,* 309–320.

Catsambis, S. (1998). *Expanding the knowledge of parental involvement in secondary education: Effects on high school academic success* (Report 27). Baltimore: Johns Hopkins University, Center for Research on the Education of Students Placed at Risk.

Catsambis, S., & Garland, J. E. (1997). *Parental involvement in students' education during middle and high school* (Report 18). Baltimore: Johns Hopkins University, Center for Research on the Education of Students Placed at Risk.

Clark, R. M. (1983). *Family life and school achievement: Why poor black children succeed or fail.* Chicago: University of Chicago Press.

Connors, L. J., & Epstein, J. L. (1994). *Taking stock: Views of teachers, parents, and students on school, family, and community partnerships in high schools* (Report 25). Baltimore: Johns Hopkins University, Center on Families, Communities, Schools, and Children's Learning.

Desimone, L. (1999). Linking parental involvement with student achievement: Do race and income matter? *Journal of Educational Research, 93,* 11–30.

Dornbusch, S. M., & Ritter, P. L. (1988). Parents of high school students: A neglected resource. *Educational Horizons, 66,* 75–77.

Epstein, J. L. (1995). School/family/community partnerships: Caring for the children we share. *Phi Delta Kappan, 76*(9), 701–712.

Epstein, J. L. (2001). *School, family, and community partnerships: Preparing educators and improving schools.* Boulder, CO: Westview Press.

Epstein, J. L., & Dauber, S. L. (1991). School programs and teacher practices of parent involvement in inner-city elementary and middle schools. *Elementary School Journal, 91*(3), 289–305.

George, P. (1995). Search Institute looks at home and school: Why aren't parents getting involved? *High School Magazine, 3*(5), 9–11.

Goyette, K., & Xie, Y. (1999). Educational expectations of Asian American youths: Determinants and ethnic differences. *Sociology of Education, 72,* 22–36.

Ho, E. S-C., & Willms, D. J. (1996). Effects of parental involvement on eighth-grade achievement. *Sociology of Education, 69,* 126–141.

Ingels, S. J., Thalji, L., Pulliam, P., Bartot, V. H., & Frankel, M. R. (1994). *National educational longitudinal study of 1988. Second follow-up: Parent component data file user's manual.* Washington, DC: Office of Educational Research and Improvement, U.S. Department of Education.

Lee, S. (1994). *Family-school connections and students' education: Continuity and change of family involvement from the middle grades to high school.* Unpublished doctoral dissertation, Johns Hopkins University, Baltimore.

Lee, S.-A. (1993). Family structure effects on student outcomes. In B. Schneider & J. S. Coleman (Eds.), *Parents, their children, and schools.* Boulder, CO: Westview Press.

Phelan, P., Davidson, A. L., & Yu, H. C. (1998). *Adolescents' worlds: Negotiating family, peers, and school.* New York: Teachers College Press.

Pong, S.-L. (1998). The school compositional effects of single parenthood on 10th-grade reading achievement. *Sociology of Education, 71,* 23–42.

Schneider, B., & Coleman, J. S. (Eds.). (1993). *Parents, their children, and schools.* Boulder, CO: Westview Press.

Simon, B. S. (2000). *Predictors of high school and family partnerships and the influence of partnerships on student success.* Unpublished doctoral dissertation, Johns Hopkins University, Baltimore.

Singh, K., Bickley, P. G., Trivette, P., Keith, T. Z., & Keith, P. B. (1995). The effects of four components of parental involvement on eighth-grade student achievement: Structural analysis of NELS-88 data. *School Psychology Review, 24,* 299–317.

Steinberg, L. (1998). Standards outside the classroom. In D. Ravitch (Ed.), *Brookings papers on education policy: 1998.* Washington, DC: The Brookings Institution.

Stevenson, D. L., & Baker, D. P. (1987). The family-school relation and the child's school performance. *Child Development, 58,* 1348–1357.

Van Voorhis, F. L. (2000). *The effects of TIPS interactive and non-interactive homework on science achievement and family involvement of middle grade students.* Unpublished doctoral dissertation, University of Florida, Gainesville.

A Goal-Oriented Approach to Partnership Programs in Middle and High Schools

Natalie Rodriguez Jansorn

Increase writing achievement. Improve attendance. Enhance math skills. These are goals that most middle and high schools set for students. Along with an effective curriculum and excellent instruction, programs of school, family, and community partnerships can help students reach these and other school improvement goals. A goal-oriented partnership program links closely with the school improvement plan to enhance students' opportunities for school success.

The following pages discuss the elements of a goal-oriented approach to partnerships and provide school, district, and state leaders with examples of partnership activities for the six types of involvement (i.e., parenting, communicating, volunteering, learning at home, decision making, and collaborating with the community) that can be selected to reach specific goals. The examples following this article may be used as overheads and handouts in workshops to help middle and high schools write goal-oriented plans for school, family, and community partnerships (see pp. 127-145 of this *Handbook*).

What Is a Goal-Oriented Approach to Partnerships?

An Action Team for Partnerships (ATP) using a goal-oriented approach to partnerships begins with this question: What are the goals this school has set for students to reach this year? The ATP reviews the school improvement plan and selects a few major goals that would benefit from family and community involvement. Goals may include

- Increasing academic achievement in reading, writing, science, math, social studies, and other subjects

- Improving attendance

- Promoting positive student behavior in school

- Ensuring successful transitions and adjustments to new schools

- Enhancing students' awareness of postsecondary opportunities

- Attaining other important academic or nonacademic goals on the school's agenda for the year

The ATP then writes a One-Year Action Plan for partnerships with family and community involvement activities that specifically link to and support the school's selected goals for improving students' academic and nonacademic progress. The comprehensive plan includes activities for all six types of involvement to engage families and community partners in many productive ways. See the One-Year Action Plan—Form G (Goals) on pages 349-352 in Chapter 9 of this *Handbook*.

Why Use a Goal-Oriented Approach?

Research shows that by middle and high school, family involvement tends to decrease. Parents continue to want to be involved, but they may not know exactly what to do. Teachers continue to believe parent involvement is important, but they may not know how to encourage parents to remain involved.

A goal-oriented approach to partnerships enables educators and families to reach out to each other and assist students with specific results in mind. For example, an ATP at one high school developed writing-related partnership activities to engage families in helping students reach the goal of increasing writing achievement. Some activities encouraged teachers, administrators, and counselors to reach out to families with more information about their students' writing curriculum and achievement in writing. The ATP also designed approaches that welcome families to communicate with teachers about their teens' work and progress in writing.

A goal-oriented partnership program makes clear to all stakeholders that school, family, and community partnerships can be designed and implemented to benefit students in the middle grades and high school. Schools using this approach effectively should find that educators, parents, students, and community partners support and sustain successful partnerships over time.

Who Chooses the Goals for the Partnership Program?

Most often the ATP chooses the goals for each year's action plan based on the school improvement plan. After selecting the goals, the ATP may recruit additional members whose work or interests relate to a particular goal. For example, a middle school in Philadelphia focusing on the goal of increasing school safety enlisted the participation of the community's police captain on its ATP. The police captain offered unique insights and resources to increase school safety through family and community involvement activities.

How Many Goals Does an ATP Choose?

For one full school year, ATPs should select four goals that will be addressed with family and community involvement activities: two academic goals, one nonacademic goal, and one overall goal for creating a school climate of partnerships. The number of goals may vary, depending on individual schools' needs, interests, and resources.

How Does an ATP Develop a Goal-Oriented Partnership Program?

First, the ATP reviews the School Improvement Plan to select the four goals that will be the basis of the One-Year Action Plan. Goals may be to increase writing achievement, increase science skills, improve student attendance, and sustain and strengthen other family and community involvement activities (e.g., positive communications with families and the community). Middle and high schools may set goals to help students make successful transitions into the first year at their new schools or to guide students toward effective postsecondary education and career plans. These and other goals for middle and high school students may best be met by including some targeted and well-implemented family and community involvement activities that support and extend the efforts of educators at the school.

Next, the ATP develops the full One-Year Action Plan using Form G (Goals) on pages 349-352 of this *Handbook*. To write the plan, the ATP should form small committees for each goal to ensure that all team members contribute to selecting, developing, and scheduling targeted family and community involvement activities.

Each small committee should select at least three specific family and community involvement activities to support its goal and provide the necessary details for implementing the action plan. The full ATP then meets to share ideas, receive feedback, and make revisions to the entire One-Year Action Plan, which includes the activities for the four selected improvement goals. The ATP should check that each of the six types of involvement is represented when the sections for four goals are combined to form a comprehensive One-Year Action Plan for partnerships.

The success of any program depends greatly on its evaluation plan. The ATP should consider carefully how the results for each goal selected for the One-Year Action Plan will be monitored, measured, and documented. Teams may choose more than one form of evaluation for each goal in order to accurately assess the quality and effects of partnership activities.

Evaluation strategies range from simply recording the number of participants for an activity or documenting the number of families who received information to more complex surveys and questionnaires or longitudinal studies to assess the effects of family involvement activities on students' standardized test scores, grades, and attendance rates. Thoughtful reflections and sound evaluations may help improve activities from year to year and may make it more likely that the ATP will be able to secure future funding, resources, and support for its activities.

The National Network of Partnership Schools offers several resources for evaluating partnership programs. The End-of-Year Evaluation–Form G (pp. 360-364 in this *Handbook*) helps ATPs reflect on the progress of their partnership programs through a series of questions about the family and community involvement activities implemented for each major goal. A second resource is *UPDATE*, the annual progress report that the National Network requires of all members. *UPDATE* guides ATPs to evaluate the quality of partnership program implementation and to think about needed improvements in family and community involvement for the next One-Year Action Plan. Schools also may participate in annual Focus on Results projects that examine relationships of particular partnership activities and changes in specific goals for students (e.g., reading achievement, math achievement, attendance, and behavior). ATPs may assess the quality of their teamwork with the Annual Review of Team Processes on page 111 in this *Handbook*. Schools' ATPs may use these guided evaluations and their own evaluation activities to assess how their work on partnerships is progressing from different perspectives.

After writing the One-Year Action Plan and after identifying evaluation strategies, the Action Team for Partnerships is ready to implement its goal-oriented partnership program with the help of others at the school.

How Does a Goal-Oriented Partnership Program Look in Action?

A Middle School's Partnership Program. A 10-member Action Team for Partnerships at an urban middle school in Tennessee includes family, school staff, and administrative, community, and student members to represent all the school's partners in learning. After reviewing the school's improvement plan, the ATP developed a One-Year Action Plan focusing on four goals:

- Improve reading and language arts achievement

- Improve mathematics achievement

- Increase attendance

- Establish a productive partnership with a community organization

The ATP used the framework of six types of involvement to select a few activities to help reach each goal. For example, to help students reach the math goal, the ATP hosted a Family Math Night at which parents and students enjoyed math activities together. This school also collaborated with its community to conduct an after-school math tutoring program and a Mathathon. The ATP included in the school newsletter, which parents receive about every six weeks, suggestions on how to help students with math, updates on the math curriculum, and recognition of students' math achievements. By keeping families informed about the math curriculum, providing guidance in how to interact with their children about math, and connecting with the community for further support, this middle school is using school, family, and community partnerships to support teachers' efforts to increase student success in math. The ATP implemented similarly well-targeted activities for the other three goals, thus creating a comprehensive goal-oriented partnership program.

A High School's Partnership Program. As another example, an urban high school in New Jersey started its partnership program midyear and focused on two goals:

- Increase writing achievement
- Improve attendance

To develop the Action Plan for Partnerships, the 18-member Action Team for Partnerships divided into two groups, each with representatives of the school, families, community, and students. At one meeting, the groups spent about 40 minutes brainstorming ideas on new and current partnership activities that could support their particular goals. The brainstorming session allowed the ATP members to be creative—with the sky as the limit—and consider many possible partnership activities without worrying about details. Then, the whole ATP came together to share ideas and receive feedback on the potential partnership activities.

Next, the ATP again divided into its two groups to make final decisions about the partnership activities that would be included in the official One-Year Action Plan for partnerships. Each group selected two to four involvement activities to support its goal. For example, the writing achievement group planned an open-mike poetry night for students to express their creativity with families invited as audience members. They also planned to invite family volunteers to be assistant coaches and judges for the student debate club. As a third activity, they planned to develop a writing achievement page in the PTA newsletter with information on the curriculum, recognition of student achievement, and suggestions for parents to help their teens with homework.

After the two groups wrote their final goal-oriented action plans, the groups came together to share their final selections and to ensure that all six types of involvement were included in the overall plan. The full ATP made a few adjustments to the comprehensive plan to incorporate all six types of involvement and to schedule the activities evenly throughout the school year. The ATP then assigned at least one member to coordinate each activity and identified other faculty, staff, parents, students, and community partners who would assist. In planning their goal-oriented partnership program, the members of this high school's ATP collaborated and shared responsibilities to design a One-Year Action Plan in which everyone felt invested. This high school's ATP took promising steps in planning a successful and sustainable partnership program.

What Are Some Examples of Partnership Activities for Different Goals?

The following pages provide a few examples of important goals for middle and high school students and lists of activities for the six types of involvement that support each goal. Action Teams for Partnerships may select and adapt activities that are appropriate for their schools' goals for students. These activities illustrate just a few of the many possible promising partnership activities for reaching specific goals at the middle and high school levels. For additional information and examples, see the "Middle and High School" section on the website of the National Network of Partnership Schools, www.partnershipschools.org.

MIDDLE SCHOOL EXAMPLES

for a One-Year Action Plan
to Reach Results for **TRANSITIONS**

TYPE 1   New students' scavenger hunt around the school for information about the school, teachers and staff, programs, curriculum, and resources, with parents invited for tour

TYPE 2   Panel discussions at "feeder" elementary schools for fifth-grade students and their parents to hear about middle school from sixth graders, middle school teachers, counselors, administrators, and parents of sixth graders

TYPE 3   Survey of parents on how they could volunteer to share their time, specific talents, or resources at school or for the school

TYPE 4   Videotapes starring current middle school students, parents, and educators that inform fifth graders and their families about ways to help students through middle school

TYPE 5   An Action Team for Partnerships committee focused on ensuring successful transitions of students and families

TYPE 6   Collaborating with feeder schools and hosting joint events

---

. . . AND MANY OTHER IDEAS FOR EACH TYPE OF INVOLVEMENT

MIDDLE SCHOOL EXAMPLES
for a One-Year Action Plan
to Reach Results for **ATTENDANCE**

TYPE 1 "Attendance Summit" for parents featuring speakers on the importance of student attendance. Speakers may include school administrators, counselors, legal experts, teachers, health service providers, students, and family members

TYPE 2 Recognition postcards for good or improved attendance

TYPE 3 Family members volunteering as attendance monitors

TYPE 4 Interactive homework for students and family partners to create a poster about why good attendance is important

TYPE 5 PTA/PTO communications for all families on school goals and requirements for student attendance and on-time arrival, and guidelines on steps to take when students return to school after illness

TYPE 6 Agreement with local businesses to post signs that students are welcome only during nonschool hours

. . . AND MANY OTHER IDEAS FOR EACH TYPE OF INVOLVEMENT

MIDDLE SCHOOL EXAMPLES

for a One-Year Action Plan
to Reach Results for **READING**

TYPE 1 Parent workshops on how to guide and encourage students in reading for pleasure at home

TYPE 2 A page of the school newsletter with information on the school's reading and language arts program, suggestions on prompting students to read aloud at home, and questions to discuss with students about things they read

TYPE 3 Family members serving as volunteer literacy tutors, reading buddies, or library aides during the school day or in after-school programs

TYPE 4 Interactive homework in reading and writing for students to share their ideas and work with a family partner

TYPE 5 PTA/PTO-supported fundraiser for books, magazines, and other reading materials for the school media center

TYPE 6 Donations from local businesses to be used as incentives for a campaign to encourage students to read many books

... AND MANY OTHER IDEAS FOR EACH TYPE OF INVOLVEMENT

HIGH SCHOOL EXAMPLES
for a One-Year Action Plan
to Reach Results for **MATH**

TYPE 1 Continuing education classes for family members only or for family members and students together (e.g., computer classes or **GED/ABE** classes)

TYPE 2 Student recognition page in the school newsletter highlighting students who improve and excel in math

TYPE 3 Parents as audience members for "math bowl" or other math competitions

TYPE 4 Information for parents on students' math requirements to prepare for entry to postsecondary education

TYPE 5 PTA/PTO support for math with the purchase of manipulatives, calculators, computers, and other materials

TYPE 6 After-school program with local college students as math tutors

... AND MANY OTHER IDEAS FOR EACH TYPE OF INVOLVEMENT

HIGH SCHOOL EXAMPLES

for a One-Year Action Plan
to Reach Results for **POSTSECONDARY PLANNING**

TYPE 1   Workshops for parents and students on course credits and requirements for high school graduation, college financial aid, college entry tests, and career planning

TYPE 2   Series of videotapes for families to borrow to learn about high school requirements and postsecondary planning

TYPE 3   Field trips for students and parents to local colleges and universities

TYPE 4   Interactive homework that requires students to discuss their academic goals and career plans with a family partner and to outline strategies for reaching these goals

TYPE 5   A postsecondary planning committee of parents, teachers, and students to implement a series of activities on college awareness and career options from 9th to 12th grade

TYPE 6   College club for linking students and families with alumni to foster knowledge and actions on postsecondary opportunities

. . . AND MANY OTHER IDEAS FOR EACH TYPE OF INVOLVEMENT

MIDDLE and HIGH SCHOOL EXAMPLES

for a One-Year Action Plan
to **CREATE A CLIMATE OF PARTNERSHIPS**

TYPE 1 Parent support groups to discuss parenting approaches and school issues with other families

TYPE 2 "Good news" postcards, phone calls, and other two-way communications (e.g., e-mail, voice mail, websites) to connect teachers and families about student progress and success

TYPE 3 Volunteers for safe schools to greet, assist, or deter visitors

TYPE 4 Quarterly interactive homework assignments for students to review report card grades with family partners and to discuss academic and behavior goals for the next grading period

TYPE 5 PTA/PTO-sponsored "Showcase the School Day" with booths and displays on school programs, student clubs, academic departments, the parent association, and partnership activities

TYPE 6 Periodic community forums for educators, students, parents, and citizens to discuss school improvement topics, family and community support for education, and other important issues

. . . AND MANY OTHER IDEAS FOR EACH TYPE OF INVOLVEMENT

WHY PARTNERSHIPS ARE IMPORTANT IN MIDDLE AND HIGH SCHOOLS

Research shows that

◆ **Students tend to do better on achievement tests, report card grades, attendance, behavior, and postsecondary plans if their parents are involved in their education.**

◆ **Adolescents are more likely to avoid risky or negative behaviors (e.g., alcohol or drug abuse, violence) if they feel connected to their families.**

◆ **Partnership activities can help create safer schools.**

◆ **Curriculum-related family involvement, such as interactive homework, can help students improve academic skills in specific subjects.**

◆ **High-performing middle and high schools inform and involve parents and community partners as a planned part of their programs.**

◆ **Parents want to be involved and influential in their teens' education.**

◆ **Students in middle and high schools want their parents involved in meaningful ways.**

◆ **When schools reach out to involve families, more parents become involved.**

For related research, visit www.partnershipschools.org and follow the links to "Middle and High Schools and Research and Publications."

SPECIAL CONSIDERATIONS FOR MIDDLE AND HIGH SCHOOLS

All schools that develop a comprehensive program of school, family, and community partnerships use the framework of six types of involvement, establish an Action Team for Partnerships, and write a One-Year Action Plan. Middle and high schools also should consider the following guidelines for their partnership programs.

Link Partnerships to School Improvement Goals

Partnership programs in middle and high schools should be goal-oriented. A school may choose four goals for an academic year from the school improvement plan: two academic goals, one behavior goal, and an overall goal of developing a climate of partnerships. Family and community involvement activities are designed to support the selected goals such as improving students' writing, enhancing science skills, increasing attendance, and developing a welcoming school environment. Use Form G (Goals) to write a goal-oriented One-Year Action Plan and to evaluate progress at the end of the year (see pp. *349-352, 360-364* in this *Handbook*).

Focus on Transition Years

Schools that emphasize family involvement for incoming students and their families are more likely to sustain school-family-community partnerships across the middle and high school years. For example, a high school that is just beginning to develop a partnership program may want to focus, first, on involving ninth graders' families and then expand to include an additional grade level each year.

Promote Early Postsecondary Planning

Early and consistent emphases on postsecondary planning will ensure that more students set and reach goals to attend college or prepare for work after high school. Middle and high school students, teachers, guidance counselors, families, and community members should create a sequential plan for the 6th through 12th grades of activities and information to help students and families identify academic and financial requirements and actions needed to fulfill students' goals for the future. Partnership activities may include workshops, informative flyers, articles in school newsletters, interactive homework on setting goals for education and careers, field trips, panel discussions with alumni, and other targeted activities.

Actively Involve Students

Students are the main actors in their own education. Students need to be involved in school, family, and community partnership activities by delivering and interpreting information to and from their families and by providing ideas and reactions for improving involvement activities. In high schools, students must be active members of the Action Team for Partnerships. Adolescents need to know that their schools and families are working together and with students to help them succeed in school. Studies indicate that adolescents develop greater independence when their parents are knowledgeable partners in their education.

Reach Out to Families

Just about all parents of middle and high school students want to know how to help their children at home and how to help them succeed at school. Studies confirm that adolescents' families need and want more information and guidance from middle and high schools. Studies also show that when schools implement well-planned practices of partnership, more families become involved in those activities.

Expand Teachers' Roles Gradually

Because many middle and high school teachers were trained as academic specialists, they may not be aware of how family and community involvement help adolescents succeed. Action Teams for Partnerships should start by implementing partnership activities that will result in important improvements and increase teachers' support for more family and community involvement activities. ATPs may encourage teachers who already conduct partnership activities to share their success stories and recruit colleagues to implement similar activities.

TRANSITIONS: INVOLVING FAMILIES WHEN STUDENTS MOVE TO NEW SCHOOLS

Transitions to new schools often confuse or concern children and parents. Research shows that family involvement drops dramatically when children move from elementary to middle school and from middle to high school. Families begin to lose touch with their children's school and, as a result, they lose touch with their children as students.

To prevent this problem, elementary, middle, and high schools need to consider how they will prepare their students *and* families for transitions to new schools. For example, one high school designed a Type 2-Communicating project that included the following series of activities to help students and families move successfully from middle school to high school.

Example: High School Transition Plan for Family Involvement

March	High school counselors and students meet during the school day with eighth-grade students *at the middle school*. **Families are invited.** Information is provided to those who could not come.
April	High school staff and a panel of high school parents meet in the evening with eighth-grade students **and families** *at the middle school*. Information is provided to those who could not come.
May	Eighth-grade students visit the high school. **Families are invited.**
August	Ninth-grade students **and families** meet with teachers *at the high school* prior to the start of school. Information is provided to those who could not come.
September	Open-house evening meeting is held for **all families** of students in Grades 9 through 12 *at the high school*. Information is provided to those who could not come.

The Type 2-Communicating committee of the Action Team for Partnerships in this high school took the challenge to provide important information to all families of incoming ninth graders, including those who could not attend the meetings held at the middle or high school. A similar plan could help children and families move from preschool to elementary school or from elementary to middle school.

ACTIVITY: On the accompanying charts, list the activities that your school will conduct to help students and their families make successful transitions *to your school* and from your school *to a new school*. Consider these questions:

- How will your school prepare *all* students and families for successful transitions to YOUR school or to a NEW school? What information do students and families need before the start of the school year? Which present activities will your school continue or improve? Which activities will you add to provide more and better information, visits, and exchanges?

- How might your school work with educators in "feeder" and "receiver" schools to develop, conduct, and evaluate transitioning activities?

Plan to Help Students and Families
Make Successful Transitions to *THIS* School

Put a * by the month when the new school year begins.

	Which transition activities will be conducted with students?	How will families be involved?	How might feeder school(s) help this activity?
January— Before Transition			
February			
March			
April			
May			
June			
July			
August			
September			
October			
Ongoing…			

Add the transitioning activities that involve families and the community to the school's One-Year Action Plan for partnerships.

Plan to Help Students and Families
Make Successful Transitions to NEW Schools

Put a * by the month when the new school year begins.

	Which transition activities will be conducted with students?	How will families be involved?	How might receiver school(s) help this activity?
January— Before Transition			
February			
March			
April			
May			
June			
July			
August			
September			
October			
Ongoing…			

Add the transitioning activities that involve families and the community to the school's One-Year Action Plan for partnerships.

Developing State and District Leadership for Partnerships

State and district leaders play important roles in determining whether and how well schools develop and maintain successful programs of family and community involvement. This chapter describes actions that state and district leaders should take to increase their own knowledge, skills, and activities on partnerships and to facilitate the work of schools' Action Teams for Partnerships (ATPs) to strengthen their programs of family and community involvement.

Organizations also may assist schools, districts, and states to develop leadership on partnerships and to implement partnership programs. Some organizations conduct activities similar to state departments of education (e.g., Parent Information Resource Centers, large regional professional development service centers). These organizations work with school districts statewide or in large regions. Other organizations conduct activities similar to school districts by assisting schools in developing or evaluating programs of partnerships. Leaders in organizations may use the information and tools in this chapter for states or districts.

In this chapter, an introductory article discusses the importance for states and districts to write clear and comprehensive policies on partnerships, support policies with actions, and conduct other leadership activities. The article presents information on costs and sources of funds for partnerships based on the work of schools, districts, and states that have started to work on these programs.

Several tools are provided to help state and district leaders understand their roles and responsibilities for promoting school, family, and community partnerships. The outlines, summaries, checklists, and templates should help state and district leaders select activities for their own annual plans, assist schools, and make presentations to help colleagues understand state and district leadership on partnerships.

For State Leaders

State Leadership Roles

Use this handout to inform colleagues of the many ways that state leaders can coordinate interdepartmental programs and activities on school, family, and community partnerships and guide districts and schools to develop partnership programs.

State Leadership Actions

Use this overhead to talk audiences through the handout on state leadership roles.

State Leadership Checklist

Take steps to increase state leadership on school, family, and community partnerships and to support districts and schools. Check when the actions are completed.

Sample State Leadership Plan for Partnerships

See one example of a state plan that focuses on three goals for leadership on partnerships. Other state plans, activities, and ideas for improving partnership programs over time are found at www.partnershipschools.org in the "States and Districts" section.

Template for States and Districts: One-Year Leadership Plan for Partnerships

This format was suggested by states and districts that have worked on improving their partnership programs. It may be adapted to fit the requirements for plans in any location.

For District Leaders

District Leadership Roles

Use this handout to inform colleagues of the many ways that district leaders can coordinate interdepartmental programs and activities on school, family, and community partnerships and facilitate all schools to establish Action Teams for Partnerships and develop their partnership programs.

District Leadership Actions

Use this overhead to talk audiences through the handout on district leadership roles.

District Leadership Checklist

Take steps to increase district leadership on school, family, and community partnerships and to support schools with their partnership programs. Check when the actions are completed.

Sample District Leadership Plan for Partnerships

See one example of a district plan that uses the six types of involvement to organize district-level activities and to facilitate the work of each school's Action Team for Partnerships. Other district plans, activities, and ideas for improving partnership programs over time are found at www.partnershipschools.org in the "States and Districts" section. Also, see above, with tools for state leaders, the template for a district's One-Year Leadership Plan for Partnerships.

What Do Facilitators Do?

Use this outline to guide and assist schools' Action Teams for Partnerships. Review and adapt periodically to meet local requirements and expectations.

Facilitators' Tasks at the Start of the School Year

Get off to a good start in the first month of the school year by helping Action Teams for Partnerships organize their work. Also, begin the school year by working effectively with others in the district office.

Summary of School Visits

Keep a record of all meetings with schools' Action Teams for Partnerships, principals, or other groups, and plan follow-up activities to assist each school. Facilitators can use this tool to summarize the contents and results of their monthly meetings at individual schools and quarterly cluster meetings with groups of schools' Action Teams for Partnerships.

Standards for Excellent Partnership Programs

Review eight essential elements of excellent partnership programs. All work on school, family, and community partnerships by state, district, and school leaders should focus on attaining these standards. Use this overhead in presentations to discuss the expectations for high-quality, ongoing programs of school, family, and community partnerships. Details on how these standards are supported by specific actions are found online at www.partnershipschools.org by linking to "In the Spotlight and Partnership Award Criteria."

State and District Leadership for School, Family, and Community Partnerships

Joyce L. Epstein

Policies at the state and district levels increasingly include goals for school, family, and community partnerships. State and district mission statements, laws, and guidelines are beginning to go beyond general statements about the importance of parent involvement to include explicit commitments for leadership and activities to assist all schools in developing comprehensive partnership programs that benefit students.

States

Some states are increasing their leadership and improving programs that guide and support districts and schools in their work on partnerships. Some have established permanent bureaus, offices, or departments of school, family, and community partnerships with directors, coordinators, and facilitators as experts on involvement. The state leaders are responsible for helping districts, schools, business leaders, and others increase knowledge, obtain resources, and improve their programs of family and community involvement.

State leadership takes many forms. Activities to promote statewide partnership programs include writing state goals and policies for partnerships, providing training in developing programs of family and community involvement, conducting conferences to share best practices, making grants to districts and schools for improving partnership practices, evaluating work and progress, recognizing and rewarding excellent practices, creating a state network on partnerships, and performing other strategies. See the outline and checklist of state leadership activities, pages 276-279 in this *Handbook*.

Districts

Some school districts have policies, goals, and guidelines on school, family, and community partnerships. Some districts, particularly large school districts, have established offices with directors and facilitators who help all elementary, middle, and high schools plan and implement programs of partnership. Each district-level facilitator can assist up to 30 schools to establish Action Teams for Partnerships and write and implement action plans for family and community involvement.

District leadership activities include writing district goals and policies for partnerships, conducting team-training workshops for schools' Action Teams for Partnerships, making school visits with principals and Action Teams for Partnerships, awarding grants to schools for initiating or improving partnership projects, conducting conferences or workshops for all schools to share best practices, and performing other leadership activities. See the outline and checklist of district leadership activities, pages 281-286 in this *Handbook*.

Ultimately, every school must take responsibility for planning, implementing, budgeting, and continually improving its own partnership program. Importantly, state and district leadership and support make a difference in whether and how well schools design and maintain programs of family and community involvement.

State and District Leadership Activities

Education leaders in states and districts across the country are taking the following actions to guide schools with their work on school, family, and community partnerships.

Write a policy that outlines and discusses state or district expectations and commitments for comprehensive programs of school, family, and community partnerships. The policy should define school, family, and community partnerships, including the six types of involvement, and explain requirements and standards for excellent partnership programs. The policy should include enactments that specify the services that the state or district will provide to help all schools enact the policy.

State and district policies concerning school, family, and community partnerships must be clear and comprehensive, but also flexible and responsive. Good policies recognize that all schools and districts start at different points in their practices of partnership. The policies should guide schools to focus family and community involvement on reaching specific school goals for student success.

Written policies are necessary but not sufficient for helping all schools create strong partnership programs. State and district policy statements must include enactments or other official commitments that describe how schools will be assisted to develop and evaluate site-specific partnership programs to reach school improvement goals with training, funds, and other assistance, encouragement, and recognition from the state and district. Policies that are unfunded and unsupported will be unwelcome and ineffective (see Epstein, 2001, for examples of state and district plans for partnerships).

Establish an office or department with an expert leader and adequate staff to facilitate the development and continuous improvement of programs of school, family, and community partnerships. Every state and large district should have a director of school, family, and community partnerships. Small districts may designate a leader to guide schools with their work on partnerships. The leaders provide information, training, and technical assistance and conduct other activities to help teams of administrators, teachers, parents, and others understand and take action on partnerships at their schools.

To be effective, state and district leaders must write their own annual plans to list and schedule the activities that they will conduct to promote and support school, family, and community partnerships (see pp. 279, 284 of this *Handbook* for an example). The leadership plans should include activities that

- Increase state or district leaders' competencies on partnerships

- Develop interdepartmental connections to strengthen leadership on partnerships in their states or districts

- Strengthen skills and increase knowledge about partnerships in their states or districts

- Facilitate the efforts of all schools to develop and maintain their goal-oriented partnership programs

Identify funds for school, family, and community partnerships to cover staff and program costs. State and district leaders must identify specific budgets to support staff salaries, training programs, small grants for partnership projects, conferences to share best practices each year, evaluation studies, and other leadership activities on partnerships. Line items for partnerships are needed to provide stable support for these activities.

State, district, and school leaders have identified the levels and sources of funds that support their partnership programs (Epstein, Sanders, Clark, & Van Voorhis, 1999). Investments vary because states, districts, and schools vary greatly in size. To account for large and small states, districts, and schools, costs for partnerships may be estimated as *per pupil expenditures* or as *lump sum* investments, as shown in Table 7.1. The table presents estimated ranges of minimum allocations for school, family, and community partnership programs at the state, district, and school levels. Funding can always be increased to expand and improve programs. The following examples illustrate the funds needed to support programs of partnerships.

- States should plan to invest from $0.15 to $1 or more per student per year to be used *at the state level* to fund the salaries and benefits of a state director of partnerships, staff, and state leadership activities and services. Funds may support initial and advanced inservice education and training, grants for districts and schools to initiate or improve partnership programs, statewide or regional conferences, and other state leadership functions to assist all districts or schools in their work on partnerships.

Table 7.1   Levels and Sources of Funds for Schools, Districts, and States in the National Network of Partnership Schools

	Schools (*N* = 356)	Districts (*N* = 45)	States (*N* = 6)
Levels of Funding	Range: $100 - $88,500 Median = $2,000 Average = $5,722 Average per pupil expenditure = $12.29	Range: $100 - $1.3 million Median = $20,000 Average = $83,871 Average per pupil expenditure = $5.63	Range: $20,000-$410,000 Median = $125,000 Average = $163,333 Average per pupil expenditure = $0.15
Major Sources of Funding	Bilingual education Drug prevention Even Start Foundation grants General funds Goals 2000 Principal's discretionary funds PTA/PTO Special education State compensatory education Title I Schoolwide Title I Targeted Assistance Title VI Title VII Other federal and state programs	Bilingual education Drug prevention Even Start Foundation grants General funds Goals 2000 School board Special education State compensatory education Superintendent's discretionary funds Title I Schoolwide Title I Targeted Assistance Title VI Title VII Other federal and state programs	Drug prevention Even Start Foundation grants General funds Goals 2000 Special education Superintendent's discretionary funds Title I Title VI Other federal programs
Other Sources of Funding	American Legion Partnership Am South Grant (FL) At-risk funds Business partnerships Center for the Revitalization of Urban Education (MI) Child First After School Program Commonwealth of Massachusetts Corporate sponsors Danforth Foundation District grants DoDEA Extra-Duty Compensation for Teacher Leaders (Dept. of Defense Schools) Eastern Michigan Univ. Grants (MI) FAST Grants (WI) Healthy Start Home and School Funds (IL) Leona Group (MI) Parents as Partners Funds (MN) Partners in Education (WV) Ready to Learn Program Grant Savings from extended day funds School fundraising activities School-generated funds Sight-impaired funds State grants Other local programs and in-kind donations	Business partners/ contributions CESA (WI) Community education funds Department of Defense Funds (DoDEA Schools) Department of Human Services (WI) District funds Family Preservation Grant (WI) Family Center Funding Jewish Education Center Lake County Education Association (Teacher's Union) BluePrint 2000 Funds (FL) Law and Justice Grant Learning Readiness Funds (MN) Maryland State Grants Massachusetts Department of Education Massachusetts State Chapter 636 grant Mentors SB65 (CA) Private businesses in communities Rockefeller Foundation School board funds (FL) Special Education Discretionary Grant State Academic Mentoring Grant (CA) State Compensatory Education Funds (MD) State DESEG Grant (MA) State of Michigan Other state grants United Way Youth development grants	Adult education and literacy Community education funds Federal Claud Pepper Act (CT) Goals 2000 Parent Resource Center Line item from legislature to board of education Martha Holden Jennings Foundation (OH) Serve America Youth Service Learning Teacher Inservice Funds (UT) Other state programs

SOURCE: Epstein, J. L., Sanders, M. G., Clark, L. A., & Van Voorhis, F. A. (1999). *1998 UPDATE survey of schools, districts, and states in the National Network of Partnership Schools*.
NOTE: Abbreviations in parentheses refer to grants and programs in specific states.

- Districts should plan to invest from $3 to $10 or more per student per year to be used *at the district level* to fund salaries of a district coordinator, facilitator(s), district programs, and services. District funds may support training and other inservice education, grants to schools, the dissemination of effective practices, and other district leadership functions to assist all schools to develop expertise and programs of school, family, and community partnerships.

- Schools should invest $5 to $15 or more per student per year to be used *at the school level* to support family and community involvement activities planned by the school's Action Team for Partnerships. Each school's program should include activities for the six types of involvement, tailored to meet school goals and involve all families. School funds may be used to support a part-time site-based coordinator, printed materials, refreshments, incentives, workshop presenters, website development, and other involvement activities in the school's One-Year Action Plan for partnerships.

The per-pupil expenditures may be translated into lump sum investments for states, districts, and schools, taking into account the number of students served and the special needs of students, families, schools, and communities. For example, a state serving 300,000 students might set an annual budget of from $45,000 to over $300,000 to cover costs for leaders and leadership activities, whereas a state serving 800,000 students needs an annual budget ranging from $120,000 to $800,000 or more. The level of funds will, of course, affect the nature and extent of services that states provide to districts and schools on partnerships (Epstein, 2001).

A small district serving 5,000 students might invest from $15,000 to $50,000 or more per year for district-level leadership and services for all schools on partnerships. By contrast, a large district serving 100,000 students would require an annual budget of $300,000 to $1,000,000 or more for facilitators to assist groups of up to 30 schools' Action Teams for Partnerships to develop their partnership programs.

A school of about 500 students needs a minimum budget of $2,500 to $7,500 or more to cover the costs of activities in a One-Year Action Plan to include the six types of involvement and to involve all families in their children's education.

These estimates indicate that all states, districts, and schools could easily afford to develop and sustain programs of school, family, and community partnerships. The costs per pupil are very low for initiating programs that will inform and involve all families in their children's education every year. Indeed, most states, districts, and schools have funds for staff and program costs for partnerships, but presently do not coordinate or target the allocations to produce the desired effects. Thus, most states, districts, and schools can apply existing funds to new tasks to better organize their programs of partnership.

Table 7.1 also reports the sources of funds for programs of school, family, and community partnerships. Major sources include federal, state, and local programs such as Title I, Title VI, Title VII, Safe and Drug-Free Schools, Even Start, special education, and other programs. Funds also come from foundations, general funds, and other sources.

Conduct ongoing inservice education on partnerships. State and district leaders should provide or support inservice education on beginning and advanced topics of school, family, and community partnerships. Inservice education includes professional development for Action Teams for Partnerships to initiate their partnership programs and advanced training to help teams continually improve the quality of their programs. (See Chapter 4 in this *Handbook* for guidelines on conducting training workshops.)

Evaluate teachers and administrators for their work on partnerships. State boards of education and district school boards should include school, family, and community partnerships on the annual evaluations of professional and paraprofessional staff. Guidelines should be provided to teachers, principals, instructional aides, superintendents, and other leaders on standards for high-quality programs and practices of partnerships. Professionals and paraprofessionals should know how their work on partnerships will be judged along with other competencies on annual reviews.

Support state, district, and school "career ladder" programs to build expertise among educators on school, family, and community partnerships. States and districts should invest in developing leaders for school, family, and community partnerships, just as professionals build expertise in academic subjects, athletic coaching, and student services. Leadership positions include state and district directors and coordinators of partnerships; district facilitators who assist schools on partnerships; and school-level leaders such as master teachers, lead teachers, or chairs and co-chairs of Action Teams for Partnerships who plan and implement activities for family and community involvement.

Develop partnership tools or products. States and districts not only may use the tools and guidelines in this *Handbook*, but also may develop or customize tools to meet the needs and goals of their states, districts, schools, families, and students. Leaders may create brochures, calendars, newsletters, and translations of communications for families with limited English skills, summaries of survey results, and other publications and products. States and districts may develop materials to involve fathers, very young parents, new arrivals to the school, and other hard-to-reach families or to explain key topics concerning attendance policies, state and district standards for student learning, new tests and assessments, and other innovations that parents and the community need to understand in order to help students succeed in school.

Encourage business, industry, and other community connections to strengthen school, family, and community partnerships. Some businesses have policies that permit and encourage employees who are parents to become involved in their own children's education and attend parent-teacher conferences. Some have policies for all employees, with or without school-aged children, to volunteer time to assist local schools. State and district leaders may work with legislators, business leaders, and community groups to draft legislation or offer various tax incentives, credits, preferred status, or other support and recognition for businesses that encourage parent and community involvement in schools.

State and district leaders also may encourage business and industry leaders to establish media centers or resource rooms to provide employees who are parents with information on infant, child, and adolescent development, parenting skills, and school, family, and community partnerships; establish child care services for preschool children, and summer after-school, holidays, and programs for school-aged children; provide substitute-parent care during children's minor illnesses; award grants to schools and community agencies for family and community involvement programs; and conduct other activities to benefit employees and their children.

Establish advisory committees so that education leaders hear from parents and the community on partnerships and other educational issues. Each state should have an advisory committee for the state superintendent on school, family, and community partnerships, comprising representatives from key stakeholders across the state. This group may provide diverse views on topics that state leaders should explain or clarify for parents and on ways to strengthen partnerships in all districts and schools. Each district should establish a district advisory council with representatives from all schools to provide district superintendents and other leaders with ideas on important topics that families need to understand and ways to strengthen partnership programs in all schools.

Establish a clearinghouse, library, or dissemination center for research and promising practices of school, family, and community partnerships. States or districts may collect and disseminate information on partnerships in the main office building, a family resource center, community agency, mobile unit, or other convenient location. State and district leaders may want to collect and share results of research on partnerships; effective approaches for organizing partnership programs; teachers' practices for involving parents in conferences, homework, extracurricular, and other activities; surveys and other evaluation tools on partnerships; forms and technologies for communicating with parents; information on child and adolescent development and parenting strategies; and other information and materials.

Support requirements for preparing new teachers and administrators to conduct excellent partnership programs. State leaders should actively press for legislation for state certification that requires preservice and advanced education to prepare teachers and administrators to conduct effective programs and practices of school, family, and community partnerships. District leaders should reinforce the importance of preparation, relevant experience, and positive attitudes toward family and community involvement when they hire new teachers and administrators (Epstein, 2001).

Support research and evaluation on the quality and effects of programs and practices of school, family, and community partnerships. State and district leaders may collect data to learn whether and how well schools have organized programs of partnership and the results of programs and activities. Some evaluations may be relatively simple, such as taking inventory of present practices to identify starting points in program development or collecting sign-in sheets and exit evaluations for suggestions for improving specific events. Other evaluations may be more complex, such as studying the extent of outreach to all families, gathering family reactions to particular policies or practices, and studying the longitudinal effects of family and community involvement activities on students' attitudes, behaviors, and achievements. State and district leaders also may work with university researchers or other evaluators to conduct formal studies of the results of partnerships. (See the Annual Review of Team Processes, p. 111, to assess the quality of planning and interactions of Action Teams for Partnerships, and see Chapter 9 for tools to evaluate the progress and quality of partnership programs and practices.)

In sum, state and district leaders are expected to fulfill responsibilities that develop and continually improve their own knowledge, skills, and activities of school, family, and community partnerships *and* that facilitate the knowledge and skills of schools' Action Teams for Partnerships so that every elementary, middle, and high school can develop its own program of partnerships.

State leaders may work with regional staff development offices, collaborate with colleagues across departments, and assist school district leaders to provide training on school, family, and community partnerships to all schools and districts across the state. District leaders must plan how they guide schools to establish and sustain a well-functioning Action Team for Partnerships and how to help every team plan, implement, evaluate, and continually improve the quality of its program of partnerships.

State and district leaders will be assisted to fulfill these responsibilities by all sections of this *Handbook.* Other information on state and district leadership is available online at www.partnershipschools.org in the "State and District Leadership" section.

References

Epstein, J. L. (2001). Strategies for action in practice, policy, and research. In *School, family, and community partnerships: Preparing educators and improving schools* (Chap. 7). Boulder, CO: Westview Press.

Epstein, J. L., Sanders, M. G., Clark, L. A., & Van Voorhis, F. L. (1999). *Costs and benefits: School, district, and state funding for programs of school, family, and community partnerships*. Paper presented at the 1999 annual meeting of the American Sociological Association, Chicago.

State Leadership Roles

FOR SCHOOL, FAMILY, AND COMMUNITY PARTNERSHIPS

1. *WRITE A POLICY* that identifies state goals for school, family, and community partnerships, including all six types of involvement. Specify enactments to assist districts and schools to understand and implement the policy.

2. *IDENTIFY A DEPARTMENT OR OFFICE* for school, family, and community partnerships, and provide adequate staff and resources for this office.

3. *ASSIGN A COORDINATOR OR DIRECTOR* who will oversee and coordinate the state department of education's work with families and communities, establish a leadership team of colleagues across departments who work on partnerships, and provide technical assistance to districts and schools to help them develop comprehensive programs of partnership.

4. *IDENTIFY A BUDGET WITH ADEQUATE FUNDS* for staff and state leadership activities and to support districts and schools to develop partnerships. Offer small grants to schools and districts to fund initial activities and special projects, and offer awards for excellent partnership programs.

5. *PROVIDE INSERVICE EDUCATION AND ANNUAL TRAINING WORKSHOPS* for district leaders, school Action Teams for Partnerships, and other educators and parents to prepare leaders and increase skills to conduct programs of partnership.

6. *CONDUCT END-OF-YEAR WORKSHOPS OR ANNUAL CONFERENCES* to celebrate and recognize excellence and to encourage statewide or regional exchanges of good practices and solutions to challenges of school, family, and community partnerships. Support district-level conferences where schools share ideas and develop plans to continue their programs.

7. *DEVELOP OR SELECT TOOLS AND PRODUCTS* that districts and schools may use or adapt to improve their partnership programs.

8. *ESTABLISH A CLEARINGHOUSE, NEWSLETTER, OR OTHER COMMUNICATIONS* to disseminate effective practices, ideas, materials, research, and other information to help districts and schools improve their programs of partnership. Share information on partnerships with the public and the media.

9. *SUPPORT RESEARCH AND EVALUATION* to learn which practices help schools produce specific results for students, parents, teachers, schools, and communities. This includes an accountability system to monitor progress in district leadership and school program development over time.

10. *WORK WITH STATE COLLEGES AND UNIVERSITIES* to set requirements for teaching and administrative credentials to prepare educators to understand and conduct programs of school, family, and community partnerships.

11. *WORK WITH BUSINESS AND INDUSTRY* to establish flexible leave policies so parents can attend conferences at their children's schools, business-school partnerships, and volunteer programs.

12. *CONDUCT OTHER STATE LEADERSHIP ACTIVITIES* to build strong and permanent programs in districts and schools statewide.

STATE LEADERSHIP ACTIONS

- Write a state policy on partnerships

- Establish an office or department and a director of school, family, and community partnerships

- Write a leadership plan for action on partnerships

- Create a leadership team to integrate involvement activities across departments

- Identify a budget, and provide funding or grants for districts and schools

- Conduct annual conferences, training workshops, and other statewide inservice education activities

- Support research and evaluation, and monitor progress on partnerships

- Work with higher education to prepare educators to conduct effective partnerships

- Develop tools and products to assist schools and districts with partnership programs

- Work with business and industry on partnerships

- Disseminate best practices

- Celebrate excellence

- Publicize progress of the state, districts, and schools on family and community involvement

---

STATE LEADERSHIP CHECKLIST

Steps in Developing Excellent Programs
of School, Family, and Community Partnerships

State coordinators write plans for state-level leadership on school, family, and community partnerships; conduct statewide partnership activities; and assist every district to develop leadership and programs for family and community involvement. States also may directly assist schools' Action Teams for Partnerships to plan, implement, and evaluate their programs of family and community involvement. The following list will help your state develop an excellent and permanent program of school, family, and community partnerships.

CHECK ☑ WHEN YOU COMPLETE THE FOLLOWING:

❑ Identify a state Leadership Team for Partnerships (LTP) of colleagues who will work on various aspects of family and community involvement.

❑ Review or develop a state policy on school, family, and community partnerships.

❑ Select state goals for school improvement and student success that will be addressed and assisted by family and community involvement.

❑ Write an annual state Leadership Action Plan for partnerships that identifies strategies, timelines, and persons responsible for accomplishing specific family and community involvement activities.

❑ Secure a budget for staff salaries and for the planned partnership program activities.

❑ Enlist districts and schools to participate in the state's partnership initiative and in the National Network of Partnership Schools at Johns Hopkins University.

❑ Conduct professional development on partnerships for the state's leadership team, for district leaders, and for schools' Action Teams for Partnerships.

❑ Introduce the state's partnership initiative and its connection with the National Network of Partnership Schools to major policy and decision-making groups in the state department of education, other state agencies, the business community, and districts and schools statewide.

❑ Facilitate the work of districts and schools with a regular schedule of ongoing professional development workshops, conferences, or other activities to continually improve program quality.

❑ Establish procedures and select tools to periodically evaluate the quality and results of the state's partnership program and the quality and results of partnership programs in districts and schools.

❑ Celebrate end-of-the-year successes and help districts and schools share good practices.

❑ Disseminate information about the state's work and districts' and schools' progress on partnerships to the media, state educators, and families.

❑ Outline strategies for program continuity in the event of changes in leadership.

SAMPLE: STATE LEADERSHIP PLAN
FOR SCHOOL, FAMILY, AND COMMUNITY PARTNERSHIPS

Goal 1.   Promote a comprehensive definition of school, family, and community partnerships

Target audience: District leaders, school leaders, community leaders

<u>**Activities**</u>

1. Send letter on partnerships from state superintendent to all district superintendents
2. Review and update policy on partnerships from State Board of Education
3. Conduct a policy forum on partnerships with statewide representation
4. Develop and distribute model policies for local boards of education
5. Join the National Network of Partnership Schools as a state member

Goal 2.   Train school-based teams to develop and maintain partnerships

Target audience: Urban schools

<u>**Activities**</u>

1. Provide three training workshops for schools' Action Teams for Partnerships
2. Provide seed grants to Action Teams for Partnerships in the selected schools
3. Provide on-site technical assistance to the selected schools
4. Provide information to the selected schools on the state's resource library on partnerships and how to use it
5. Collaborate with other organizations in the state to increase knowledge and training on partnerships

Goal 3.   To serve as a resource and link for partnerships

Target audience: Other state agencies and organizations

<u>**Activities**</u>

1. Establish resource library and clearinghouse for information on partnerships
2. Establish a database for tracking the dissemination of information
3. Link with other organizations for training, presentations, and conferences
4. Serve on a "linkage team" for state agencies on partnerships
5. Publish semiannual newsletter on partnerships to distribute statewide

The authors thank the leadership team at the Connecticut State Department of Education for sharing this example of a Leadership Action Plan for partnerships.

ONE-YEAR LEADERSHIP PLAN
FOR SCHOOL, FAMILY, AND COMMUNITY PARTNERSHIPS

YEAR OF PLAN: _____ TO _____

Reproduce this page for each major goal that will be addressed this year.

GOAL:

OBJECTIVES:

Person(s) Responsible and Helping	Costs and Resources	Begin Date	End Date	Activities, Strategies Steps to Implement	Evaluations Accomplishments Comments

District Leadership Roles

FOR SCHOOL, FAMILY, AND COMMUNITY PARTNERSHIPS

1. *WRITE A POLICY* that identifies district-level and school-level goals for school, family, and community partnerships, including all six types of involvement. Specify the district's commitments to enact the policy and to assist schools to implement it.

2. *ASSIGN A DIRECTOR (large districts) AND FACILITATOR(S) (all districts)* who will oversee the district's work on partnerships and assist all schools with their plans to develop programs of partnership.

3. *IDENTIFY A BUDGET WITH ADEQUATE FUNDS* for district staff, leadership activities, and support for school programs, awards for excellent activities or improvement, and small grants for initial activities and special projects.

4. *GUIDE EACH SCHOOL TO FORM AN ACTION TEAM FOR PARTNERSHIPS* consisting of teachers, parents, administrators, and others who will plan, implement, and evaluate the school's partnership program.

5. *PROVIDE INSERVICE EDUCATION* for teachers, parents, and administrators and *TRAINING WORKSHOPS* for Action Teams for Partnerships to help each school plan and implement its partnership program.

6. *HELP EACH ACTION TEAM WRITE A ONE-YEAR ACTION PLAN* to involve all families in their children's education. Each school's plans should link family and community connections directly to its goals and objectives, and include practices for all six types of involvement.

7. *CONDUCT END-OF-YEAR CELEBRATION WORKSHOPS* for action teams to share ideas, discuss progress, solve problems, and plan ahead and to recognize excellent programs and practices.

8. *DEVELOP OR SELECT TOOLS AND PRODUCTS* that schools may use or adapt to improve their partnership programs.

9. *ESTABLISH A DISTRICT NEWSLETTER, LIBRARY, OR OTHER COMMUNICATIONS* to disseminate effective practices, ideas, materials, research, and other information that will help schools' action teams improve their programs of partnership. Share information on partnerships with the public and media.

10. *WORK WITH BUSINESSES AND OTHER COMMUNITY GROUPS AND ORGANIZATIONS* to establish partnerships to improve the curriculum and programs for students.

11. *SUPPORT RESEARCH AND EVALUATION* to learn which practices help schools produce specific results for students, parents, teachers, the school, and the community.

12. *CONDUCT OTHER DISTRICT LEADERSHIP ACTIVITIES* to build strong and permanent programs of partnership in all schools at the district level.

DISTRICT LEADERSHIP ACTIONS

- Write a district policy on partnerships
- Establish an office or program and director in large districts
- Write a leadership plan for action on partnerships
- Assign facilitator(s) to assist schools
- Identify a district budget, and provide funding and grants for schools
- Conduct annual conferences, training workshops, and other districtwide activities
- Provide schools with ongoing facilitation

- Integrate partnership activities across programs and departments
- Develop tools and products to assist schools with partnerships
- Work with business and industry on partnerships
- Support research and evaluation, and monitor schools' progress on partnerships
- Disseminate best practices
- Celebrate excellence
- Publicize progress of the district and schools on family and community involvement

DISTRICT LEADERSHIP CHECKLIST

Steps in Developing Excellent Programs of School, Family, and Community Partnerships

District facilitators write plans for district-level leadership on partnerships, conduct districtwide partnership activities, and assist every school's Action Team for Partnerships to plan, implement, and evaluate a school-based program of family and community involvement. The following list will help your district to develop an excellent and permanent program of school, family, and community partnerships.

CHECK ☑ WHEN YOU COMPLETE THE FOLLOWING:

❑ Identify a district Leadership Team for Partnerships of colleagues who will work on various aspects of family and community involvement.

❑ Review or develop a district policy on school, family, and community partnerships.

❑ Select the district's goals for school improvement and student success that will be addressed and assisted by family and community involvement.

❑ Write an annual district Leadership Action Plan for partnerships that identifies strategies, timelines, and persons responsible for accomplishing specific family and community involvement activities.

❑ Secure a budget to implement the planned partnership activities.

❑ Enlist schools to participate in the district's partnership initiative and in the National Network of Partnership Schools at Johns Hopkins University.

❑ Conduct staff development for the district's leadership team and training workshops for all schools' Action Teams for Partnerships.

❑ Introduce the district's partnership initiative and its connection with the National Network of Partnership Schools to major policy and decision-making groups in the district, schools, and community.

❑ Facilitate the work of each school's Action Team for Partnerships on a regular schedule to help school-based programs succeed.

❑ Establish procedures and select tools to periodically evaluate the quality and results of the district and schools' partnership programs.

❑ Celebrate end-of-the-year successes and help schools share good practices.

❑ Disseminate information about the district's work and schools' progress on partnerships to the media, educators throughout the district, and families.

❑ Outline strategies for program continuity in the event of changes in leadership.

SAMPLE: DISTRICT LEADERSHIP PLAN FOR SCHOOL, FAMILY, AND COMMUNITY PARTNERSHIPS

Districts May Organize Their Leadership Activities by the Six Types of Involvement
(Use the template on p. 280 to outline the details for achieving each goal.)

TYPE 1

- Offer parenting classes
- Assist parents to communicate with students about the importance of education

TYPE 2

- Provide information about districtwide events for family and community involvement
- Schedule training workshops for schools' Action Teams for Partnerships (ATPs)
- Conduct other leadership workshops for principals, assistant principals, and other leaders on partnerships
- Facilitate the work of all ATPs by visiting schools monthly and by conducting quarterly cluster meetings with the chairs of ATPs
- Conduct end-of-year celebrations for schools' ATPs to share ideas with each other

TYPE 3

- Organize and provide training to some parent and community volunteers to assist schools
- Invite parent volunteers to assist with districtwide events

TYPE 4

- Help schools involve families with students on learning activities at home (e.g., TIPS interactive homework, see Chapter 8 of this *Handbook*)
- Help schools guide families and students in selecting schools, programs, and courses
- Help schools guide families and students in preparing postsecondary plans

TYPE 5

- Increase parent participation in decision making at the district and school levels by providing leadership training for parent leaders
- Provide opportunities for all parents to give ideas about school programs, district policies, and decisions that affect students

TYPE 6

- Assist schools and families in accessing community programs and services and in developing business partners

What Do Facilitators Do?

HOW DISTRICT-LEVEL FACILITATORS HELP *EVERY SCHOOL* DEVELOP A STRONG PROGRAM OF SCHOOL, FAMILY, AND COMMUNITY PARTNERSHIPS

Facilitators help their schools set a course, stay on course, reach their goals, share ideas with one another, and continue their plans and programs of partnership. Facilitators conduct training, planning, networking, and technical assistance activities, including the following:

- Help each school establish an Action Team for Partnerships (ATP)
- Provide training to ATPs to help them understand the framework of the six types of involvement
- Help ATPs use the framework to develop *Three-Year Outlines* to set a vision for long-term goals for partnerships
- Help ATPs use the framework to write *One-Year Action Plans* for improving partnerships
- Help schools tailor practices of partnership to reach specific school improvement goals, such as improving attendance, achievement, behavior, and a school climate of partnership
- Help schools focus on meeting specific challenges that affect the success of their practices of partnership
- Help schools assess the results of their practices of partnership in activity-specific and annual evaluations
- Meet with ATP leaders and team members at least once a month or more as requested or needed
- Conduct quarterly cluster meetings that bring small groups of schools' ATP leaders together to share best practices and to discuss problems and solutions
- Meet individually with principals at the start of the school year to clarify the work of the facilitator and how the principal will support the work of the ATP
- Conduct End-of-Year Celebration Workshops with all schools' ATPs to celebrate progress, share problems, and continue planning
- Conduct other activities to assist the ATPs with their work, such as presentations to teachers, families, School Improvement Teams, or others

Facilitators also conduct other *meetings and presentations*:

- Meet with the district administrators to discuss their expectations for the program, for facilitators, and to clarify how they will encourage principals to support the work of their schools' Action Teams for Partnerships
- Make presentations to groups of principals, superintendents, the school board, other district leaders, parents, or other groups interested in improving partnerships

The success of a district's program of partnerships depends on the work of the Action Team for Partnerships and others at each school, responsive technical assistance from the district-level facilitator, support from each school's principal, and support from district and state leaders.

FACILITATORS' TASKS
AT THE START OF THE SCHOOL YEAR

At each school

- Schedule a meeting with each principal and the chair or cochairs of the Action Team for Partnerships (ATP) to discuss the school's One-Year Action Plan, goals for partnership, and how the facilitator will assist the school.
- If invited to do so, present information on the school, family, and community partnership program at back-to-school nights and at meetings of the faculty, parent organization, school council, or other groups. Or, attend these meetings to support the chair or cochairs of the ATP.

With the chair or cochairs of each Action Team for Partnerships

- Set the date for the first meeting of the full ATP to review the school's One-Year Action Plan (see p. 108 of this *Handbook*).
- Help the ATP replace members who left the school and select leaders for the team and committees.
- Review and discuss activities in the One-Year Action Plan for partnerships that are scheduled for September and October.
- Discuss the responsibilities of team members and others to ensure that the planned activities are well implemented and on schedule.
- Provide assistance, as needed, to the full ATP and to ATP committees that are implementing activities in September and October.

In the district office

- Meet periodically with the director of school, family, and community partnerships or your immediate supervisor.
- Attend and participate in the superintendent's meetings of principals, community and parent groups, or other groups, as requested.
- Contribute to the district newsletter with a column on school, family, and community partnerships with reports on district-level activities and the work of schools' ATPs.
- Provide your supervisor or office staff with your schedule of work and school visits so that you can be located every day.
- Provide a monthly report of activities and progress to the director of school, family, and community partnerships or to your immediate supervisor.
- Conduct other district leadership activities on school, family, and community partnerships (see pp. 281-287 in this *Handbook*).

Summary of School Visits

School, Family, and Community Partnerships

Facilitator:_____   Date:_____

School: _____   Time of visit: _____ to _____

Who initiated the visit? _____

_____

With whom did you meet? _____

_____

What issues and/or challenges were discussed during this visit?

_____

_____

_____

_____

_____

_____

What progress and/or decisions were made about these issues and/or challenges?

_____

_____

_____

_____

_____

_____

What are your next steps to assist this school with its program of school, family, and community partnerships?

_____

_____

_____

_____

_____

STANDARDS
FOR EXCELLENT
PARTNERSHIP PROGRAMS

- **Leadership**

- **Teamwork**

- **Plans for Action**

- **Implementation and Facilitation**

- **Evaluation**

- **Funding**

- **Support**

- **Network Connections**

For details on these standards, visit www.partnershipschools.org and follow the links to "In the Spotlight" and "Criteria for Partnership Awards."

8

Implementing Teachers Involve Parents in Schoolwork (TIPS)

This chapter presents background information and guidelines on two research-based approaches for increasing family involvement in students' education. These practical programs were designed, developed, and tested to help educators systematically, equitably, and productively involve families at home and in school to improve student learning.

TIPS Interactive Homework

Teachers Involve Parents in Schoolwork (TIPS) interactive homework enables teachers to design and use homework assignments to connect school and home on curriculum-related activities. TIPS activities guide students to share their work and ideas with a family partner. The assignments improve parents' understanding of what their children are learning; promote positive conversations about schoolwork at home; and, if well implemented, improve students' homework completion, subject-matter skills, and readiness for classwork.

In this chapter, the purposes of homework are outlined. Then, the goals and components of TIPS interactive homework in language arts, math, and science are discussed. Sample assignments are given for the elementary, middle, and high school grades. Steps for implementing TIPS interactive homework are explained.

TIPS Volunteers in Social Studies and Art

Teachers Involve Parents in Schoolwork Volunteers in Social Studies and Art creates a corps of volunteers who discuss famous art prints with social studies classes in middle schools. The presentations integrate art and history, increase students' knowledge and appreciation of art, and ensure that volunteers assist teachers and students in productive ways.

In this chapter, the rationale for and components of TIPS Volunteers in Social Studies and Art are explained, and steps for implementing this process are described. A sample presentation for DaVinci's *Mona Lisa* is included.

The information in this chapter is supported by prototype lessons, manuals, videos, workshops, and other resources that are listed as references. For additional information visit www.partnershipschools.org and follow the links to "TIPS."

How to Implement Teachers Involve Parents in Schoolwork (TIPS) Processes

Interactive Homework and Volunteers in Social Studies and Art

Joyce L. Epstein and Frances L. Van Voorhis

Why Build School and Family Partnerships?

If enough studies show the same result, you begin to believe it. That is how it is with school, family, and community partnerships. Research is accumulating that shows that particular parent involvement practices improve student achievement, attitudes, homework, report card grades, and aspirations. Surveys of parents indicate that most families want to talk with, monitor, encourage, and guide their children as students, but many say they need more information from the schools about how to help their children at home.

Studies also demonstrate that when teachers guide parent involvement and interaction, more parents become involved in ways that benefit their children. For example, when teachers frequently use practices to involve families in reading, students gain more in reading than do similar students whose teachers do not involve families. This suggests an important connection between parent involvement in particular subjects and student success in those subjects. These findings also confirm the important roles teachers play in helping families become involved in schoolwork at home.

There are other benefits to school, family, and community partnerships. Families say they need more information from the schools about how to help their children at home. When parents are assisted by the schools, they become more aware of their children's education and they interact with their children more. When students see that their parents and teachers are in contact, they become aware that they can talk to someone at home about schoolwork and school decisions.

Students also need guidance about how to keep their families aware of and involved in the work they do in school. Over time, students learn that their teachers want their families to know about what they are learning and participate in homework.

There are two TIPS processes—one that increases family involvement *at home* on interactive homework assignments and one that increases family involvement *at school* as volunteers.

1. TIPS Interactive Homework

Family Involvement at Home

Of all the types of involvement, the one that most parents want to know about is this: How do I help my own child at home? This request is at the top of parents' wish lists, because they want to do what they can to help their children succeed in school. Yet, this type of involvement is the one that schools have the most difficulty organizing. It requires every teacher at every grade level to communicate with all families about how to work and interact with their children on learning activities at home.

To meet this need, researchers worked with teachers to design, implement, and test a process called Teachers Involve Parents in Schoolwork (TIPS) interactive homework. With TIPS, any teacher can help all families stay informed and involved in their children's learning activities at home. With TIPS, students complete homework designed to promote their success in school. TIPS activities are homework assignments that require students to talk to someone at home about something interesting that they are learning in class.

TIPS helps solve some important problems with homework:

- TIPS enables all families to become involved, not just those who already know how to discuss math, science, or other subjects.

- TIPS makes homework the student's responsibility and does not ask parents to teach subjects or skills that they are not prepared to teach.

- TIPS asks students to share and enjoy their work, ideas, and progress with their families.

- TIPS allows families to comment and request other information from teachers in a section for home-to-school communication.

With TIPS, homework becomes a three-way partnership involving students, families, and teachers at the elementary, middle, or high school levels. Families immediately recognize and appreciate the efforts of teachers to keep them informed and involved. The TIPS activities keep school on the agenda at home so that children know that their families believe schoolwork is important and worth talking about.

Teachers' Roles in Designing Homework

Designing homework is the responsibility of teachers, but many teachers report that they feel unprepared to design effective homework activities. Well-designed homework assignments should be designed to meet specific purposes, and the content and format of assignments should help teachers advance students' skills in specific subjects. Epstein identified ten broad purposes (or 10-Ps) of homework: *practice, preparation, participation, personal development, parent-child relations, parent-teacher communications, peer interactions, policy, public relations,* and *punishment* (Epstein, 2001; Epstein & Van Voorhis, 2001). All are valid purposes except punishment.

Each purpose of homework yields different results for student learning and development, for parent information and involvement, and for teaching and administrative practice. For example, the TIPS interactive homework process fulfills several purposes. Each assignment is designed to extend student learning time, provide students with opportunities to *practice* skills and *participate* actively in learning, *prepare* for the next day's lessons, increase *parent-teacher communication* about the curriculum, and improve *parent-child connections* on learning activities at home.

Overcoming Obstacles

Jump Hurdle 1: Homework Should NOT Always Be Done Alone

Some teachers believe that all homework should be completed in a quiet place, away from the family or other people. Its purpose is to allow students to practice what was taught in class, to study for a quiz, or to complete other work *on their own*. While SOME homework is assigned for these purposes, OTHER homework should fulfill other goals. TIPS homework—given once a week or twice a month in math, science, or language arts—is designed specifically to keep students and their families talking about schoolwork at home. More than quarterly report cards, lists of required skills, or other occasional explanations, TIPS brings school home on a regular schedule of homework that requires students to talk with their parents and other family partners.

Jump Hurdle 2: Just ANY Homework Won't Do

Some homework is rather boring; it requires students' time, but not much thinking. TIPS activities are designed to be challenging and engaging—the type of homework that students will want to explain and share with their families. TIPS includes higher-level thinking skills and interactions with family members that make students think, write, gather information, collect suggestions, explain, demonstrate, draw, sketch or construct things, and conduct other interactive activities with parents and other family partners at home.

Purposes of Homework

PRACTICE	To give each student an opportunity to demonstrate mastery of skills taught in class; to increase speed, mastery, and maintenance of skills.
PREPARATION	To ensure readiness for the next class; to complete activities and assignments that are not finished in class.
PARTICIPATION	To increase each student's individual involvement in applying specific skills and knowledge, and in enjoying learning.
PERSONAL DEVELOPMENT	To build student responsibility, perseverance, time management, self-confidence, and feelings of accomplishment; to develop and recognize students' diverse talents and skills that may not be taught in class.
PARENT-CHILD RELATIONS	To establish communications between parent and child on the importance of schoolwork, and the application of school skills in real-life situations and experiences.

Purposes of Homework, continued

PARENT-TEACHER COMMUNICATIONS

To enable teachers to inform families and involve them in children's curricular activities, and to keep families aware of topics that are taught in class, how their children are progressing, and how to support their children's work and progress at home.

PEER INTERACTIONS

To encourage students to work together on assignments or projects to motivate and learn from each other.

POLICY

To fulfill directives from administrators at the district or school levels for a prescribed amount of homework per day or week.

PUBLIC RELATIONS

To demonstrate to the general public that a school has rigorous standards for student work in school and at home, and to establish a base for productive business and community partnerships for student learning.

~~PUNISHMENT~~

To correct problems in conduct or productivity. (Not a defensible purpose.)

SOURCE: Epstein, 2001; Epstein & Van Voorhis, 2001

What Are TIPS Interactive Homework Activities?

TIPS prototype activities are examples of homework assignments that teachers can use or adapt to match their curricula and learning objectives for students. There are TIPS prototype activities in language arts, math, and science.

TIPS LANGUAGE ARTS provides a format for students to share skills in writing, reading, thinking, grammar, and related language activities. The students do the work—reading and writing—but students and parents enjoy thinking together, discussing, sharing, and exchanging ideas. Family members may listen to what their children write, help students edit their writing, think about words, react to writing, and provide ideas, memories, their own experiences, and other interactions. TIPS Language Arts homework should be assigned once a week to keep families aware of and involved in students' work and progress in language arts.

Goals for TIPS Language Arts

- Encourage teachers to design homework that builds students' skills in reading, writing, speaking, and listening through communications with family partners.

- Guide students to conduct, discuss, and enjoy language arts activities at home.

- Enable parents to stay informed about their children's language arts work and progress.

- Encourage parents to communicate with teachers about their observations and questions concerning their children's homework and progress in language arts.

TIPS Format—Language Arts

1. **Letter to Parent, Guardian, or Family Partner** explains the purpose of the activity. The student writes in the due date and signs the letter.

2. **Objectives** explain the learning goal of the activity (if this is not clear from the title and letter).

3. **Materials** are listed if more than paper and pen are needed. In writing activities, prewriting gives the student space to plan a letter, essay, or story by outlining, brainstorming, listing, designing language nets and webs, or performing other planning activities.

4. **Interactions,** such as a family survey or an interview, guide the student to interview someone for ideas or memories, read work aloud for reactions, edit their work based on responses, practice a speech, take turns with others in giving ideas, or carry out other interactions.

5. **Home-to-School Communication** invites the family partner to share comments and observations with language arts teachers about whether the child understood the homework, whether they both enjoyed the activity, and whether the parent gained information about the student's work in language arts.

6. **Parent Signature** is requested on each activity.

TIPS MATH provides a format for students to share what they are learning about a specific math skill. The TIPS format allows students to show parents exactly how they learned a skill in class. Then, students complete regular math homework activities and obtain reactions from parents. TIPS Math emphasizes the mastery of basic and advanced math skills. The activities may include challenges in games or other extensions of skills, or finding examples of specific math skills in real life. TIPS Math homework should be assigned once a week to keep students and families talking about math at home on a regular schedule.

Goals for TIPS Math

- Illustrate clearly how the teacher taught the skill in class.

- Allow students to demonstrate, discuss, and celebrate their mastery of new math skills.

- Enable parents to stay informed about their children's math work.

- Encourage parents to communicate with teachers about their observations and questions concerning their children's homework and progress in math.

TIPS Format—Math

1. **Look This Over** shows an example of a skill that was taught in class and allows the student to explain the skill to a parent or family partner. The answer to this example is given.

2. **Now Try This** presents another example for the student to demonstrate how to do the particular skill, with the answer on the back of the page.

3. **Practice and More Practice** are regular homework problems for the student to master the skill.

4. **Let's Find Out or In the Real World** may be added to help the student and family partner discover and discuss how the math skill is used at home or in common situations. Games or other interactions may be included to reinforce the math skill.

5. **Home-to-School Communication** invites the family partner to record an observation, comment, or question for the math teacher about the skill the student demonstrated.

6. **Parent Signature** is requested on each activity.

TIPS SCIENCE provides a format for students to conduct and discuss hands-on lab or data collection activities related to the science topics they study in class. Some TIPS Science activities require students to discuss topics, gather reactions, or collect data from family members on issues of health and student development. The hands-on science activities help students and their families see that science topics are enjoyable, enriching, and part of everyday life.

In science, it is important that TIPS activities require only inexpensive or no-cost materials that are readily available at home. Special equipment, if it is needed, should be provided by the school. TIPS Science activities include a brief letter to parents explaining the topic. Then, the activities outline objectives, materials, space for lab reports or data charts, challenges, discussion questions, conclusions, and home-to-school communications. TIPS Science homework should be assigned on a regular schedule (e.g., once a week or twice a month) to keep students and families discovering and talking about science at home.

Goals for TIPS Science

- Encourage teachers to introduce science topics in class and follow up with discussions or demonstrations after the TIPS interactive homework assignments are completed.

- Guide students to conduct and discuss science activities at home.

- Enable parents to stay informed about their children's science work and progress.

- Encourage parents to communicate with teachers about their observations and questions concerning their science homework and progress.

TIPS Format—Science

1. **Letter to Parent, Guardian, or Family Partner** briefly explains the topic and specific science skills involved in the activity. The student writes in the due date and signs the letter.

2. **Objectives** explain the learning goal(s) of the activity.

3. **Materials** are common, inexpensive, and immediately available at home or easily obtained. If they are not, the school should provide the materials.

4. **Procedure** guides the students, step by step. Each assignment includes hands-on actions that require the student to think and act like a scientist. The teacher may change, simplify, or increase the difficulty of activities to meet the special needs of students.

5. **Lab Report or Data Chart** gives space for the student to report findings.

6. **Conclusions** guide the student to discuss results and real-world applications of science with family partners.

7. **Home-to-School Communication** invites the family partner to share comments and observations with science teachers about whether the child understood the homework, whether they both enjoyed the activity, and whether the family partner gained information about the student's work in science.

8. **Parent Signature** is requested on each activity.

Some TIPS prototype assignments may be useful just as they are. But, because homework must match the teachers' own learning objectives, teachers may adapt the TIPS prototypes or create their own TIPS activities. Teachers who see TIPS activities usually say, "I can do that!" It is, indeed, possible for every teacher in every grade level to implement an interactive homework program for their students and families.

Goals for TIPS Interactive Homework

- Build students' confidence by requiring them to show their work, share ideas, gather reactions, interview parents, or conduct other interactions with a family partner

- Link schoolwork with real-life situations

- Help parents understand more about what their children are learning in school

- Encourage parents and children to talk regularly about schoolwork and progress

- Enable parents and teachers to frequently communicate about children's work, progress, and problems

Why Does the TIPS Process Work?

- Can be used with any text or curriculum

- Helps teachers organize homework into manageable, focused segments

- Emphasizes connections between school and home

- Involves the child as an active learner and guides students to share and demonstrate their skills to show parents what they are learning

- Offers opportunities to link homework to the real world experiences of children and families

- Provides families with the information they ask for on how to help at home each year

- Emphasizes mastery of basic and advanced skills

How Do You Develop and Implement TIPS Homework?

Teachers may develop a TIPS program in seven steps:

1. Select the subject(s) for TIPS interactive homework.

The faculty should discuss the subjects and grade levels for which the TIPS process will be used. A team of teachers should be identified for each TIPS subject and grade level.

2. Select the skills for weekly or bimonthly TIPS assignments.

The team of teachers that will work on TIPS should consider the sequence of skills that are taught in each unit throughout the school year. Teachers should identify one skill or learning objective each week or every other week that lends itself to enjoyable and useful student-parent interactions. These will be the topics for the TIPS interactive homework assignments.

3. Adapt and develop TIPS activities to match the curriculum.

Teachers should work together during the summer months to examine existing TIPS manuals and prototype activities. Teachers must decide which of the available TIPS assignments will be useful to them for the skills they teach, or they must design new interactive homework to match the learning objectives in their curricula.

4. Orient students and families to the TIPS interactive homework process.

Teachers must explain the TIPS process and purposes to students and to their parents or other family partners. This may be done in letters to the home, discussions with students in class, presentations at parent meetings, and other ways. Special attention is needed to inform and involve parents with limited reading proficiency or who speak languages other than English at home. Guidance is needed for students so they will involve family partners effectively, regardless of family culture or educational background.

5. Assign TIPS on a regular, family-friendly schedule.

Teachers assign TIPS activities to students weekly or every other week. Teachers give students several days or a weekend to complete each assignment to allow time for students to work with a family partner. Students follow directions to share their skills and activities with their parents or another family partner.

6. Evaluate student work and respond to family questions.

Teachers grade and comment on TIPS activities just as they would any other homework assignment. Teachers also respond to the family feedback in the Home-to-School Communication section to encourage open channels of communication about students' needs and progress.

7. Revise and improve activities as needed.

Teachers note any problems with particular sections of assignments throughout the year and revise activities or develop new activities as needed.

The Importance of Teacher Collaboration in the TIPS Process

One way to develop TIPS is for a school or district to provide salaries for teams of teachers from each grade level to work together during the summer months. Support is needed for each teacher for two to four weeks to develop, edit, and produce the TIPS homework that will be used throughout the school year.

TIPS homework must be enjoyable as well as challenging for students. This takes careful thinking about the design of homework and about how to build in students' communications with parents or other family members. It helps for two or more teachers to work together discussing, writing, and editing their ideas. It also helps if this work is guided by a curriculum supervisor, department chair, assistant principal, master or lead teacher, school-family coordinator, or other individual who understands good curricular designs and who will guide the development and implementation of TIPS.

Once tested, TIPS homework designs may be shared with other teachers who follow the same curriculum objectives. If teachers save the activities on a computer, they may be easily shared and adapted by other teachers. Support for a few teachers in the summer, then, yields materials that can be used or adapted by many teachers for many years. The TIPS process is very cost-effective.

How Do All Partners Participate in TIPS Homework?

Teachers, students, parents, and administrators all have responsibilities for the success of TIPS:

- **Teachers** design the homework assignments or select those that match their classwork, orient parents to the process, explain TIPS and family involvement to students, conduct follow-up activities in class, and maintain homework records.

- **Students** complete the TIPS assignments and involve their parents or other family partners as directed in the activities.

- **Parents** learn about the TIPS process, set aside time each week to discuss TIPS homework activities with their children, and complete the home-to-school communications.

- **Principals** help teachers orient parents to the program and support and recognize teachers, students, and families who use TIPS well.

To introduce parents to TIPS, teachers may send letters, explain the TIPS process at parent-teacher conferences and meetings, and include an article in the school newsletter. Teachers may conduct classroom or grade-level meetings to show parents examples of the TIPS activities on an overhead projector and describe how parents should proceed when their children bring TIPS activities home.

Students must be oriented to the program and reminded about the importance of involving a family partner each time TIPS assignments are made. Teachers must reinforce that they want the student to talk with someone at home about the work and that they believe it is important for families to be aware of what children are learning in school.

How Do Teachers Evaluate TIPS Homework?

There are two main goals for TIPS:

1. To encourage students to complete their homework well and to improve attitudes, behaviors, and achievements

2. To create good information and interactions at home between students and their families about schoolwork

TIPS homework comes with two built-in evaluations. First, students are expected to complete the TIPS activities just as they do any homework. Teachers grade, return, and discuss TIPS just as they do other homework. Second, every TIPS activity includes a section called "Home-to-School Communication" so that parents can provide observations and reactions to their children's work. This section asks parents to check whether their children understood the homework or need extra help from the teacher, whether the assignment was enjoyable for parents and students at home, and if the activity informed parents about schoolwork in a particular subject. Teachers monitor parents' reactions and respond to questions with phone calls, notes, or individual meetings.

When educators use TIPS, they must evaluate whether and how the process helps them reach their goals for school and family connections. Follow-up activities are needed to learn whether students or parents need more information, explanations, or guidance in the use of TIPS at home for positive interactions about schoolwork. This may be done through discussions with students and informal interviews, phone calls, class or grade-level meetings with parents, and formal surveys. Researchers have conducted formal evaluations of the effects of TIPS on parent involvement and student learning (Balli, 1995; Balli, Demo, & Wedman, 1998; Epstein, Simon, & Salinas, 1997; Epstein & Van Voorhis, 2001; Van Voorhis, 2000, 2001).

How Do Parents, Students, and Teachers React to TIPS Homework?

One school using TIPS reported a parent's reaction: "When I see that yellow paper, I know that is important homework for my son to complete with me."

In one study, interviews and surveys of parents, students, and teachers in the middle grades revealed overwhelmingly positive reactions. Parents said they get to talk about things with their children that they would otherwise not discuss. For example, when students worked on TIPS Language Arts, parents wrote,

- I can tell from Jenneaka relating the story to me that she really enjoyed reading it.

- Anthony is improving every day. I believe his report card will be better.

- This blue paper is a learning experience for me.

- Very interesting assignment. I enjoyed this and it brought back good memories.

When students worked on TIPS Science, parents wrote,

- We are still working on neatness.

- Althea's thought process was more mature than what I knew.

- I think she could have done a better job with the consequences.

- This opened up an easier way of communicating.

Students said that they like TIPS because they do not have to copy the homework from the board, because it is not boring, and because they learn something from or about their parents or families that they did not know before. Most teachers reported that more children complete TIPS than other homework.

Sample TIPS Interactive Homework Activities

The pages that follow include four sample TIPS activities:

It is best to keep the length of the TIPS activities to two sides of one page. This keeps copy costs down and requires teachers to focus their attention on the quality of questions, rather than on quantity. Second, all activities should be clear and attractive with computer graphics, where relevant. Finally, all the activities may be produced on colored paper to help students and families identify and enjoy the activities. For example, a math teacher assigning TIPS weekly may choose to copy each assignment on blue paper. Other sample TIPS activities and templates are available in print and on CD. For more information, visit www.partnershipschools.org in the "TIPS" section.

Subject	Grade Level	Title	Topic
TIPS Math	Middle Grades	"I Mean It!"	Finding averages
TIPS Science	Middle Grades	"On Your Mark, Get Set, Go!"	Explaining viscosity
TIPS Language Arts	Elementary	"Hairy Tales"	Improving writing skills
TIPS Social Studies	High School	"Why Do We Need Government"	Understanding social services

TIPS MATH - MIDDLE GRADES

Student's Name _____ Date _____

TIPS: I MEAN IT!

Dear Family Partner:
In math, we are finding and using averages to discuss some common facts. I hope you enjoy this activity with me. This assignment is due _____.

Sincerely,

_____
Student's signature

LOOK THIS OVER: Explain this example to your family partner.

Remember: To find the average (mean) for a set of data:
1) add all of the data;
2) divide the number of pieces of data; and
3) round to the nearest whole number if necessary.
DATA: 4, 9, 5, 6, 11
ADD: 4 + 9 + 5 + 6 + 11 = 35
    5 pieces of data
DIVIDE by Number of Items in Set: 35 ÷ 5 = 7
    AVERAGE (MEAN) = 7

NOW TRY THIS: Show your family member how you do this example.

DATA: 7, 13, 23, 3, 17, 9, 12
ADD:
DIVIDE by Number of Items:
    AVERAGE (MEAN) =

PRACTICE SECTION: Complete these examples on your own. Show your work. Explain one example to your family partner.

1. List the ages of all your family and find the mean age.
   DATA:
   ADD:
   DIVIDE by Number of Items
   AVERAGE (MEAN) =   Is your age close to the mean? _____

2. Find the mean shoe size for all of your family (round half sizes up).
   DATA:
   ADD:
   DIVIDE by Number of Items
   AVERAGE (Mean) =   Is your shoe size close to the mean? _____

3. Find the mean height (in inches) of all of your family.
   DATA:
   ADD:
   DIVIDE by Number of Items
   AVERAGE (Mean) =   Is your height close to the mean? _____

People use averages or means to report survey results. Poll four family members or friends. Include at least one family member.

ASK: How many hours each day do you <u>work</u> (at school, at a job, or at home)?
How many hours each night do you <u>sleep</u>? (Fill in the chart below with your data.)

Names of people you surveyed	Number of hours of work each day (at school, at a job, or at home)	Number of hours of sleep each day
1.		
2.		
3.		
4.		
	AVERAGE (MEAN) =	AVERAGE (MEAN) =

Find the average (mean) amount of time the people you selected work and sleep each day.

WORK SPACE:

Explain your results to a family member. Discuss with your family member:
Would I find the same means if I surveyed only friends my age? Why or why not?

_____

_____

ANSWER TO "NOW TRY THIS":

ADD: 7 + 13 + 23 + 3 + 17 + 9 + 12 = 84
DIVIDE by Number of Items: 84 ÷ 7 = 12
AVERAGE (MEAN) = 12

HOME-TO-SCHOOL COMMUNICATION:

Dear Parent/Family Partner,
Please give me your reactions to your child's work on this activity.
Write YES or NO for each statement.
_____My child understood the homework and was able to complete it.
_____My child and I enjoyed the activity.
_____This assignment helped me know what my child is learning in math.

Any other comments: _____

Parent's signature: _____

Epstein, J. L., Salinas, K. C., & Jackson, V. (revised 2000). *Teachers Involve Parents in Schoolwork (TIPS) Interactive Homework for the Middle Grades.* Baltimore: Johns Hopkins University, Center on School, Family, and Community Partnerships.

TIPS SCIENCE - MIDDLE GRADES

Student's Name _____ Date _____

TIPS: ON YOUR MARK, GET SET, GO!

Dear Family Partner:

In science, we are studying the phases of matter. This activity focuses on liquids to help build skills in observing, recording, and drawing conclusions. I hope you enjoy this activity with me. This activity is due _____.

Sincerely,

_____
Student's signature

OBJECTIVE: To understand <u>viscosity</u>—a liquid's resistance to <u>flow</u>

MATERIALS: ONE TEASPOON of 3-5 liquids that have different thicknesses—such as catsup, mustard, water, syrup, honey, milk, or others that your family partner will allow you to use.

Also, baking pan, teaspoon, clock with second hand or count seconds.

PROCEDURE:

1. Explain the following to a family partner to share what we are learning in class:
   Who is working with you? _____

   Some liquids are thicker and <u>more viscous</u> than others. They <u>flow slowly</u>.
   Some liquids are thin and <u>less viscous</u> than others. They <u>flow quickly</u>.

2. With your family partner decide: Which 3-5 liquids will you test?

   a. _____ d. _____
   b. _____ e. _____
   c. _____

3. Tilt the pan and prop it up against something like a phone book so that it is at an angle (between $45^0 - 60^0$). At about what angle is your pan tilted? _____

   One of you will put each liquid in the pan and identify the finish line. The other will serve as the timer. You can check each other to get an accurate observation.

   Start each teaspoon of a new liquid <u>at the same level at the top of the pan</u> at least one inch away from the previous liquid. Make sure the pan remains tilted at the same angle for each test. When you are ready with all of the materials, do these steps:
   a. Place one teaspoon of liquid at the top of your pan.
   b. <u>Time the seconds</u> it takes for the liquid to reach the "finish line" at the <u>bottom of the pan</u>.
   c. Record the information on the Data Chart.
   d. Continue until you have tested each teaspoon of liquid.

DATA CHART:

LIQUID	SECONDS TO "FINISH" LINE	OBSERVATION HOW VISCOUS IS IT?
_____	_____	_____
_____	_____	_____
_____	_____	_____
_____	_____	_____
_____	_____	_____

CONCLUSIONS:

1. Which liquid finished
   First (fastest) _____
   Midway _____
   Last (slowest) _____
2. Which liquid has high viscosity? _____
3. Which liquid has low viscosity? _____
4. Why was it important that your pan remained at the same angle for each test?
   _____

FAMILY SURVEY:

ASK: Can you think of any foods or other products that use viscosity (how fast or slow the flow) as part of the advertising to get you to buy it?
Family member's idea_____
My idea_____
Why is high viscosity (slow flow) a good feature (or a bad feature) of a product you use?

_____

_____

Why is low viscosity (quick flow) a good feature (or a bad feature) of a product you use?

_____

_____

HOME-TO-SCHOOL COMMUNICATION:

Dear Parent/Family Partner,
Please give me your reactions to your child's work on this activity.
Write YES or NO for each statement.
_____My child understood the homework and was able to complete it.
_____My child and I enjoyed the activity.
_____This assignment helped me know what my child is learning in science.
Any other comments:_____
Parent's signature: _____

Epstein, J. L., Salinas, K. C., Jackson, V., & Van Voorhis, F. L. (revised 2000). Teachers Involve Parents in Schoolwork (TIPS) Interactive Homework for the Middle Grades. Baltimore: Johns Hopkins University, Center on School, Family, and Community Partnerships.

TIPS LANGUAGE ARTS - ELEMENTARY

Student's Name _____   Date _____

TIPS: HAIRY TALES

Dear Family Partner:

In language arts I am working on using information gathered from others to write explanations. For this assignment, I am comparing today's hairstyles with those of the past.   I hope you enjoy this activity with me. This activity is due _____.

Sincerely,

_____

Student's signature

FAMILY INTERVIEW

FIND A FAMILY MEMBER TO INTERVIEW.
Who is it? _____
Ask:

1) In what decade were you born? (1960s, 1970s, etc.) _____

2) What is one hairstyle that was popular when you were my age?
For boys: _____
For girls: _____

3) What hairstyle did you have when you were my age?   _____

4) Did your family agree with your choice of hairstyle? _____

5) What is your favorite current hairstyle and why? _____

6) What is your least favorite current hairstyle and why? _____

Ask your family member to show you a picture of a hairstyle from the past. Draw a picture of the hairstyle here.

First Draft

Use the information from your interview to write a paragraph about hairstyles.
Remember to:
- Give a paragraph a title.
- Be sure all of your sentences relate to your topic.
- Use descriptive words to help explain the ideas.
- If you compare hairstyles, tell how they are alike and how they are different.

WRITE YOUR PARAGRAPH HERE

Title: _____

_____

_____

_____

_____

_____

_____

_____

_____

Read your paragraph aloud to your family partner.
Revise or add sentences, as needed.

EXTENSION ACTIVITY

Select another topic for comparison—for example, clothing styles, ways to have fun, or rules at home or school. What topic did you choose? _____

Next to each "Q" line, write a question about your topic. Use your questions to interview a family member. Write the family member's answer next to each "A" line.

1. Q: _____

    A: _____

2. Q: _____

    A: _____

3. Q: _____

    A: _____

HOME-TO-SCHOOL COMMUNICATION

Dear Parent/Family Partner,
Please give me your reactions to your child's work on this activity.
Write YES or NO for each statement.
_____My child understood the homework and was able to complete it.
_____My child and I enjoyed the activity.
_____This assignment helped me know what my child is learning in language arts.

Any other comments: _____
Parent's signature: _____

Epstein, J. L., Salinas, K. C., Jackson, V., & Van Voorhis, F. L. (revised 2000). Teachers Involve Parents in Schoolwork (TIPS) Interactive Homework for the Elementary Grades. Baltimore: Johns Hopkins University, Center on School, Family, and Community Partnerships.

TIPS SOCIAL STUDIES - HIGH SCHOOL

Student's Name _____   Date _____

TIPS: WHY DO WE NEED GOVERNMENT?
How have social conditions changed over time?

Interview a parent or other family partner who is at least 20 years older than you.
Ask the following **three** questions. You record your family partner's opinions.

1. Compared to twenty years ago, have the following social conditions gotten better, stayed the same, or gotten worse? Please tell me <u>in what way</u>.

SOCIAL CONDITIONS	Got Better	Stayed the Same	Got Worse	IN WHAT WAY?
Education	____	____	____	_____
Environment	____	____	____	_____
Crime/violence	____	____	____	_____
Taxes	____	____	____	_____
Unemployment	____	____	____	_____
Poverty	____	____	____	_____
Health care	____	____	____	_____
Race relations	____	____	____	_____
Standard of living	____	____	____	_____
Individual freedom	____	____	____	_____
Family values	____	____	____	_____
Foreign relations	____	____	____	_____

2. Which TWO of the above topics do you think have been helped by governmental programs over the past 20 years, and **IN WHAT WAY?** You record your family partner's opinions.

TWO areas helped by government   **IN WHAT WAY?**

1. _____   _____

   _____

2. _____   _____

   _____

3. Which TWO of the above topics do you think could use **MORE** or **LESS** help from governmental programs over the next 5 or 10 years, and **IN WHAT WAY?** You record your family partner's opinions.

TWO areas that you think need
MORE OR LESS help from government   **IN WHAT WAY?**
(circle one)

MORE or LESS_____   _____

   _____

MORE or LESS_____   _____

STUDENT VIEW

   _____

Use a separate page to write your views, based on your interview of a family partner. Attach your work to this assignment.

   a. Write a short summary of your views on how social conditions have changed over the past 20 years.

   b. Choose TWO social conditions from the list on the first page. Discuss your views: Should there be more or less attention over the next 5-10 years from federal, state, or local government on the two social conditions you selected, and why?

HOME-TO-SCHOOL COMMUNICATION

Please ask your family partner for his/her views:

___Yes ___No   This assignment helped me know what my student is learning in Government/Social Studies.

COMMENTS: _____

Family Partner's Signature: _____

Epstein, J.L. (2000). Teachers Involve Parents in Schoolwork (TIPS) Interactive Homework for High Schools. Baltimore: Johns Hopkins University, Center on School, Family, and Community Partnerships. (Assignment suggested by Chesapeake High School, Baltimore County.)

2. TIPS Social Studies and Art Volunteers

Family Involvement at School

A second TIPS process—Teachers Involve Parents in Schoolwork (TIPS) Volunteers in Social Studies and Art—addresses the problem of organizing volunteers, especially in the middle grades. This process establishes a teacher-volunteer partnership to enrich the social studies curriculum for all students.

The TIPS Volunteers in Social Studies and Art process integrates art with social studies in the middle grades. The process brings volunteers (parents, other family members, or members of the community) to the school on a regular schedule to introduce artists and artwork to students in their social studies classes. When students study American history, for example, they see and learn about American artists; world history is linked to the work of artists from around the world; government and citizen participation is linked to artwork on themes of government and citizenship.

How Does TIPS Social Studies and Art Work?

Volunteers introduce a new art print to students each month from October to May. Over three middle grades (e.g., 6-8 or 7-9) students are introduced to the work of at least 24 artists with different styles, media, and topics who lived at different times and places in history.

Presentations by parents or other volunteers on each art print require only 20 minutes of class time. Each presentation includes information on the artist's life, style and technique, the specific artwork, connections to social studies, and topics for class discussion, writing, and artwork. Research for the presentations may be conducted by parents who cannot volunteer at school, but who want to contribute time and ideas to improve school programs. Discussions include anecdotes and interesting information about the artist and artwork that should interest middle grades students.

Why Implement TIPS Volunteers in Social Studies and Art?

TIPS Volunteers in Social Studies and Art is designed to increase connections of art with history, geography, and issues of importance in society. The TIPS process helps to solve three common problems in the middle grades: the need for integrated or interdisciplinary curricula, the need for more productive parent volunteers, and the need for students to learn something about art as an important part of cultural literacy. The process is adaptable to other grade levels, other social studies units, and other subjects (e.g., art may be linked to English or literature, foreign language classes, or other subjects).

Prototype presentations in American History (14 artists), World Cultures (14 artists), and Government and Citizen Participation (12 artists) are available, along with a manual that outlines the work of teachers and parents to organize, implement, and evaluate the program. The presentations were designed by parents and other volunteers in partnership with teachers and researchers, tested by middle grades teachers, and evaluated by researchers. The manual includes prototype worksheets for students to use on field trips to art museums, sample quizzes to assess students' knowledge and reactions to the program, and questionnaires for teachers and volunteers about the program.

How Do You Implement TIPS Volunteers in Social Studies and Art?

The implementation process follows 10 easy steps.

1. **Select a teacher-coordinator.** This may be the chair of the social studies department, a team leader, or a social studies teacher who is committed to implementing an interdisciplinary program and who supports community volunteers.

2. **Select a parent-coordinator.** This person will coordinate the schedules of the parent volunteers and help train the volunteers. There should also be an assistant parent-coordinator who will assume leadership of the program in the next school year.

3. **Order the prints** that fit the social studies curricula at each grade level. Prints that are drymounted and laminated may be obtained at a reasonable price from

   Shorewood Fine Art Reproductions
   129 Glover Avenue, Norwalk, CT 06850
   Telephone: (800) 677-6947 Fax: (203) 846-2105

   You may find the Shorewood and other art reproduction collections online at www.liebermans.net

   Order enough prints for the monthly rotations among teachers.

4. **Select the art prints** to be presented and discussed each month by the volunteers.

5. **Recruit volunteers** to make classroom presentations once a month from October to May.

6. **Train the volunteers** so they are comfortable about making their presentations to students in their assigned social studies class(es). The manual for TIPS Volunteers in Social Studies and Art describes how to conduct the orientation session for volunteers in about an hour.

7. **Schedule monthly presentations** at times mutually convenient for the volunteers and the teachers. Volunteers will meet with the same classes each month.

8. **Check with volunteers** after the first visit and periodically through the year to see that the program is working as planned.

9. **Evaluate the program** to determine if students gain knowledge of the artists and artwork and develop an understanding and appreciation of art.

10. **Make necessary improvements** in the implementation process and continue the program.

These steps run smoothly as the parent-coordinator and teacher-coordinator become familiar with their roles and if all volunteers and teachers work in partnership.

Sample TIPS Social Studies and Art Presentation

This section illustrates a sample TIPS Social Studies and Art Presentation on the painting *Mona Lisa* by Leonardo da Vinci in the World Cultures Series. All prototype presentations include information on the artist's life, style of painting, and characteristics or stories of the painting. Also included are suggestions for tying the print to social studies lessons, other prints, and other school subjects. Finally, all prototypes present ideas for art experiences and writing across the curriculum that teachers may use to supplement the volunteers' presentations.

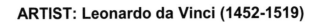

ARTIST: Leonardo da Vinci (1452-1519)

PAINTING: Mona Lisa, also called La Giaconda

PERSONAL

Leonardo da Vinci was born in 1452. He was Leonardo from Vinci—the city where he was born—or, in Italian, Leonardo da Vinci.

He received art training in Florence—a famous art city in Italy. For seventeen years, he worked at the Court of Milan.

Da Vinci was talented in many ways. The King of France once said, "No man knows more than da Vinci." Although primarily a painter, he was also a scientist, musician, inventor, engineer, mathematician, architect, and writer.

Today, we call a person who has many abilities a "Renaissance man or woman." Da Vinci lived during the Renaissance, an age of genius, new ideas, new ways of thinking, and exploration. With his many talents, he really was a Renaissance man.

STYLE

Leonardo da Vinci believed that in order to paint objects or people, an artist had to understand their structure—how they are formed or put together. He was able to study things and understand them clearly. He figured out and drew diagrams to explain how birds fly—several centuries before slow motion cameras showed the same ideas.

Da Vinci believed that an artist could show emotions in portraits. He did this with a technique called *sfumato* (smoke), in which he painted a color that turned slowly from light to dark tones to give off a kind of misty glow or smokey mystery. He tried to paint portraits that showed emotions, not just a blank stare.

IN THIS PAINTING

The *Mona Lisa* is the most famous portrait in the world. In the *Mona Lisa*, da Vinci painted an elegant woman gazing at you with a strangely calm yet haunting look. The mysterious quality of the portrait is achieved by the use of the technique of *sfumato* (smoke). You can see a 3-D quality that comes from the soft background that makes the horizon look very far away.

Da Vinci was so interested in perfect form that he painted some other woman's hands to go with the face of the *Mona Lisa.*

Notice the use of portrait and landscape together in the picture. This combination was an invention of da Vinci.

The smile of the *Mona Lisa* seems to glow from within. Is the smile in her mouth or in her eyes? Cover her mouth. Do you think her eyes are smiling?

Not long ago, some art historians proposed a new theory about the *Mona Lisa.* They believe that the *Mona Lisa* was really based on a self-portrait of da Vinci. They looked under the paint with a type of x-ray machine and discovered lines and drawings *under* the picture you see. A computer researcher compared a self-portrait by da Vinci with the painting and found that the eyes, hair, cheeks, nose, and famous smile were very similar. These lines and drawings supported the art historians' theory. Others insist she is Monna Lisa Gherardini del Giocardo, the wife of an Italian nobleman.

The painting is so popular that officials of the Louvre Museum in Paris say that people even write letters and send New Year's greetings to "Madame Mona Lisa." About 3 million people visit the museum to see the *Mona Lisa* every year.

Some say that the *Mona Lisa* looks at you wherever you are standing. Test this in class with people who are in different parts of the room. Some people say, "She's very plain." Others say, "She has an interesting face." What do you think?

TYING THIS PRINT TO SOCIAL STUDIES

Columbus and other explorers were conducting their adventures around the world at the same time that Leonardo da Vinci was painting and inventing things in Italy. *Perspective painting* was invented, which allowed artists to control their view of the world, much as explorers controlled their travels across oceans. It was an AGE OF EXPLORATION in life and in art.

During the time da Vinci painted, Italy was a collection of city-states, not a unified nation. A city-state was a small, self-contained political area—something like a big city or small country today. People pledged their allegiances and worked and paid taxes to the city-state in which they lived. Da Vinci's name shows the strong connections between the people and where they lived, as he was from Vinci.

In da Vinci's time, educated people needed to learn how to read Latin and to understand and appreciate art and literature. Artists and their work became an important part of everyday life during the Renaissance.

A new class called the "middle class" was developing, in addition to the nobles and peasants. The middle class began to earn enough money to purchase art. The increasing amounts of money available for purchasing art created more opportunities for artists.

Geography: Locate Italy and the cities of Milan and Florence.

TYING THIS PRINT TO OTHER SCHOOL SUBJECTS

Math: DaVinci borrowed and used the shape of the pyramid from his knowledge of math to give strength to his paintings. Ask the students where they "see" a pyramid form in the picture (e.g., the shape of the head and shoulders of Mona Lisa).

Advertising: The *Mona Lisa* has been used as a trademark for Spanish olive oil, Italian hair pins, a West Berlin restaurant called The Smile, computer companies, and many other businesses.

TYING THIS PRINT TO OTHER PRINTS

Compare with other portraits—for example, Gainsborough's *Blue Boy.* What does da Vinci do differently from later artists? How do the different pictures make the viewer feel? Which print conveys deeper emotion? Which print do you like more and why?

WHERE YOU CAN SEE ORIGINAL WORK BY DA VINCI

National Gallery of Art, Washington, D.C., has a portrait called *Ginevra de Benci,* the only original painting by da Vinci in a U.S. museum. It was purchased for 5 million dollars in 1967.

The *Mona Lisa* is in the Louvre in Paris, but many galleries in the United States have copies of it.

Check local museums and galleries for original art or reproductions by Leonardo da Vinci.

Art  Experiences

1. Choose one color crayon or pencil and draw a square. Use the crayon to fill the square with color going very slowly from light to dark. Start at the bottom of the square with very, very light color and gradually get darker and darker as you reach the top of the square. Does the color "glow"? This is called "sfumato."

2. Da Vinci liked to sketch almost anything he saw in order to learn from his drawings. He sketched buildings, animals, hands, trees, rocks, inventions, and even knots of rope to learn about shape, line, light, and shadow. His notebooks, filled with sketches, became famous. (Students may be able to locate the notebooks or books about them in a public library.) Pick a common object in school, at home, or outside to sketch. Try to sketch the same object 3 or 4 times to see if you learn about its form by drawing it from different angles.

3. Draw a portrait of yourself or another person that shows emotion.

Writing
Across the Curriculum

1. The *Mona Lisa* is probably the world's best-known and most famous portrait. It may be the most famous painting in the world. Why do you think people even like this painting? What does the painting "say" to you?

2. You may see the *Mona Lisa* today. For example, some commercials for modern products have used the *Mona Lisa* in their advertisements. Why would they do this (e.g., to connect the product with a "masterpiece," to connect the product with the world's definition of "beautiful" or "mysterious")? What product would you link with the *Mona Lisa* and why? Draw your advertisement to show how you would use the *Mona Lisa* to sell a product.

3. Write a paragraph that tells how a portrait that is drawn or painted is different from a photograph.

4. Write a paragraph explaining why you think art is important in your education. Can someone be "educated" without understanding and having an appreciation for art?

How Do You Get Started With TIPS Interactive Homework or TIPS Volunteers?

Many professional development tools and materials are available to help district leaders and teachers understand and implement the TIPS processes. Manuals, prototype printed homework assignments and prototypes as computer (CD) files, PowerPoint presentations, and workshop materials are disseminated from Johns Hopkins University's Center on School, Family, and Community Partnerships. See information and address below.

TIPS Interactive Homework

Manuals, Prototype Activities

There are manuals for teachers and prototype activities in print form and on CD for TIPS interactive homework in math (Grades K-5) and science (Grade 3) in the elementary grades and language arts, science, and math in the middle grades (Grades 6-8).

TIPS CD

A TIPS CD (for Windows) includes background information on TIPS and all interactive homework assignments that are available in print form for the elementary and middle grades. The CD contains over 500 TIPS activities in math, science, and language arts in Adobe Acrobat (exactly the same as the printed copies) and in Microsoft Word to enable teachers to adapt the assignments to their own curriculum objectives.

Teacher Manual (elementary grades for math and science) (J. Epstein and K. Salinas)	$8.00
TIPS **Math, Kindergarten**	$10.00
TIPS **Math, Grade 1**	$6.00
TIPS **Math, Grade 2**	$6.00
TIPS **Math, Grade 3**	$10.00
TIPS **Math, Grade 4**	$6.00
TIPS **Math, Grade 5**	$6.00
TIPS **Science, Grade 3**	$3.00
TIPS **Elementary Grades Set 1** -Includes all items listed above	$50.00

Teacher Manual (middle grades for language arts, science/health, and math) (J. Epstein, K. Salinas, and V. Jackson)	$8.00
TIPS **Language Arts, Grade 6**	$8.00
TIPS **Language Arts, Grade 7**	$8.00
TIPS **Language Arts, Grade 8**	$8.00
TIPS **Science/Health, Grade 6**	$8.00
TIPS **Science/Health, Grade 7**	$8.00
TIPS **Science/Health, Grade 8**	$8.00
TIPS **Science Set from Pikesville Middle School-Prototype Activities for Grades 6-8**	$12.00
TIPS **Math (Basic Skills)**	$4.00
TIPS **Middle Grades Set** Includes all items listed above	$65.00
TIPS **CD.** ALL the printed assignments listed above are on the TIPS CD (for Windows) in Adobe Acrobat and Microsoft Word for local adaptation. Includes over 500 TIPS Math, Science, and Language Arts interactive homework activities for the elementary and middle grades.	$60.00

TIPS programs require the manual for teachers and the prototype activities or CD. Costs include shipping and handling.

Transparency and PowerPoint Presentations

The National Network of Partnership Schools (NNPS) offers information on Teachers Involve Parents in Schoolwork (TIPS) interactive homework on color transparencies and in PowerPoint for educators to use in professional development team-training workshops and other presentations. The transparencies and PowerPoint presentation include the same information on the following topics: purposes of homework, student-parent interactions, components of TIPS interactive homework, and designing your TIPS homework activities. For more information about prices and ordering, visit the National Network of Partnership Schools' website (www.partnershipschools.org, click on "TIPS") or contact the Network staff at Johns Hopkins University: (410) 516-8061).

TIPS Interactive Homework Leadership Development Workshop

The National Network of Partnership Schools periodically offers members the opportunity to attend a one-day workshop on the TIPS interactive homework process. Contact the National Network staff at Johns Hopkins University at (410) 516-8061 for more information about the next TIPS Interactive Homework Workshop.

TIPS Interactive Homework Video

ASCD (Association for Supervision and Curriculum Development) produced a 15-minute video titled "How to Make Homework More Meaningful by Involving Parents," featuring the TIPS interactive homework process. For more information, visit the ASCD website (www.ascd.org) or call (800) 933-2723 (press 2).

TIPS Volunteers in Social Studies and Art

Manual and Prototype Activities

There are manuals and training materials for teachers and parent coordinators and 40 prototype presentations of art prints for use with units on American History, World Cultures, and Government and Citizen Participation.

Teacher Manual Volunteers in Social Studies and Art (middle grades) (J. Epstein and K. Salinas)	$6.00
TIPS Presentations for Art Prints for **American History (14 prototype presentations)**	$6.00
World Cultures (14 prototype presentations)	$6.00
Government and Citizen Participation (12 prototype presentations)	$6.00
TIPS **Social Studies and Art Set** Includes all items listed above	$20.00

TIPS programs require the manual for teachers and the prototype activities. Costs include shipping and handling.

To order any of the TIPS materials or to obtain a free list of available reports and materials, contact:

Diane Diggs
Publications
Center on School, Family, and Community Partnerships
Johns Hopkins University, 3003 N. Charles Street, Suite 200
Baltimore, MD 21218
Telephone: (410) 516-8808

Note: Research and development of TIPS interactive homework was supported by grants from the U.S. Department of Education-OERI, the Disney Learning Partnership, and the Edna McConnell Clark Foundation. Research and development of TIPS Social Studies and Art Volunteers was supported by grants from OERI and the National Endowment for the Arts.

References

Assocation of Supervision and Curriculum Development. (2001). *How to make homework more meaningful* [Video]. Alexandria, VA: Author.

Balli, S. J. (1995). *The effects of differential prompts on family involvement with middle-grades homework.* Unpublished doctoral dissertation, University of Missouri, Columbia.

Balli, S. J., Demo, D. H., & Wedman, J. F. (1998). Family involvement with children's homework: An intervention in the middle grades. *Family Relations, 47,* 149-157.

Epstein, J. L. (2001). *School, family, and community partnerships: Preparing educators and improving schools.* Boulder, CO: Westview Press.

Epstein, J. L., Salinas, K. C., & Jackson, V. E. (1992, 1995, revised a). *Manual for teachers and prototype activities: Teachers Involve Parents in Schoolwork (TIPS) Language Arts, Science/Health, and Math Interactive Homework in the middle grades.* Baltimore: Johns Hopkins University, Center on School, Family, and Community Partnerships.

Epstein, J. L., Salinas, K. C., & Jackson, V. E. (1992, 1995, revised b). *TIPS Language Arts, Math, and Science Prototype Activities for Grades 6, 7, and 8.* Baltimore: Johns Hopkins University, Center on School, Family, and Community Partnerships.

Epstein, J. L., Simon, B. S., & Salinas, K.C. (1997). Effects of Teachers Involve Parents in Schoolwork (TIPS) Language Arts Interactive Homework in the middle grades. *Phi Delta Kappa Research Bulletin, 18*(September), 1-4.

Epstein, J. L., & Van Voorhis, F. L. (2000). *Teachers Involve Parents in Schoolwork (TIPS) interactive homework training materials.* Baltimore: Authors.

Epstein, J. L., & Van Voorhis, F. L. (2001). More than minutes: Teachers' roles in designing homework. *Educational Psychologist, 36*(3), 181-193.

Van Voorhis, F. L. (2000). *The effects of TIPS interactive and non-interactive homework on science achievement and family involvement of middle grade students.* Unpublished dissertation, University of Florida, Gainesville.

Van Voorhis, F. K. (2001). Interactive science homework: An experiment in home and school connections. *National Association of Secondary Schools Bulletin, 85* (627, October), 20-32.

Planning and Evaluating Your Partnership Program

This chapter provides tools to help Action Teams for Partnerships (ATP) plan, implement, and evaluate their work. All ATPs should do the following annually to improve their partnership programs every year:

- Complete an inventory of present practices of school, family, and community partnerships.

- Outline or update a vision of how practices of partnership will develop and improve over three years.

- Prepare a detailed One-Year Action Plan for partnerships indicating how the ATP and others will schedule and conduct involvement activities to reach specific results during the school year.

- Evaluate the school, family, and community partnership program each year in order to improve practices in the next school year.

The following forms enable schools' Action Teams for Partnerships to complete these four tasks.

Starting Points

This inventory (see pp. 208-211 in Chapter 5) helps your Action Team for Partnerships (ATP) identify the *present* practices conducted in your school for each of the six types of involvement and the grade levels that conduct the activities. The checklist should help the ATP think about how to increase, improve, or maintain activities for a comprehensive program of partnerships. *Starting Points* may be used from year to year to monitor the progress of your program. Or, see the *Measure of School, Family, and Community Partnerships,* which follows, for another way to conduct an annual review of activities in your school's partnership program.

Measure of School, Family, and Community Partnerships

This inventory helps your ATP assess how strongly your school focuses on various activities and approaches for the six types of involvement. The measure also refers to strategies for meeting key challenges to involve all families. Used annually, the *Measure of School, Family, and Community Partnerships* promotes insights and ideas about how to sustain good practices and continually improve programs of family and community involvement.

Planning and Evaluation Tools

Alternative forms of three planning and evaluation tools are provided to identify long-term goals, write annual plans, and conduct end-of-year assessments of progress. Three tools are labeled "Form T" for use in programs that organize partnerships around the six TYPES of involvement. Three tools are labeled "Form G" for use in programs that organize partnerships around four major school improvement GOALS.

Action Teams for Partnerships that write a Three-Year Outline—Form T should also use the One-Year Action Plan—Form T and assess progress with the End-of-Year Evaluation—Form T. Similarly, Three-Year Outline—Form G, One-Year Action Plan—Form G, and End-of-Year Evaluation—Form G should be used in concert.

Three-Year Outline: A Vision Statement Form T (Types) or Form G (Goals)

This broad outline asks your Action Team for Partnerships to set long-term goals for family and community involvement. There are two versions of the Three-Year Outline:

- **Three-Year Outline—Form T (Types)** focuses the ATP on developing a comprehensive program including practices for all six types of involvement. It asks the following: *How will your school increase, improve, or maintain practices for each of the six types of involvement for the next three years?*

- **Three-Year Outline—Form G (Goals)** focuses the ATP on how family and community involvement activities link to the major goals in a school improvement plan (e.g., improving attendance, reading, achievement, safety). It asks the following: *Which practices of the six types of involvement will help reach your school's major goals for student achievement, behavior, and school climate for the next three years?*

Your ATP may use *either* the Three-Year Outline Form T *or* Form G. To complete the outline of long-term goals, the ATP should review the school's inventory (*Starting Points*), school improvement goals, and practices for the six types of involvement that will produce desired results. After completing the Three-Year Outline, the ATP should discuss its vision with the School Improvement Team, full faculty, parent organization, students, and others who have important ideas about the directions that partnerships should take over time. Each spring, the Action Team for Partnerships should update the Three-Year Outline with input from others to maintain a long-term perspective on family and community involvement.

Note: If your school has written three- or five-year plans that include specific goals to improve school, family, and community partnerships, there is no need to write another three-year vision statement. If a long-term vision for partnerships has not been written, the Three-Year Outline (Form T *or* Form G) will guide your ATP to complete that task.

One-Year Action Plan
Form T (Types) or Form G (Goals)

This form asks for specific information about the work that your Action Team for Partnerships will do to oversee and conduct activities for all six types of involvement to reach partnership goals or to support important school improvement goals for the next school year. There are two versions of the One-Year Action Plan:

- **One-Year Action Plan—Form T (Types)** focuses the ATP on the six types of involvement. It asks the following: *For each type of involvement, which activities will your school continue or add this year?*

- **One-Year Action Plan—Form G (Goals)** focuses the ATP on how partnerships link to the major goals in a school improvement plan. It asks the following: *Which practices of the six types of involvement will you choose to help reach the major goals your school has set for students and for school climate this year?* The One-Year Action Plan—Form G focuses on four select goals: two academic or curricular goals for student achievement, one nonacademic behavioral goal for students, and one goal for other partnerships and a welcoming school climate.

The One-Year Action Plan asks the ATP to be clear about the dates, preparation, helpers, and expected results for each family and community involvement activity that will be implemented. The ATP should check that the work scheduled from month to month during the year is reasonable and clearly targeted to important goals and results.

Note: Even if your school writes a school improvement plan, the ATP must complete a One-Year Action Plan for partnerships each year to ensure that leadership and schedules for each activity are clearly defined. The One-Year Action Plan for partnerships should be appended to the school improvement plan each year.

End-of-Year Evaluation
Form T (Types) or Form G (Goals)

This form helps an Action Team for Partnerships review and document the school's progress in developing a comprehensive and effective program of school, family, and community partnerships.

- **End-of-Year Evaluation—Form T (Types)** should be used if your school used Form T of the One-Year Action Plan to organize its partnership program. Form T asks the ATP to rate the quality of the overall program and each type of involvement. It also guides the ATP to reflect on the quality of specific activities that were implemented for the six types of involvement and to discuss ideas for improvements in the next school year.

- **End-of-Year Evaluation—Form G (Goals)** should be used if your school used Form G of the One-Year Action Plan to organize its partnership program. Form G asks the ATP to rate the quality of the overall program and to estimate how well family and community involvement activities are connecting to four select goals—two academic or curricular goals, one nonacademic or behavior goal, and one overall goal for good connections in a welcoming school climate. This form also guides the ATP to reflect on the quality of specific activities that were implemented to attain the selected goals and to discuss ideas for improvements in the next school year.

The End-of-Year Evaluation Form T or Form G should be completed each spring by the Action Team for Partnerships before writing a new One-Year Action Plan for the next school year.

The following charts illustrate how the three forms should be used as linked planning and evaluation tools. ATPs that use forms marked T should organize ATP committees to address the six types of involvement. Teams that use forms marked G should organize ATP committees to focus on selected school goals. See pages 87-90 on the structures of Action Teams for Partnerships.

Partnership programs organized by the six types of involvement use forms marked "T-(Types)"
Three-Year Outline—Form T (Types)
One-Year Action Plan—Form T (Types)
End-of-Year Evaluation—Form T (Types)

Partnership programs organized around school improvement goals use forms marked "G-(Goals)"
Three-Year Outline—Form G (Goals)
One-Year Action Plan—Form G (Goals)
End-of-Year Evaluation—Form G (Goals)

Measure of School, Family, and Community Partnerships

Karen Clark Salinas, Joyce L. Epstein, & Mavis G. Sanders, Johns Hopkins University,
Deborah Davis & Inge Aldersbaes, Northwest Regional Educational Laboratory

This instrument is designed to measure how your school is reaching out to involve parents, community members, and students in a meaningful manner. The measure is based on the framework of six types of involvement. At this time, your school may conduct all, some, or none of the activities or approaches listed. Not every activity is appropriate at every grade level. The selected items show that your school is meeting challenges to involve all families in many different ways that will improve the school climate, strengthen families, and increase student success in school. Your school may be conducting other activities for each type of involvement. These may be added and rated to account for all major partnership practices that your school presently conducts.

Directions: Carefully examine the scoring rubric below before rating your school on the six types of involvement. As you review each item, please circle the response that comes closest to describing your school. A score of 4 or 5 indicates that the activity or approach is strong and prominent. A score of 1, 2, or 3 indicates that the activity is not yet part of the school's program, or needs improvement. The results provide information on the strength of current practices of partnership and insights about possible future directions or needed improvements in your school's partnership program.

Scoring Rubric:

1 – Never: Strategy does not happen at our school.

2 – Rarely: Occurs in only one or two classes. Receives isolated use or little time. Clearly not emphasized in this school's parental involvement plan.

3 – Sometimes: Occurs in some classes. Receives minimal or modest time or emphasis across grades. Not a prevalent component of this school's parental involvement plan.

4 – Often: Occurs in many but not all classes or grade levels. Receives substantive time and emphasis. A prevalent component of this school's parental involvement plan.

5 – Frequently: Occurs in most or all classes or grade levels. Receives substantive time and emphasis. A highly prevalent component of this school's parental involvement plan.

I. PARENTING: Help all families establish home environments to support children as students.

Our School:	Rating				
	Never	Rarely	Sometimes	Often	Frequently
1. Conducts workshops or provides information for parents on child or adolescent development.	1	2	3	4	5
2. Provides information, training, and assistance to all families who want it or who need it, not just to the few who can attend workshops or meetings at the school building.	1	2	3	4	5
3. Produces information for families that is clear, usable, and linked to children's success in school.	1	2	3	4	5
4. Asks families for information about children's goals, strengths, and talents.	1	2	3	4	5
5. Sponsors home visiting programs or neighborhood meetings to help families understand schools and to help schools understand families.	1	2	3	4	5
6. Provides families with information on developing home conditions or environments that support learning.	1	2	3	4	5
7. Respects the different cultures represented in our student population.	1	2	3	4	5
Other Type 1-Parenting activities: _____	1	2	3	4	5
_____	1	2	3	4	5

II. COMMUNICATING: Design effective forms of school-to-home and home-to-school communications about school programs and children's progress.

Our School:	Rating				
	Never	Rarely	Sometimes	Often	Frequently
1. Reviews the readability, clarity, form, and frequency of all memos, notices, and other print and nonprint communications.	1	2	3	4	5
2. Develops communications with parents who do not speak or read English well, or need large type.	1	2	3	4	5
3. Provides written communication in the language of the parents and translators as needed.	1	2	3	4	5
4. Has clear two-way channels for communications from home to school and from school to home.	1	2	3	4	5
5. Conducts a formal conference with every parent at least once a year.	1	2	3	4	5
6. Conducts annual survey for families to share information and concerns about student needs, reactions to school programs, and satisfaction with their involvement in school and at home.	1	2	3	4	5
7. Conducts an orientation for new parents.	1	2	3	4	5
8. Sends home folders of student work weekly or monthly for parent review and comment.	1	2	3	4	5
9. Provides clear information about the curriculum, assessments, achievement levels, and report cards.	1	2	3	4	5
10. Contacts families of students having academic or behavior problems.	1	2	3	4	5
11. Develops school's plan and program of family and community involvement with input from educators, parents, and others.	1	2	3	4	5
12. Trains teachers, staff, and principals on the value and utility of family involvement and ways to build positive ties between school and home.	1	2	3	4	5
13. Builds policies that encourage all teachers to communicate frequently with parents about curriculum plans, expectations for homework, and how parents can help.	1	2	3	4	5
14. Produces a regular school newsletter with up-to-date information about the school, special events, organizations, meetings, and parenting tips.	1	2	3	4	5
Other Type 2-Communicating activities: _____	1	2	3	4	5
_____	1	2	3	4	5

III. VOLUNTEERING: Recruit and organize parent help and support.

Our School:	Rating				
	Never	Rarely	Sometimes	Often	Frequently
1. Conducts an annual survey to identify interests, talents, and availability of parent volunteers in order to match their skills and talents with school and classroom needs.	1	2	3	4	5
2. Provides a parent or family room for volunteers and family members to work, meet, and access resources about parenting, childcare, tutoring, and related topics.	1	2	3	4	5
3. Creates flexible volunteering opportunities and schedules, enabling employed parents to participate.	1	2	3	4	5
4. Schedules school events at different times during the day and evening so that all families can attend.	1	2	3	4	5
5. Reduces barriers to parent participation by providing transportation and child care, and by addressing the needs of English language learners.	1	2	3	4	5
6. Trains volunteers so they use their time productively.	1	2	3	4	5
7. Recognizes volunteers for their time and efforts.	1	2	3	4	5
8. Encourages families and the community to be involved with the school in a variety of ways (assisting in classroom, giving talks, monitoring halls, leading activities, etc.).	1	2	3	4	5
Other Type 3-Volunteering activities: _____	1	2	3	4	5
_____	1	2	3	4	5

IV. LEARNING AT HOME: Provide information to families about how to help students at home with homework and other curriculum-related activities, decisions, and planning.

Our School:	Rating				
	Never	Rarely	Sometimes	Often	Frequently
1. Provides information to families on how to monitor and discuss schoolwork at home.	1	2	3	4	5
2. Provides information to families on required skills in all subjects.	1	2	3	4	5
3. Provides ongoing and specific information to parents on how to assist students with skills that they need to improve.	1	2	3	4	5
4. Makes parents aware of the importance of reading at home, and asks parents to listen to their child read or read aloud with their child.	1	2	3	4	5
5. Assists families in helping students set academic goals and select courses and programs.	1	2	3	4	5
6. Schedules regular interactive homework that requires students to demonstrate and discuss what they are learning with a family member.	1	2	3	4	5
Other Type 4-Learning at Home activities: _____	1	2	3	4	5
_____	1	2	3	4	5

V. DECISION MAKING: Include parents in school decisions to develop leaders and representatives.

Our School:	Rating				
	Never	Rarely	Sometimes	Often	Frequently
1. Has active PTA, PTO, or other parent organization.	1	2	3	4	5
2. Includes parent representatives on the school's advisory council, improvement team, or other committees.	1	2	3	4	5
3. Has parents represented on district-level advisory council and committees.	1	2	3	4	5
4. Involves parents in organized, ongoing, and timely ways in planning, reviewing, and improving school programs.	1	2	3	4	5
5. Involves parents in revising school and district curricula.	1	2	3	4	5
6. Includes parent leaders from all racial, ethnic, socioeconomic, and other groups in the school.	1	2	3	4	5
7. Develops formal networks to link all families with their parent representatives.	1	2	3	4	5
8. Includes students (with parents) in decision-making groups.	1	2	3	4	5
9. Deals with conflict openly and respectfully.	1	2	3	4	5
10. Asks involved parents to make contact with parents who are less involved to solicit their ideas and report back to them.	1	2	3	4	5
Other Type 5-Decision Making activities: _____	1	2	3	4	5
_____	1	2	3	4	5

VI. COLLABORATING WITH THE COMMUNITY: Identify and integrate resources and services from the community to strengthen school programs, family practices, and student learning and development.

Our School:	Rating				
	Never	Rarely	Sometimes	Often	Frequently
1. Provides a resource directory for parents and students with information on community services, programs, and agencies.	1	2	3	4	5
2. Involves families in locating and using community resources.	1	2	3	4	5
3. Works with local businesses, industries, libraries, parks, museums, and other organizations on programs to enhance student skills and learning.	1	2	3	4	5
4. Provides "one-stop" shopping for family services through partnership of school, counseling, health, recreation, job training, and other agencies.	1	2	3	4	5
5. Opens its building for community use after school hours.	1	2	3	4	5
6. Offers after-school programs for students with support from community businesses, agencies, and volunteers.	1	2	3	4	5
7. Solves turf problems of responsibilities, funds, staff, and locations for collaborative activities to occur.	1	2	3	4	5
Other Type 6-Collaborating With the Community activities: _____	1	2	3	4	5
_____	1	2	3	4	5

A. What major factors *contributed to the success* of your school's family and community involvement efforts this year?

B. What major factors *limited the success* of your school's family and community involvement efforts this year?

C. What is *one* of your school's major goals for improving its program of school, family, and community partnerships over the next three years?

SCHOOL _____

Three-Year Outline From _____ to _____

VISION: A COMPREHENSIVE PROGRAM OF SIX TYPES OF INVOLVEMENT

Outline the activities that might help your school improve all six types of involvement over the next three years. What steps might your Action Team for Partnerships (ATP) take in Year 1, Year 2, and Year 3 to improve Parenting, Communicating, Volunteering, Learning at Home, Decision Making, and Collaborating With the Community? Use this form *after* completing *Starting Points* and *before* completing the *One-Year Action Plan Form T (Types)*.

Type 1—PARENTING: Assist families with parenting skills, family support, understanding child and adolescent development, and setting home conditions to support learning at each age and grade level. Obtain information from families to help schools understand children's strengths, talents, and needs, and families' backgrounds, cultures, and goals for their children.

VISION: What is your ATP's broad goal for improving Type 1—Parenting over the next three years? _____

Which ACTIVITIES might your school conduct over three years to reach this vision for Type 1—Parenting?

Year 1 _____

Year 2 _____

Year 3 _____

Type 2—COMMUNICATING: Communicate with families about school programs and student progress using school-to-home and home-to-school communications. Create two-way channels so that families can easily contact and respond to teachers and administrators.

VISION: What is your ATP's broad goal for improving Type 2—Communicating over the next three years? _____

Which ACTIVITIES might your school conduct over three years to reach this vision for Type 2—Communicating?

Year 1 _____

Year 2 _____

Year 3 _____

School, Family, and Community Partnerships by J. L. Epstein et al., © 2002 Corwin Press, Inc.
Photocopying permissible for local school use only.

Type 3—VOLUNTEERING: Improve recruitment, training, activities, and schedules to involve families as volunteers and audiences at the school or in other locations to support students and the school's programs.

VISION: What is your ATP's broad goal for improving Type 3—Volunteering over the next three years? _____

_____

Which ACTIVITIES might your school conduct over three years to reach this vision for Type 3—Volunteering?

Year 1 _____

Year 2 _____

Year 3 _____

Type 4—LEARNING AT HOME: Involve families with their children in academic learning activities at home including homework, goal setting, and other curriculum-related activities and decisions.

VISION: What is your ATP's broad goal for improving Type 4—Learning at Home over the next three years? _____

_____

Which ACTIVITIES might your school conduct over three years to reach this vision for Type 4—Learning at Home?

Year 1 _____

Year 2 _____

Year 3 _____

Type 5—DECISION MAKING: Include families as participants in school decisions, governance, and advocacy activities through school councils, committees, teams, PTA/PTO, and other parent associations. Assist family representatives to obtain information from and give information to those they represent.

VISION: What is your ATP's broad goal for improving Type 5—Decision Making over the next three years? _____

Which ACTIVITIES might your school conduct over three years to reach this vision for Type 5—Decision Making?

Year 1 _____

Year 2 _____

Year 3 _____

Type 6—COLLABORATING WITH THE COMMUNITY: Coordinate the work and resources of community businesses, agencies, cultural and civic organizations, and other groups to strengthen school programs, family practices, and student learning and development. Enable students, staff, and families to contribute service to the community.

VISION: What is your ATP's broad goal for improving Type 6—Collaborating With the Community over the next three years? _____

Which ACTIVITIES might you conduct over three years to reach your vision for Type 6—Collaborating With the Community?

Year 1 _____

Year 2 _____

Year 3 _____

School _____

Three-Year Outline From _____ to _____
VISION: REACHING SCHOOL GOALS WITH
SCHOOL, FAMILY, AND COMMUNITY PARTNERSHIPS

- On these **4** pages, select **4** major goals: **2** academic goals for students, **1** behavioral goal for students, and **1** overall goal for creating a school climate of partnership.
- Next, list **specific, measurable results** for each goal for Year 1, Year 2, and Year 3.
- Finally, list activities for **school, family, and community partnerships** that will help reach the desired results for EACH goal in Years 1, 2, and 3.

NOTE: All six types of involvement need not be addressed for every goal, but all types should be included on some goal(s) every year.

GOAL 1—ACADEMIC. Select ONE curricular goal for students, such as improving reading, math, writing, science, or other skills that the school will address over three years: _____

_____

DESIRED RESULTS FOR THIS GOAL by the end of YEAR 1: _____

_____

Links with School, Family, and Community Partnerships:
Which practices of partnership will help reach the desired results for THIS goal in **Year 1**?
Type 1—Parenting: _____
Type 2—Communicating: _____
Type 3—Volunteering: _____
Type 4—Learning at Home: _____
Type 5—Decision Making: _____
Type 6—Collaborating With the Community: _____

DESIRED RESULTS FOR THIS GOAL by the end of YEAR 2: _____

_____

Links with School, Family, and Community Partnerships:
Which practices of partnership will help reach the desired results for THIS goal in **Year 2**?
Type 1—Parenting: _____
Type 2—Communicating: _____
Type 3—Volunteering: _____
Type 4—Learning at Home: _____
Type 5—Decision Making: _____
Type 6—Collaborating With the Community: _____

DESIRED RESULTS FOR THIS GOAL by the end of YEAR 3: _____

_____

Links with School, Family, and Community Partnerships:
Which practices of partnership will help reach the desired results for THIS goal in **Year 3**?
Type 1—Parenting: _____
Type 2—Communicating: _____
Type 3—Volunteering: _____
Type 4—Learning at Home: _____
Type 5—Decision Making: _____
Type 6—Collaborating With the Community: _____

GOAL 2—ACADEMIC. Select ANOTHER curricular goal for students, such as improving reading, math, writing, science, or other skills that the school will address over three years: _____

_____

DESIRED RESULTS FOR THIS GOAL by the end of YEAR 1: _____

_____

Links with School, Family, and Community Partnerships:

Which practices of partnership will help reach the desired results for THIS goal in **Year 1**?

Type 1—Parenting: _____

Type 2—Communicating: _____

Type 3—Volunteering: _____

Type 4—Learning at Home: _____

Type 5—Decision Making: _____

Type 6—Collaborating With the Community: _____

DESIRED RESULTS FOR THIS GOAL by the end of YEAR 2: _____

_____

Links with School, Family, and Community Partnerships:

Which practices of partnership will help reach the desired results for THIS goal in **Year 2**?

Type 1—Parenting: _____

Type 2—Communicating: _____

Type 3—Volunteering: _____

Type 4—Learning at Home: _____

Type 5—Decision Making: _____

Type 6—Collaborating With the Community: _____

DESIRED RESULTS FOR THIS GOAL by the end of YEAR 3: _____

_____

Links with School, Family, and Community Partnerships:

Which practices of partnership will help reach the desired results for THIS goal in **Year 3**?

Type 1—Parenting: _____

Type 2—Communicating: _____

Type 3—Volunteering: _____

Type 4—Learning at Home: _____

Type 5—Decision Making: _____

Type 6—Collaborating With the Community: _____

GOAL 3—BEHAVIORAL. Select ONE goal for students, such as improving behavior, attendance, respect for others, safety, or another quality that requires improvement over three years:

_____

DESIRED RESULTS FOR THIS GOAL by the end of YEAR 1: _____

_____

Links with School, Family, and Community Partnerships:

Which practices of partnership will help reach the desired results for THIS goal in **Year 1**?

Type 1—Parenting: _____

Type 2—Communicating: _____

Type 3—Volunteering: _____

Type 4—Learning at Home: _____

Type 5—Decision Making: _____

Type 6—Collaborating With the Community: _____

DESIRED RESULTS FOR THIS GOAL by the end of YEAR 2: _____

_____

Links with School, Family, and Community Partnerships:

Which practices of partnership will help reach the desired results for THIS goal in **Year 2**?

Type 1—Parenting: _____

Type 2—Communicating: _____

Type 3—Volunteering: _____

Type 4—Learning at Home: _____

Type 5—Decision Making: _____

Type 6—Collaborating With the Community: _____

DESIRED RESULTS FOR THIS GOAL by the end of YEAR 3: _____

_____

Links with School, Family, and Community Partnerships:

Which practices of partnership will help reach the desired results for THIS goal in **Year 3**?

Type 1—Parenting: _____

Type 2—Communicating: _____

Type 3—Volunteering: _____

Type 4—Learning at Home: _____

Type 5—Decision Making: _____

Type 6—Collaborating With the Community: _____

GOAL 4—CLIMATE OF PARTNERSHIPS (Required goal). Identify ALL OTHER family and community partnership activities for the six types of involvement that the school will conduct to create a welcoming school environment, not covered in GOALS 1, 2, and 3. Check *Starting Points* for activities that will create a climate of partnership over the next three years:

Strengthen the six types of family and community involvement

DESIRED RESULTS FOR THIS GOAL by the end of YEAR 1: _____

_____

_____

Links with School, Family, and Community Partnerships:

Which practices of partnership will help reach the desired results for THIS goal in **Year 1**?

Type 1—Parenting: _____

Type 2—Communicating: _____

Type 3—Volunteering: _____

Type 4—Learning at Home: _____

Type 5—Decision Making: _____

Type 6—Collaborating With the Community: _____

DESIRED RESULTS FOR THIS GOAL by the end of YEAR 2: _____

_____

Links with School, Family, and Community Partnerships:

Which practices of partnership will help reach the desired results for THIS goal in **Year 2**?

Type 1—Parenting: _____

Type 2—Communicating: _____

Type 3—Volunteering: _____

Type 4—Learning at Home: _____

Type 5—Decision Making: _____

Type 6—Collaborating With the Community: _____

DESIRED RESULTS FOR THIS GOAL by the end of YEAR 3: _____

_____

Links with School, Family, and Community Partnerships:

Which practices of partnership will help reach the desired results for THIS goal in **Year 3**?

Type 1—Parenting: _____

Type 2—Communicating: _____

Type 3—Volunteering: _____

Type 4—Learning at Home: _____

Type 5—Decision Making: _____

Type 6—Collaborating With the Community: _____

School: _____

One-Year Action Plan

SCHEDULE OF ACTIVITIES FOR THE SIX TYPES OF INVOLVEMENT

School Year: _____

For the One-Year Action Plan, the Action Team for Partnerships should list the activities that are *presently* conducted at the school that will be continued, as well as *new activities* that will strengthen all six types of involvement.

Type 1—PARENTING: Assist families with parenting skills, family support, understanding child and adolescent development, and setting home conditions to support learning at each age and grade level. Obtain information from families to help schools understand children's strengths, talents, and needs, and families' backgrounds, cultures, and goals for their children.

Type 1—Committee Chair or Cochairs: _____

TYPE 1 ACTIVITY (continuing or new)	Date of Activity	Grade Level(s)	What Needs to Be Done for Activity & When?	Persons in Charge and Helping	What RESULTS & How Measured?

Any extra funds, supplies, or resources needed for these activities? _____

You may add pages to show more activities that support THIS type of involvement or to provide detailed plans for the work that must be done THIS YEAR.

Type 2—COMMUNICATING: Communicate with families about school programs and student progress using school-to-home and home-to-school communications. Create two-way channels so that families can easily contact teachers and administrators.

Type 2—Committee Chair or Cochairs: _____

TYPE 2 ACTIVITY (continuing or new)	Date of Activity	Grade Level(s)	What Needs to Be Done for Activity & When?	Persons in Charge and Helping	What RESULTS & How Measured?

Any extra funds, supplies, or resources needed for these activities? _____

You may add pages to show more activities that support THIS type of involvement or to provide detailed plans for the work that must be done THIS YEAR.

Type 3—VOLUNTEERING: Improve recruitment, training, activities, and schedules to involve families as volunteers and audiences at the school or in other locations to support students and the school's programs.

Type 3—Committee Chair or Cochairs: _____

TYPE 3 ACTIVITY (continuing or new)	Date of Activity	Grade Level(s)	What Needs to Be Done for Activity & When?	Persons in Charge and Helping	What RESULTS & How Measured?

Any extra funds, supplies, or resources needed for these activities? _____

You may add pages to show more activities that support THIS type of involvement or to provide detailed plans for the work that must be done THIS YEAR.

Type 4—LEARNING AT HOME: Involve families with their children in academic learning activities at home including homework, goal setting, and other curriculum-related activities and decisions.

Type 4—Committee Chair or Cochairs: _____

TYPE 4 ACTIVITY (continuing or new)	Date of Activity	Grade Level(s)	What Needs to Be Done for Activity & When?	Persons in Charge and Helping	What RESULTS & How Measured?

Any extra funds, supplies, or resources needed for these activities? _____

You may add pages to show more activities that support THIS type of involvement or to provide detailed plans for the work that must be done THIS YEAR.

Type 5—DECISION MAKING: Include families as participants in school decisions, governance, and advocacy activities through PTA/PTO, committees, councils, and other parent organizations. Assist family representatives to obtain information from and give information to those they represent.

Type 5—Committee Chair or Cochairs: _____

TYPE 5 ACTIVITY (continuing or new)	Date of Activity	Grade Level(s)	What Needs to Be Done for Activity & When?	Persons in Charge and Helping	What RESULTS & How Measured?

Any extra funds, supplies, or resources needed for these activities? _____

You may add pages to show more activities that support THIS type of involvement or to provide detailed plans for the work that must be done THIS YEAR.

Type 6—COLLABORATING WITH THE COMMUNITY: Coordinate the work and resources of community businesses, agencies, and cultural, civic, and other organizations to strengthen school programs, family practices, and student learning and development. Enable students, staff, and families to contribute service to the community.

Type 6—Committee Chair or Cochairs: _____

TYPE 6 ACTIVITY (continuing or new)	Date of Activity	Grade Level(s)	What Needs to Be Done for Activity & When?	Persons in Charge and Helping	What RESULTS & How Measured?

Any extra funds, supplies, or resources needed for these activities? _____

You may add pages to show more activities that support THIS type of involvement or to provide detailed plans for the work that must be done THIS YEAR.

School: _____

One-Year Action Plan

SCHEDULE OF SCHOOL, FAMILY, AND COMMUNITY PARTNERSHIPS TO REACH SCHOOL GOALS

School Year: _____

- On these **4** pages, select **4** major goals: **2** academic goals for students, **1** behavioral goal for students, and **1** goal for creating a school climate of partnership.
- List the specific, **measurable results** that will show you have reached EACH goal.

GOAL 1—ACADEMIC. Select ONE curricular goal for students, such as improving reading, math, writing, science, or other skills that the school will address in the next school year: _____

Desired result(s) for THIS goal: _____

How will you measure the result(s)? _____

- Which practices of school, family, and community partnerships will help you reach THIS goal? (Choose activities from more than one type of involvement.)
- How will you organize and schedule the family and community involvement activities that support THIS goal?

ACTIVITY (continuing or new)	Type (1-6)	Date of Activity	Grade Level(s)	What Needs to Be Done for Activity & When?	Persons in Charge and Helping

Any extra funds, supplies, or resources needed for these activities? _____

You may add pages to show more activities that support THIS goal or to provide detailed plans for the work that must be done THIS YEAR.

GOAL 2—ACADEMIC. Select ANOTHER curricular goal for students, such as improving reading, math, writing, science, or other skills that the school will address in the next school year: _____

Desired result(s) for THIS goal: _____

How will you measure these result(s)?

- Which practices of school, family, and community partnerships will help you reach THIS goal? (Choose activities from more than one type of involvement.)
- How will you organize and schedule the family and community involvement activities that support THIS goal?

ACTIVITY (continuing or new)	Type (1-6)	Date of Activity	Grade Level(s)	What Needs to Be Done for Activity & When?	Persons in Charge and Helping

Any extra funds, supplies, or resources needed for these activities? _____

You may add pages to show more activities that support THIS goal or to provide detailed plans for the work that must be done THIS YEAR.

GOAL 3—BEHAVIORAL. Select ONE goal for students, such as improving behavior, attendance, respect for others, safety, or another quality that requires improvement in the next school year: _____

Desired result(s) for THIS goal: _____

How will you measure these result(s)? _____

- Which practices of school, family, and community partnerships will help you reach THIS goal? (Choose activities from more than one type of involvement.)
- How will you organize and schedule the family and community involvement activities that support THIS goal?

ACTIVITY (continuing or new)	Type (1-6)	Date of Activity	Grade Level(s)	What Needs to Be Done for Activity & When?	Persons in Charge and Helping

Any extra funds, supplies, or resources needed for these activities? _____

You may add pages to show more activities that support THIS goal or to provide detailed plans for the work that must be done THIS YEAR.

GOAL 4—CLIMATE OF PARTNERSHIPS (Required goal). Identify ALL OTHER family and community partnership activities for the six types of involvement that the school will conduct to create a welcoming school environment, not covered in GOALS 1, 2, and 3. Check *Starting Points* for activities that will help create a climate of partnership in the next school year:

Strengthen the six types of family and community involvement

Desired result(s) for THIS goal: _____

How will you measure these result(s)? _____

- Which practices of school, family, and community partnerships will help you reach THIS goal? (Choose activities from more than one type of involvement.)
- How will you organize and schedule the family and community involvement activities that support THIS goal?

ACTIVITY (continuing or new)	Type (1-6)	Date of Activity	Grade Level(s)	What Needs to Be Done for Activity & When?	Persons in Charge and Helping

Any extra funds, supplies, or resources needed for these activities? _____

You may add pages to show more activities that support THIS goal or to provide detailed plans for the work that must be done THIS YEAR.

School Name _____   School Year_____

End-of-Year Evaluation
School, Family, and Community Partnerships—Six Types of Involvement

This annual report helps your Action Team for Partnerships evaluate its progress in developing its comprehensive program of school, family, and community partnerships. The End-of-Year Evaluation—Form T contains one set of general questions on the overall partnership program, and one page for each of the six types of involvement.

The entire Action Team for Partnerships (ATP) should discuss and complete the general questions on the first page. The chair or cochairs who oversee committees on each of the six types of involvement may complete the page about the type of involvement for which they are responsible and then discuss progress with the full team. Add pages if you need more space to document progress.

This report should assist the ATP with its One-Year Action Plan for the next school year.

General Questions:
1. **What has changed most in the past year as a result of the work on school, family, and community partnerships?** _____
   _____

2. **Overall, how would the ATP rate the quality of this school's program of school, family, and community partnerships?**

   This school's partnership program is:

   _____ a. **Weak/Just Starting: Not well developed and needs a great deal of work**

   _____ b. **Fair: Implemented but needs improvement and expansion**

   _____ c. **Good: Well developed and covers all six types of involvement and addresses the needs of most families at most grade levels**

   _____ d. **Excellent: Well developed and implemented, covers all six types of involvement, and addresses the needs of all families at all grade levels**

3. **Who are the members of your Action Team for Partnerships this year? Mark * next to the names of members who are completing their terms or leaving the school and who will be replaced by new members.**

ATP members for this school year	Position (teacher, parent, etc., and note chairs or cochairs of team and committees)	Responsible for or helping with which type of involvement?
1. _____	_____	_____
2. _____	_____	_____
3. _____	_____	_____
4. _____	_____	_____
5. _____	_____	_____
6. _____	_____	_____
7. _____	_____	_____
8. _____	_____	_____

If you have more than eight members on the ATP, please continue this list on another page.

Evaluation of Type 1—PARENTING Activities: Type 1 activities help *families* understand their children's development and improve their parenting skills and help *schools* understand their students' families (workshops on parenting skills, GED classes, children's clothing swaps, etc.).

1. From the ATP's One-Year Action Plan—Form T (Types), <u>review</u> the Type 1—Parenting activities that were implemented during this school year. List two or three that are (or will be) particularly helpful at your school:

    _____

    _____

    _____

2. Overall, how would you rate the quality of all Type 1 activities that your school presently conducts? (Check one)
    _____ a. Weak/Just Starting: Not well developed and need a great deal of work
    _____ b. Fair: Implemented but need improvement and expansion
    _____ c. Good: Well developed and reach most families at most grade levels
    _____ d. Excellent: Well developed and implemented, reach all families at all grade levels, and meet other major challenges

3. Select one Type 1—Parenting activity to describe in detail (i.e., one that reflects your school's best effort this year) and answer the following questions.

    One effective Type 1 activity implemented this year: _____

    About how many were involved?   # of families _____   # of teachers _____
    # of students _____   # of others _____

    Which grade levels were involved? _____

    What was the main goal of this activity? _____

    _____

    How well was the activity implemented this year? Was it a new initiative or an improvement of an existing practice?

    _____

    _____

    _____

    What result(s) did this activity produce this year for students, teachers, parents, and the community? How were the results measured?

    _____

    _____

    _____

    What might be done to make this activity even more successful next year? Were there parents, teachers, or students who were *not* involved? How might they be involved in the future? Could other aspects of the practice be improved? Explain.

    _____

    _____

    _____

Evaluation of Type 2—COMMUNICATING Activities: Type 2 activities include school-to-home and home-to-school communications about school and classroom programs and children's progress (newsletter, website, parent-teacher-student conferences, phone calls, etc.).

1.   From the ATP's One-Year Action Plan—Form T (Types), <u>review</u> the Type 2—Communicating activities that were implemented during this school year. List two or three that are (or will be) particularly helpful at your school:

   _____

   _____

   _____

2.   Overall, how would you rate the quality of all Type 2 activities that your school presently conducts? (Check one)

          _____ a. Weak/Just Starting: Not well developed and need a great deal of work

          _____ b. Fair: Implemented but need improvement and expansion

          _____ c. Good: Well developed and reach most families at most grade levels

          _____ d. Excellent: Well developed and implemented, reach all families at all grade levels, and meet other major challenges

3.   Select one Type 2—Communicating activity to describe in detail (i.e., one that reflects your school's best effort this year) and answer the following questions.

   One effective Type 2 activity implemented this year: _____

   About how many were involved?   # of families _____   # of teachers _____

                                             # of students _____   # of others _____

   Which grade levels were involved? _____

   What was the main goal of this activity? _____

   _____

   How well was the activity implemented this year? Was it a new initiative or an improvement of an existing practice?

   _____

   _____

   _____

   What result(s) did this activity produce this year for students, teachers, parents, and the community? How were the results measured?

   _____

   _____

   _____

   What might be done to make this activity even more successful next year? Were there parents, teachers, or students who were *not* involved? How might they be involved in the future? Could other aspects of the practice be improved? Explain.

   _____

   _____

   _____

Evaluation of Type 3—VOLUNTEERING Activities: Type 3 activities enable families to give their time and talents to support the school, teachers, and children. Volunteers may conduct activities at school, at home, or in the community (volunteer training, volunteer tutors, office assistants, readers, etc.).

1. From the ATP's One-Year Action Plan—Form T (Types), <u>review</u> the Type 3—Volunteering activities that were implemented during this school year. List two or three that are (or will be) particularly helpful at your school:

    _____

    _____

    _____

2. Overall, how would you rate the quality of all Type 3 activities that your school presently conducts? (Check one)

    _____ a. Weak/Just Starting: Not well developed and need a great deal of work
    _____ b. Fair: Implemented but need improvement and expansion
    _____ c. Good: Well developed and reach most families at most grade levels
    _____ d. Excellent: Well developed and implemented, reach all families at all grade levels, and meet other major challenges

3. Select one Type 3—Volunteering activity to describe in detail (i.e., one that reflects your school's best effort this year) and answer the following questions.

    One effective Type 3 activity implemented this year: _____

    About how many were involved?   # of families _____   # of teachers _____
                                              # of students _____   # of others _____

    Which grade levels were involved? _____

    What was the main goal of this activity? _____

    _____

    How well was the activity implemented this year? Was it a new initiative or an improvement of an existing practice?

    _____

    _____

    _____

    What result(s) did this activity produce this year for students, teachers, parents, and the community? How were the results measured?

    _____

    _____

    _____

    What might be done to make this activity even more successful next year? Were there parents, teachers, or students who were not involved? How might they be involved in the future? Could other aspects of the practice be improved? Explain.

    _____

    _____

    _____

Evaluation of Type 4—LEARNING AT HOME Activities: Type 4 activities provide information and ideas to families about the academic work their children do in class, how to help their children with homework, and other curriculum-related activities and decisions (interactive homework, summer learning packets, reading at home, etc.).

1. From the ATP's One-Year Action Plan—Form T (Types), <u>review</u> the Type 4—Learning at Home activities that were implemented during this school year. List two or three that are (or will be) particularly helpful at your school:

    _____

    _____

    _____

2. Overall, how would you rate the quality of all Type 4 activities that your school presently conducts? (Check one)
    _____ a. **Weak/Just Starting:** Not well developed and need a great deal of work
    _____ b. **Fair:** Implemented but need improvement and expansion
    _____ c. **Good:** Well developed and reach most families at most grade levels
    _____ d. **Excellent:** Well developed and implemented, reach all families at all grade levels, and meet other major challenges

3. Select one Type 4—Learning at Home activity to describe in detail (i.e., one that reflects your school's best effort this year) and answer the following questions.

    One effective Type 4 activity implemented this year: _____

    About how many were involved? # of families _____   # of teachers _____
                                    # of students _____   # of others _____

    Which grade levels were involved? _____

    What was the main goal of this activity? _____

    _____

    How well was the activity implemented this year? Was it a new initiative or an improvement of an existing practice?

    _____

    _____

    _____

    What result(s) did this activity produce this year for students, teachers, parents, and the community? How were the results measured?

    _____

    _____

    _____

    What might be done to make this activity even more successful next year? Were there parents, teachers, or students who were not involved? How might they be involved in the future? Could other aspects of the practice be improved? Explain.

    _____

    _____

    _____

Evaluation of Type 5—DECISION MAKING Activities: Type 5 activities enable families to participate in decisions about school programs that affect their own and other children (leadership training, parents on school council, PTA/PTO, action team, etc.).

1. From the ATP's One-Year Action Plan—Form T (Types), <u>review</u> the Type 5—Decision Making activities that were implemented during this school year. List two or three that are (or will be) particularly helpful at your school:

   _____

   _____

   _____

2. Overall, how would you rate the quality of all Type 5 activities that your school presently conducts? (Check one)

   _____ a. Weak/Just Starting: Not well developed and need a great deal of work
   _____ b. Fair: Implemented but need improvement and expansion
   _____ c. Good: Well developed and reach most families at most grade levels
   _____ d. Excellent: Well developed and implemented, reach all families at all grade levels, and meet other major challenges

3. Select one Type 5—Decision Making activity to describe in detail (i.e., one that reflects your school's best effort this year) and answer the following questions.

   One effective Type 5 activity implemented this year: _____

   About how many were involved?   # of families _____   # of teachers _____
                                      # of students _____   # of others _____

   Which grade levels were involved? _____

   What was the main goal of this activity? _____

   _____

   How well was the activity implemented this year? Was it a new initiative or an improvement of an existing practice?

   _____

   _____

   _____

   What result(s) did this activity produce this year for students, teachers, parents, and the community? How were the results measured?

   _____

   _____

   _____

   What might be done to make this activity even more successful next year? Were there parents, teachers, or students who were not involved? How might they be involved in the future? Could other aspects of the practice be improved? Explain.

   _____

   _____

   _____

Evaluation of Type 6—COLLABORATING WITH THE COMMUNITY Activities: Type 6 activities facilitate cooperation and collaboration among schools, families, and community groups, organizations, agencies and individuals (business partnerships, community resource book, on-site health services, job shadowing, etc.).

1. From the ATP's One-Year Action Plan—Form T (Types), <u>review</u> the Type 6—Collaborating With the Community activities that were implemented during this school year. List two or three that are (or will be) particularly helpful at your school:

   _____

   _____

   _____

2. Overall, how would you rate the quality of all Type 6 activities that your school presently conducts? (Check one)

   _____ a. Weak/Just Starting: Not well developed and need a great deal of work

   _____ b. Fair: Implemented but need improvement and expansion

   _____ c. Good: Well developed and reach most families at most grade levels

   _____ d. Excellent: Well developed and implemented, reach all families at all grade levels, and meet other major challenges

3. Select one Type 6—Collaborating With the Community activity to describe in detail (i.e., one that reflects your school's best effort this year) and answer the following questions.

   One effective Type 6 activity implemented this year: _____

   About how many were involved?   # of families _____   # of teachers _____

                                                       # of students _____   # of others _____

   Which grade levels were involved? _____

   What was the main goal of this activity? _____

   _____

   How well was the activity implemented this year? Was it a new initiative or an improvement of an existing practice?

   _____

   _____

   _____

   What result(s) did this activity produce this year for students, teachers, parents, and the community? How were the results measured?

   _____

   _____

   _____

   What might be done to make this activity even more successful next year? Were there parents, teachers, or students who were not involved? How might they be involved in the future? Could other aspects of the practice be improved? Explain.

   _____

   _____

   _____

School Name _____

School Year _____

End-of-Year Evaluation

School, Family, and Community Partnerships Focused on School Goals

This annual report helps your Action Team for Partnerships (ATP) discuss and rate the quality of your school's partnership program. It also asks ATP committees to consider *how well* activities were implemented and *how to improve* activities in the next school year to meet targeted school improvement goals.

This End-of-Year Evaluation—Form G includes one page of questions on the overall partnership program and a separate page of questions for each goal that was targeted in the *One-Year Action Plan—Form G* for this school year. If more than four goals were targeted, the ATP should make a copy of a "goals page" for each additional goal. This evaluation should assist the ATP with its *One-Year Action Plan—Form G* for the next school year.

Overall Program Evaluation

1. What has changed most in the past year as a result of your work on school, family, and community partnerships?

_____

Overall, how would you rate the quality of your school's program of school, family, and community partnerships?
Our school's partnership program is:

___ WEAK/JUST STARTING: Not well developed and needs a great deal of work

___ FAIR: Implemented, but needs improvement and expansion

___ GOOD: Well developed, is focused on school improvement goals, covers all six types of involvement, and addresses the needs of *most* families at *most* grade levels

___ EXCELLENT: Well developed and implemented, is focused on school improvement goals, covers all six types of involvement, and addresses the needs of *all* families at *all* grade levels

2. Who are the members of your Action Team for Partnerships this year? Mark * next to the names of members who are completing their terms or leaving the school and who will be replaced by new members.

ATP members for this school year	Position (teacher, parent, etc.)	Role on Action Team (e.g., chair, cochair, committee member working on which goal[s])
1.		
2.		
3.		
4.		
5.		
6.		
7.		
8.		

If you have more than eight members on the ATP, please continue this list on another page.

Goal 1—ACADEMIC: Which curricular goal for improving student learning and achievement was selected in the One-Year Action Plan—Form G?

Was Goal 1 reached this year? ☐ YES or ☐ NO
Will Goal 1 be continued or expanded in the One-Year Action Plan—Form G for the next school year? ☐ YES or ☐ NO

PROGRESS IN REACHING GOAL 1—ACADEMIC

Use *Excellent (E)*, *Good (G)*, *Fair (F)*, or *Poor (P)* to rate the **partnership activities** that were conducted to help reach GOAL 1 in each category. Explain the next steps that will be taken to maintain or improve the partnership activities in the next school year. Use additional pages if more than three family and community involvement activities were conducted to reach this goal.

| Partnership Activity | Action Team Support
How helpful and active were ATP members? | Other Support
How helpful were family, students, community members, and others? | Implementation
How well was the activity planned and implemented? | Overall Success of Activity
Did the activity reach its targeted audience?
Did it produce desired result(s)? |
|---|---|---|---|---|
| 1. _____ | ☐ | ☐ | ☐ | ☐ |

Will this partnership activity be continued in the next school year? YES or NO. If NO, why not? _____

If YES, what might be done to improve the support, implementation, or overall success of this activity? _____

Partnership Activity	Action Team Support	Other Support	Implementation	Overall Success of Activity
2. _____	☐	☐	☐	☐

Will this partnership activity be continued in the next school year? YES or NO. If NO, why not? _____

If YES, what might be done to improve the support, implementation, or overall success of this activity? _____

Partnership Activity	Action Team Support	Other Support	Implementation	Overall Success of Activity
3. _____	☐	☐	☐	☐

Will this partnership activity be continued in the next school year? YES or NO. If NO, why not? _____

If YES, what might be done to improve the support, implementation, or overall success of this activity? _____

Goal 2—ACADEMIC: Which other curricular goal for improving student learning and achievement was selected in the One-Year Action Plan—Form G?

Was Goal 2 reached this year? ❑ YES or ❑ NO
Will Goal 2 be continued or expanded in the One-Year Action Plan—Form G for the next school year? ❑ YES or ❑ NO

PROGRESS IN REACHING GOAL 2—ACADEMIC

Use *Excellent (E)*, *Good (G)*, *Fair (F)*, or *Poor (P)* to rate the **partnership activities** that were conducted to help reach GOAL 2 in each category. Explain the next steps that will be taken to maintain or improve the partnership activities in the next school year. Use additional pages if more than three family and community involvement activities were conducted to reach this goal.

| Partnership Activity | Action Team Support
How helpful and active were ATP members? | Other Support
How helpful were family, students, community members, and others? | Implementation
How well was the activity planned and implemented? | Overall Success of Activity
Did the activity reach its targeted audience?
Did it produce desired result(s)? |
|---|---|---|---|---|
| 1. _____ | ❑ | ❑ | ❑ | ❑ |

Will this partnership activity be continued in the next school year? YES or NO. If NO, why not?
_____

If YES, what might be done to improve the support, implementation, or overall success of this activity?
_____

Partnership Activity	Action Team Support	Other Support	Implementation	Overall Success of Activity
2. _____	❑	❑	❑	❑

Will this partnership activity be continued in the next school year? YES or NO. If NO, why not?
_____

If YES, what might be done to improve the support, implementation, or overall success of this activity?
_____

Partnership Activity	Action Team Support	Other Support	Implementation	Overall Success of Activity
3. _____	❑	❑	❑	❑

Will this partnership activity be continued in the next school year? YES or NO. If NO, why not?
_____

If YES, what might be done to improve the support, implementation, or overall success of this activity?
_____

Goal 3—BEHAVIORAL: Which goal for improving student attendance, attitudes, or other behaviors was selected in the One-Year Action Plan—Form G?

Was Goal 3 reached this year? ☐ YES or ☐ NO
Will Goal 3 be continued or expanded in the One-Year Action Plan—Form G for the next school year? ☐ YES or ☐ NO

PROGRESS IN REACHING GOAL 3—BEHAVIORAL

Use *Excellent (E), Good (G), Fair (F),* or *Poor (P)* to rate the **partnership activities** that were conducted to help reach GOAL 3 in each category. Explain the next steps that will be taken to maintain or improve the partnership activities in the next school year. Use additional pages if more than three family and community involvement activities were conducted to reach this goal.

Partnership Activity	Action Team Support How helpful and active were ATP members?	Other Support How helpful were family, students, community members, and others?	Implementation How well was the activity planned and implemented?	Overall Success of Activity Did the activity reach its targeted audience? Did it produce desired result(s)?
1. _____	☐	☐	☐	☐

Will this partnership activity be continued in the next school year? YES or NO. If NO, why not? _____

If YES, what might be done to improve the support, implementation, or overall success of this activity? _____

Partnership Activity	Action Team Support	Other Support	Implementation	Overall Success of Activity
2. _____	☐	☐	☐	☐

Will this partnership activity be continued in the next school year? YES or NO. If NO, why not? _____

If YES, what might be done to improve the support, implementation, or overall success of this activity? _____

Partnership Activity	Action Team Support	Other Support	Implementation	Overall Success of Activity
3. _____	☐	☐	☐	☐

Will this partnership activity be continued in the next school year? YES or NO. If NO, why not? _____

If YES, what might be done to improve the support, implementation, or overall success of this activity? _____

Goal 4—CLIMATE OF PARTNERSHIPS (Required goal): ALL OTHER family and community involvement activities that contribute to a welcoming school environment. _Strengthen the six types of family and community involvement_

Was Goal 4 reached this year? ☐ YES or ☐ NO
Will Goal 4 be continued or expanded in the One-Year Action Plan—Form G for the next school year? ☐ YES or ☐ NO

PROGRESS IN REACHING GOAL 4—CLIMATE OF PARTNERSHIP

Use *Excellent (E)*, *Good (G)*, *Fair (F)*, or *Poor (P)* to rate the **partnership activities** that were conducted to help reach GOAL 4 in each category. Explain the next steps that will be taken to maintain or improve the partnership activities in the next school year. Use additional pages if more than three family and community involvement activities were conducted to reach this goal.

Partnership Activity	Action Team Support How helpful and active were ATP members?	Other Support How helpful were family, students, community members, and others?	Implementation How well was the activity planned and implemented?	Overall Success of Activity Did the activity reach its targeted audience? Did it produce desired result(s)?
1. _____	☐	☐	☐	☐

Will this partnership activity be continued in the next school year? YES or NO. If NO, why not? _____

If YES, what might be done to improve the support, implementation, or overall success of this activity? _____

Partnership Activity	Action Team Support	Other Support	Implementation	Overall Success of Activity
2. _____	☐	☐	☐	☐

Will this partnership activity be continued in the next school year? YES or NO. If NO, why not? _____

If YES, what might be done to improve the support, implementation, or overall success of this activity? _____

Partnership Activity	Action Team Support	Other Support	Implementation	Overall Success of Activity
3. _____	☐	☐	☐	☐

Will this partnership activity be continued in the next school year? YES or NO. If NO, why not? _____

If YES, what might be done to improve the support, implementation, or overall success of this activity? _____

10

Networking for Best Results on Partnerships

You may use this *Handbook* on your own to develop a comprehensive program of school, family, and community partnerships. Or, your school, district, or state may join the National Network of Partnership Schools (NNPS) at Johns Hopkins University. This chapter includes two resources that will help you and your colleagues decide whether to link with leaders in other schools, districts, and states across the country who are improving family and community involvement to increase students' success.

National Network of Partnership Schools at Johns Hopkins University

Review the mission, benefits, services, requirements, and how to join the National Network of Partnership Schools. Benefits include leadership development workshops, newsletters to guide progress in program development, annual collections of best practices, annual evaluations of results of partnerships, annual awards for excellent programs, and ongoing professional development through phone, e-mail, and website connections with the researchers at Johns Hopkins University.

www.partnershipschools.org
NNPS Website

This dynamic website serves the members of the National Network of Partnership Schools with 15 sections of information and exchanges to improve leadership and programs of school, family, and community partnerships. The website includes summaries of research; program guidelines for elementary, middle, and high schools and for state and district leaders; and avenues for questions, answers, and idea exchanges with the Network staff and other leaders in schools, districts, states, and organizations working on partnerships.

National Network of Partnership Schools

at Johns Hopkins University

Joyce L. Epstein, Director

Educators and families agree that school-family-community partnerships are essential for children's success. Based on more than two decades of research and the work of many educators, parents, students, and others, we know that it is possible for all elementary, middle, and high schools to develop and sustain strong programs of partnerships that help students succeed in school.

States and districts can establish policies and leadership activities that help all schools develop programs of partnerships.

As a member of the National Network of Partnership Schools, you will be guided, supported, and recognized in your efforts to improve and maintain goal-oriented school, family, and community connections.

What is the National Network of Partnership Schools?

Established by researchers at Johns Hopkins University in 1996, the National Network of Partnership Schools brings together schools, districts, and states that are committed to developing and maintaining strong programs of school, family, and community partnerships. Each Partnership School strengthens its program by addressing six types of involvement and by using an Action Team approach. Districts and states assist schools to develop and sustain excellent programs of partnerships.

Why Become a Member of the National Network?

Membership has its benefits! Members of the Network are assisted to develop their partnership program. Each school, district, and state that joins the National Network receives the following:

★ Comprehensive handbook to guide partnership program development
★ Certificate of membership
★ Invitations to attend leadership development workshops
★ *Type 2*, Network newsletter
★ Annual collection, *Promising Partnership Practices*
★ Colorful posters of six "keys" to successful partnerships
★ Technical assistance by phone, e-mail, and website
★ Opportunities to participate in research and evaluation projects
★ Other benefits and services

Members benefit from the experiences of others in the National Network. In every issue of the newsletter, at workshops, and through the Network's website, members have opportunities to share creative solutions for improving school, family, and community partnerships.

Who May Join the National Network of Partnership Schools?

Membership is open to all schools, districts, and states that agree to the requirements listed on the following page.

NATIONAL NETWORK OF
Partnership Schools
JOHNS HOPKINS UNIVERSITY

Membership Requirements

Members work with the National Network of Partnership Schools to improve connections with students, families, and communities. Schools, districts, and states must meet a few requirements.

At the SCHOOL LEVEL, each Partnership School will:

✓ Create an Action Team for Partnerships.
✓ Use the framework of six types of involvement to plan and implement a program of partnerships.
✓ Allocate an annual budget for the work and activities of the school's Action Team for Partnerships.
✓ Allocate time for an initial day-long team training workshop, and at least one hour per month for the Action Team for Partnerships to plan, coordinate, and evaluate activities.

At the DISTRICT LEVEL, each Partnership District will:

✓ Assign the equivalent of one full-time facilitator to assist 15 to 30 schools to create their Action Teams for Partnerships. Part-time coordinators may work in districts with fewer than 15 schools.
✓ Allocate an annual budget for the district facilitators' salaries and activities to develop, strengthen, and maintain programs of partnership in all schools.
✓ Assist each participating school to fulfill the requirements listed above for the school level.

At the STATE LEVEL, each Partnership State will:

✓ Create or identify an Office or Department for School, Family, and Community Partnerships.
✓ Assign the equivalent of one full-time coordinator and adequate staff to conduct state-wide leadership activities for school, family, and community partnerships.
✓ Allocate an annual budget for the work of this office and for the activities to support districts and schools to develop excellent partnership programs.
✓ Assist districts and schools to fulfill the membership requirements listed above.

ALL MEMBERS will:

✓ Complete an annual UPDATE survey to report progress and to renew membership in the National Network.

To join the Network, there is a $100 processing fee for schools; $200 for districts, states, and organizations. Annual renewal fees are $100 for schools and $200 for districts, states, and organizations. ***RENEWAL FEES ARE WAIVED FOR ALL MEMBERS THAT RETURN THE ANNUAL UPDATE SURVEY.***

If your school, district, or state is ready to develop strong school, family, and community partnerships for student success, you are invited to join the National Network of Partnership Schools. For more information and membership forms for schools, districts, states, or for organization/university partners, write to:
Dr. Joyce Epstein, Director, Center on School, Family, and Community Partnerships, Johns Hopkins University
3003 N. Charles Street, Suite 200, Baltimore, MD 21218
Or contact Karen Clark Salinas at tel: 410-516-8818 fax: 410-516-8890 or e-mail: nnps@csos.jhu.edu

Visit us on the Internet at www.partnershipschools.org

www.partnershipschools.org

About NNPS   Search   Meet the Staff   Links   What's New

What is a Partnership Program?

Join the Network

In the Spotlight

Publications and Products

Research Briefs

Q & A

Bulletin Board

TIPS-Teachers Involve Parents in Schoolwork

Districts and States

Middle and High Schools

National Network of Partnership Schools
at Johns Hopkins University

What is a Partnership Program?
Learn about the six types of involvement, the Action Team approach, meeting challenges, expected results from partnerships, and other key features of successful programs of school, family, and community partnerships.

In the Spotlight
Read activities from annual collections of *Promising Partnership Practices* submitted by school, district, and state members of the Network. Also learn about the Network's standards for excellent partnership programs that guide the annual Partnership Awards.

Publications and Products
View lists of publications and products available from the National Network. Read *Type 2*, the Network's newsletter; learn about the latest Transparency/Power Point tools for training; and shop for Network Rewards and Recognition items, including posters, t-shirts, pens, and mugs.

Q & A
Explore Frequently Asked Questions to learn how to solve challenges to good partnerships. Post your questions and ideas on the Network's Bulletin Board. Or, cast your vote on a "hot topic" in the Quick Survey.

TIPS-Teachers Involve Parents in Schoolwork
Learn how interactive homework promotes student success at all grade levels. Download sample TIPS activities and blank templates to design homework assignments that match your school's curriculum. See how to order TIPS manuals, prototype activities, and workshop materials.

Districts and States
Review promising practices from district and state members, share ideas and post questions for district, state, and organization leaders, and get information about leadership development opportunities.

Middle and High Schools
Learn how middle and high schools can develop goal-oriented partnership programs to improve students' reading and math skills, increase attendance, smooth transitions across school levels, and plan postsecondary pathways. Read about successful family and community involvement activities submitted by Network members in middle and high schools across the country.

369

Index

ORDER FORM

To order more copies of this book fill out the form below!　　D2702

CORWIN PRESS, INC.
A Sage Publications Company

CALL
Toll Free
(800) 818-7243
Monday-Friday: 6 am–7 pm PT

MAIL
2455 Teller Road
Thousand Oaks, CA 91320-2218

FAX
Toll Free
(800) 417-2466

ONLINE
www.corwinpress.com

BILL TO (if different)　*Please attach original purchase order.*

☐ Purchase Order #_____

Name:_____

Title:_____

Organization:_____

Address:_____

City:_____ State:_____

Zip Code:_____

Telephone
Required: ☐☐☐-☐☐☐-☐☐☐☐

SHIP TO

Name:_____

Title:_____

Organization:_____

Address:_____

City:_____ State:_____

Zip Code:_____

Qty.	Book#	Title	Unit Price	Total Price
	0-7619-7666-3 (Paper)	School, Family, and Community Partnerships Your Handbook for Action, 2nd Edition	$36.95	
	0-7619-7665-5 (Cloth)	School, Family, and Community Partnerships Your Handbook for Action, 2nd Edition	$81.95	
Attach a sheet of paper for additional books ordered.		☐ Please send your latest catalog	FREE	FREE

Total Book Order	
Sales Tax Add appropriate sales tax in IL, MA, CA, NY Add appropriate GST & HST in Canada	
Shipping and Handling $3.50 for first book, $1.00 for each additional book Canada: $10.00 for first book, $2.00 each additional book	
Total Amount Due $ Remit in US dollars	

DISCOUNTS ARE AVAILABLE
for large quantity orders —
CALL (800) 818-7243
and ask for a sales manager.

Professional books may be tax-deductible.
Federal ID Number 77-0260369

All orders are shipped Ground Parcel.
For other shipping methods and cost, **call (800) 818-7243**

Payment Method

☐ Check # _____ Payable to Corwin Press

CREDIT CARD

☐ **VISA**　☐ **MasterCard**　☐ **DISCOVER**　☐ **AMERICAN EXPRESS**

Credit Card #:
☐☐☐☐-☐☐☐☐-☐☐☐☐-☐☐☐☐
☐☐/☐☐
month/year
Signature: _____

In case we have questions...

Telephone: ☐☐☐-☐☐☐-☐☐☐☐

Fax: ☐☐☐-☐☐☐-☐☐☐☐

E-mail:_____

☐ Yes, you may e-mail other Corwin Press offers to me.
Your email address will NOT be released to any third party.